Learning OpenDaylight

The art of deploying successful networks

Reza Toghraee

BIRMINGHAM - MUMBAI

Learning OpenDaylight

First published: May 2017

Production reference: 1260517

Published by Packt Publishing Ltd.
Livery Place
35 Livery Street
Birmingham
B3 2PB, UK.
ISBN 978-1-78217-452-3

www.packtpub.com

Credits

Author
Reza Toghraee

Reviewers
Pradeeban Kathiravelu
Moiz Raja

Commissioning Editor
Kartikey Pandey

Acquisition Editor
Rahul Nair

Content Development Editor
Sweeny Dias

Technical Editor
Prashant Chaudhari

Copy Editor
Gladson Monteiro

Project Coordinator
Virginia Dias

Proofreader
Safis Editing

Indexer
Francy Puthiry

Graphics
Kirk D'Penha

Production Coordinator
Shraddha Falebhai

About the Author

Reza Toghraee, CCIE 22518, is a network and security expert. For the last 15 years, he has designed and deployed many large campus and data center projects, leveraging his skills in networking, security, virtualization, compute, and storage. He has worked with all networking vendors. In 2013, he started exploring the hardware and software of Ethernet switches and was inspired to build an Audio Video Bridging (AVB) Ethernet switch by designing hardware and software protocols. Soon, he discovered SDN and early SDN controllers, and dedicated his time to promoting and contributing to SDN and the OpenNetworking community. He works as a freelance consultant for SDN, NFV, network automation, network virtualization, and cloud projects.

He can be reached via his e-mail: `Reza@Toghraee.com`.

Acknowledgments

First of all, I would like to thank all of you readers. Thanks for reading this book, and I hope it can help you start your SDN journey. Since this is my first book, it might not be perfect-- there may be a few mistakes. Please accept them as my first book-authoring experience.

Thanks to Packt Publishing, who gave me the opportunity to write this book. Thanks to all members of the editorial team for their contributions that made this book what it is.

I would like to thank the London OpenDaylight meetup group, a very friendly group with amazing folks. Special thanks to Stace Hipperson, Giles Heron, and Nathan Sowatskey for all their contribution to the group.

A big thanks to Aseem and Aneeta Gupta for their inspiration that helped me build a new me.

I will use this opportunity to thank folks from the Linux Foundation, who are in charge of OpeDaylight and OPNFV.

Thanks to the great people form Inverse for their support and providing the PacketFence SDN-NAC plugin for OpenDaylight.

At the end, a big thanks to my wife, Neda, and my daughter, Hanna, for their motivation and allowing me to spend lots of family time on this book.

About the Reviewers

Pradeeban Kathiravelu is an open source evangelist. He is a PhD researcher at INESC-ID Lisboa/Instituto Superior Técnico, Universidade de Lisboa, Portugal, and Université Catholique de Louvain, Belgium. He is a Fellow of Erasmus Mundus Joint Degree in Distributed Computing (EMJD-DC), researching a software-defined approach to quality of service and data quality in multi-tenant clouds. He holds a master of science degree, Erasmus Mundus European Master in Distributed Computing (EMDC), from Instituto Superior Técnico, Portugal and KTH Royal Institute of Technology, Sweden. He also holds a first class bachelor of science in engineering (Hons) degree, majoring in computer science and engineering, from the University of Moratuwa, Sri Lanka. His research interests include software-defined networking (SDN), distributed systems, cloud computing, web services, big data in biomedical informatics, and data mining. He is very interested in free and open source software development and has been an active participant of the Google Summer of Code (GSoC) program since 2009, as a student and as a mentor. He has also reviewed OpenDaylight Cookbook (ISBN: 978-1-78646-230-5).

I would like to thank Prof. Luís Veiga, my MSc and PhD advisor, for his continuous guidance and encouragement throughout my 5 years at Instituto Superior Técnico.

Moiz Raja is a software developer with more than 20 years' experience in building enterprise software. His primary experience is in building highly scalable distributed applications, but he also has years of experience building front-end software for Windows and the Web.

Moiz has worked at several large enterprise software companies, such as Avaya and Cisco. At Avaya, he built the Contact Center software, which included the Avaya Interaction Center and Avaya one-X Agent. At Cisco, Moiz served as a committer on the OpenDaylight controller project, where he contributed to building the MD-SAL distributed data store. He was voted a top-10 developer 2 years in a row while working on OpenDaylight and was also a presenter at the OpenDaylight summit in 2015.

Moiz is currently employed as a principal engineer at Viptela, which is a leading SD-WAN software startup, where he is helping build a highly scalable network management controller.

www.PacktPub.com

For support files and downloads related to your book, please visit www.PacktPub.com.

Did you know that Packt offers eBook versions of every book published, with PDF and ePub files available? You can upgrade to the eBook version at www.PacktPub.com and as a print book customer, you are entitled to a discount on the eBook copy. Get in touch with us at service@packtpub.com for more details.

At www.PacktPub.com, you can also read a collection of free technical articles, sign up for a range of free newsletters and receive exclusive discounts and offers on Packt books and eBooks.

https://www.packtpub.com/mapt

Get the most in-demand software skills with Mapt. Mapt gives you full access to all Packt books and video courses, as well as industry-leading tools to help you plan your personal development and advance your career.

Why subscribe?

- Fully searchable across every book published by Packt
- Copy and paste, print, and bookmark content
- On demand and accessible via a web browser

Customer Feedback

Thanks for purchasing this Packt book. At Packt, quality is at the heart of our editorial process. To help us improve, please leave us an honest review on this book's Amazon page at `https://www.amazon.com/dp/1782174524`.

If you'd like to join our team of regular reviewers, you can e-mail us at `customerreviews@packtpub.com`. We award our regular reviewers with free eBooks and videos in exchange for their valuable feedback. Help us be relentless in improving our products!

To my parents, Bahman and Soheyla, who have always been supporting me in all situations without any expectations.

Table of Contents

Preface

OpenDaylight is an open source, software-defined network controller based on standard protocols. It aims to accelerate the adoption of software-defined networking (SDN) and create a solid foundation for network functions virtualization (NFV).

SDN is a vast subject; many network engineers find it difficult to get started with using and operating different SDN platforms. This book will give you a practical bridge from legacy networking and SDN theory to the practical, real-world use of SDN in data centers and by cloud providers.

The book will help you understand the features and use cases for SDN, NFV, and OpenDaylight. It also provides hands-on examples to build and use OpenDaylight in a test and lab environment on your computer.

NFV uses virtualization concepts and techniques to create virtual network functions such as routers, firewalls, and load balancers using standard x86 servers. Used together, SDN and NFV can elevate the agility of your network architecture; generic hardware-saving costs and the advanced and abstracted software will give you the freedom to evolve your network in the future without having to invest more in costly equipment.

By the end of this book, you will have learned how to design and deploy OpenDaylight networks. You will also have mastered basic network programming over the SDN fabric.

What this book covers

Chapter 1, *Introduction to SDN - Transformation from Legacy to SDN*, explains SDN basics and covers SDN controllers and the position of OpenDaylight in the SDN ecosystem. It will help transform a traditional, legacy networking mind into an SDN mindset. It also covers a translation of how legacy network features, terms, protocols, and functions such as routing, switching, VLANs, and link aggregations are implemented in SDN.

Chapter 2, *Overview of OpenDaylight*, is about the OpenDaylight project and its components, history, and versions. OpenDaylight is a complex project based on multiple components that are tightly integrated. The aim is to make you familiar with the architecture of OpenDaylight in order to have a better understanding of how OpenDaylight works and the logic behind it.

Chapter 3, *OpenDaylight Installation and Deployment*, provides step-by-step installation instructions for OpenDaylight in a virtual environment. You will learn how to install it from scratch and in a Docker container.

Chapter 4, *Building a Virtual SDN Test Lab with Virtual Switches*, helps you build a virtual lab using mininet virtual-SDN-enabled switches.

Chapter 5, *Basic Networking with OpenDaylight*, is dedicated to performing basic network operations using OpenDaylight and SDN. You will learn basic networking operations and managing the fabric using OpenDaylight.

Chapter 6, *Overview of OpenDaylight Applications*, is about OpenDaylight applications. You will learn about OpenDaylight application programming using model-driven SAL (MD-SAL) in very basic steps.

Chapter 7, *Building SDN Applications for OpenDaylight*, helps you build an SDN application on top of OpenDaylight. We will go through SDN-based network access control (NAC) to understand how to hook up to OpenDaylight and take control of packet flow decision process.

Chapter 8, *Network Function Virtualization NFV*, gets you familiar with the role of OpenDaylight in an NFV ecosystem. You will learn about network function virtualization (NFV) basics, the OPNFV framework, and existing NFV projects. You will also learn about service chaining, which is one of the main use cases of SDN and OpenDaylight.

Chapter 9, *Building a Software-Driven Data Center with OpenDaylight*, summarizes and uses all the learning of this book by integrating it into a responsive software-driven data center use case. You will learn how to integrate and automate networking tasks from OpenStack to OpenDaylight, as well as understanding the role of network orchestration in a service-provider network by evolving OSS and BSS.

What you need for this book

In order to keep up with the book, you will need to spend some time learning basic coding. Ensure that you have the following software installed:

- Oracle VirtualBox Or VMware workstation
- Ubuntu 16 server as base operating system for installation of OpenDaylight
- Mininet virtual appliance
- OpenDaylight Beryllium-SR4
- VTN coordinator
- PacketFence module for OpenDaylight

Who this book is for

This book is for network professionals, network automation engineers, and developers who are working on software defined networking, network orchestration, and the cloud, in both service-provider and enterprise segments. This book tries to transform a legacy networking mindset to a software-defined networking one. Knowledge of networking is required.

Conventions

In this book, you will find a number of text styles that distinguish between different kinds of information. Here are some examples of these styles and an explanation of their meaning.

Code words in text, database table names, folder names, filenames, file extensions, pathnames, dummy URLs, user input, and Twitter handles are shown as follows: "We can include other contexts through the use of the `include` directive."

A block of code is set as follows:

```
01 <?xml version="1.0" encoding="UTF-8" standalone="no"?>
02 <flow xmlns="urn:opendaylight:flow:inventory">
03    <flow-name>Flow1</flow-name>
04    <id>258</id>
05    <instructions>
```

When we wish to draw your attention to a particular part of a code block, the relevant lines or items are set in bold:

```
01 <?xml version="1.0" encoding="UTF-8" standalone="no"?>
02 <flow xmlns="urn:opendaylight:flow:inventory">
03    <flow-name>Flow1</flow-name>
04    <id>258</id>
05    <instructions>
```

Any command-line input or output is written as follows:

```
scp $path/controller-upgrade-2013.02.13.0921.pkg images@192.168.67.141:"
```

New terms and important words are shown in bold. Words that you see on the screen, for example, in menus or dialog boxes, appear in the text like this: "Clicking the Next button moves you to the next screen."

 Warnings or important notes appear in a box like this.

Tips and tricks appear like this.

Reader feedback

Feedback from our readers is always welcome. Let us know what you think about this book-what you liked or disliked. Reader feedback is important for us as it helps us develop titles that you will really get the most out of.

To send us general feedback, simply e-mail feedback@packtpub.com, and mention the book's title in the subject of your message.

If there is a topic that you have expertise in and you are interested in either writing or contributing to a book, see our author guide at www.packtpub.com/authors.

Customer support

Now that you are the proud owner of a Packt book, we have a number of things to help you to get the most from your purchase.

Downloading the example code

You can download the example code files for this book from your account at http://www.packtpub.com. If you purchased this book elsewhere, you can visit http://www.packtpub.com/ support and register to have the files e-mailed directly to you.

You can download the code files by following these steps:

1. Log in or register to our website using your e-mail address and password.
2. Hover the mouse pointer on the SUPPORT tab at the top.
3. Click on Code Downloads & Errata.
4. Enter the name of the book in the Search box.
5. Select the book for which you're looking to download the code files.
6. Choose from the drop-down menu where you purchased this book from.
7. Click on Code Download.

You can also download the code files by clicking on the Code Files button on the book's webpage at the Packt Publishing website. This page can be accessed by entering the book's name in the Search box. Please note that you need to be logged in to your Packt account.

Once the file is downloaded, please make sure that you unzip or extract the folder using the latest version of:

- WinRAR / 7-Zip for Windows
- Zipeg / iZip / UnRarX for Mac

7-Zip / PeaZip for Linux

The code bundle for the book is also hosted on GitHub at `https://github.com/PacktPublishing/Learning-OpenDaylight`. We also have other code bundles from our rich catalog of books and videos available at `https://github.com/PacktPublishing/`. Check them out!

Downloading the color images of this book

We also provide you with a PDF file that has color images of the screenshots/diagrams used in this book. The color images will help you better understand the changes in the output. You can download this file from `https://www.packtpub.com/sites/default/files/downloads/LearningOpenDaylight_ColorImages.pdf`.

Errata

Although we have taken every care to ensure the accuracy of our content, mistakes do happen. If you find a mistake in one of our books-maybe a mistake in the text or the code-we would be grateful if you could report this to us. By doing so, you can save other readers from frustration and help us improve subsequent versions of this book. If you find any errata, please report them by visiting `http://www.packtpub.com/submit-errata`, selecting your book, clicking on the **Errata Submission Form** link, and entering the details of your errata. Once your errata are verified, your submission will be accepted and the errata will be uploaded to our website or added to any list of existing errata under the Errata section of that title.

To view the previously submitted errata, go to `https://www.packtpub.com/books/content/support` and enter the name of the book in the search field. The required information will appear under the **Errata** section.

Piracy

Piracy of copyrighted material on the Internet is an ongoing problem across all media. At Packt, we take the protection of our copyright and licenses very seriously. If you come across any illegal copies of our works in any form on the Internet, please provide us with the location address or website name immediately so that we can pursue a remedy.

Please contact us at `copyright@packtpub.com` with a link to the suspected pirated material.

We appreciate your help in protecting our authors and our ability to bring you valuable content.

Questions

If you have a problem with any aspect of this book, you can contact us at `questions@packtpub.com`, and we will do our best to address the problem.

1
Introduction to SDN - Transformation from Legacy to SDN

You might have heard about **Software-Defined Networking** (**SDN**). If you are in the networking industry this is a topic that you probably have studied initially when you heard about the SDN for the first time.

To understand the importance of the SDN and SDN controller, let's look at Google. Google silently built its own networking switches and controller called **Jupiter**, a home grown project that is mostly software driven and supports such massive scale of Google.

Similar to all other technologies, we were in a hype for SDN for the last three years, everyone was talking about it, while it was still un-matured enough. The technology hype is a cycle for each and every new technology being introduced to the world. You can recall other hypes such as SD-WAN and IOT, where marketing and people start talking about them and industry leaders start giving ideas, publishing papers, and developing the idea while still there is not enough maturity in technology to become as a product.

The IT and computing industry is all about change. It changes its models, forms, or services from time to time. Even it goes back to a previous model where it was deprecated and ceased by a technology successor. For example, computers back in the 1970s, were all a central computing system in the form of a main frame, with multiple terminals. People were using a central system for executing their day to day computing requirements. This model slowly evolved by introducing micro and personal computers in the late 1980s and started to become a distributed computing. Mainframes started ceasing off, and were deprecated and replaced by standalone servers.

In the last five years, by explosion of the cloud, again we are going back to a central model, a model where a central cloud will perform all the computing, storage, networking, and security, without the need of any on-premises infrastructure.

Similarly, in the networking world, we are evolving to a *central brain* model. In the networking industry, we had standard protocols for more than 20 years. BGP, OSPF, ISIS, spanning tree, and so on are protocols and concepts that you deal with on a daily basis. These protocols were built on a very important basis, *no one has a full picture of a network*. However, in SDN, we are changing the basis. The SDN base is *There is a controller who knows the whole network*.

OpenDaylight (**ODL**) is an SDN controller. In other words, it's the central brain of the network.

Going back to SDN and this book, we will go for a practical experience with SDN and we will learn:

- What is and what is not SDN
- Difference between SDN and overlay
- The SDN controllers
- BUM (broadcast, unknown, and multicast)
- OpenDaylight as an SDN controller
- Understanding the flows, tables, and flow mappings

Traditional networking terms and features in the SDN world.

Why are we going towards SDN?

Everyone who is hearing about SDN should ask the question why we are talking about SDN? What problem is it trying to solve?

If we look at traditional networking (layer 2 and layer 3 with routing protocols such as BGP and OSPF), we are completely dominated by what is called **protocols**.

These protocols in fact have been very helpful to the industry. They are mostly standard. Different vendors and products can communicate using standard protocols with each other. A Cisco router can establish a BGP session with a Huawei switch or an open source Quagga router can exchange OSPF routes with a Juniper firewall.

The routing protocol is a constant standard with solid bases. If you need to override something in your network routing, you have to find a trick to use protocols, even by using a static route.

Further more the legacy networking and switching gears are based on a tied control plane and forwarding plane on a single box. Each switch or router runs a control software (AKA firmware or operating system) which includes components such as spanning tree, BGP, OSPF, link aggregation, LLD, and so on. Each device uses these protocols to build a network from its own perspective.

This tide integration between software and hardware, or control and data plane limits the scalability of the network because of a lack of having a single, know all, network brain.

This integration also has a cost impact as each vendor will charge extra for a software running on their switches.

One of the main objectives of SDN is to dis-aggregate the control and data plane. That means to have a single control plane software (the SDN controller) and multiple bare metal SDN-enabled data plane gears (such as pure OpenFlow switches).

SDN can help us to come out of the routing protocol cage, look at different ways to forward traffic. SDN can directly program each switch or even override a route that is installed by routing protocols.

There are high-level benefits of using SDN, a few of which we have explained in the following list:

- **An integrated network**: We used to have a standalone concept in traditional networks. Each switch was managed separately; each switch was running its own routing protocol instance and was processing routing information messages from other neighbors. In SDN, we are migrating to a centralized model, where the SDN controller becomes the single point of configuration of the network, where you will apply the policies and configuration.
- **Scalable layer 2 across layer 3**: Having a layer 2 network across multiple layer 3 networks is something that all network architects are interested in and until now we have been using proprietary methods such as OTV or by using a service provider VPLS service. With SDN, we can create layer 2 networks across multiple switches or layer 3 domains (using VXLAN) and expand the layer 2 networks. In many cloud environments, where the virtual machines are distributed across different hosts in different data centers, this is a major requirement.

- **Third-party application programmability**: This is a very generic term, isn't it? But what I'm referring to is to let other applications communicate with your network. For example, in many new distributed IP storage systems, the IP storage controller has the ability to talk to networks to provide the best, shortest path to the storage node. With SDN we are letting other applications control the network. Of course this control has limitations and SDN doesn't allow an application to scrap the whole network.
- **Flexible application based network**: In SDN, everything is an application. L2/L3, BGP, VMware Integration, and so on all are applications running in the SDN controller.
- **Service chaining**: On the fly you add a firewall in the path or a load balancer. This is **service insertion**.
- **Unified wired and wireless**: This is an ideal benefit, to have a controller that supports both wired and wireless network. OpenDaylight is the only controller that supports CAPWAP protocols that allows integration with wireless access points.

Components of an SDN

A software-defined network infrastructure has two main key components:

- The SDN controller (only one, could be deployed in a highly available cluster)
- The SDN-enabled switches (multiple switches, mostly in a Clos topology in a data center) as shown in the following figure:

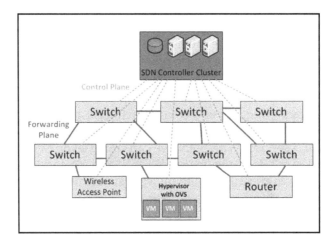

An SDN controller is the single brain of the SDN domain. In fact, an SDN domain is very similar to a chassis-based switch. You can imagine the supervisor or management module of a chassis-based switch as an SDN controller and the rest of the line card and I/O cards as SDN switches. The main difference between an SDN network and a chassis-based switch is that you can scale out the SDN with multiple switches, where in a chassis-based switch you are limited to the number of slots in that chassis:

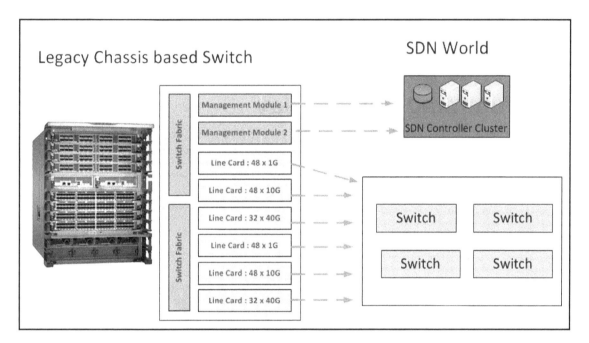

Controlling the fabric

It is very important that you understand the main technologies involved in SDN. These methods are used by SDN controllers to manage and control the SDN network.

In general, there are two methods available for controlling the fabric:

- **Direct fabric programming**: In this method, the SDN controller directly communicates with SDN-enabled switches via southbound protocols such as OpenFlow, NETCONF, and OVSDB. The SDN controller programs each switch member with related information about fabric, and how to forward the traffic. Direct fabric programming is the method used by OpenDaylight.

- **Overlay**: In the overlay method, the SDN controller doesn't rely on programming the network switches and routers. Instead it builds a virtual overlay network on top of the existing underlay network. The underlay network can be an L2 or L3 network with traditional network switches and router, just providing IP connectivity. The SDN controller uses this platform to build the overlay using encapsulation protocols such as VXLAN and NVGRE. VMware NSX uses overlay technology to build and control the virtual fabric.

Difference between direct fabric programming and overlay

Let's look at how the standard switch or router performs a frame forwarding. For our understanding we will look at a generic layer 3 switch (1G or 10G) from any vendor:

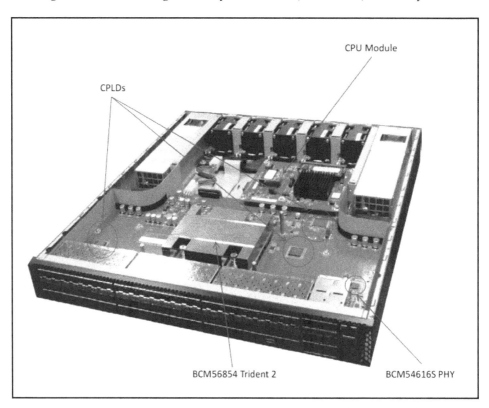

An Ethernet switch is a very simple device, it's just a silicon chipset, which is from one of the large silicon manufacturers such as Broadcom or Marvel, a CPU (which is either a x86 or a low power ARM-based processor), which runs the vendor's software (vendor here is referring to switch vendor such as Cisco or Juniper or Arista, and so on.):

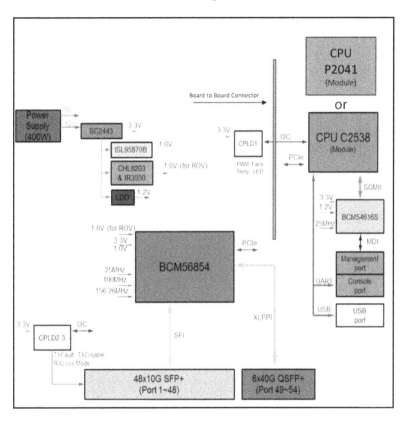

The switch silicon is like a comparison table. It maps the frames to ports. When a switch receives a packet, it looks into its **content-addressable memory** (**CAM**) table to find out what needs to be done to this frame received on port *X*. The CAM table, which is already programmed and filled by the switch software, will have an entry to tell the switch silicon what needs to be done on that frame. For example, send it out of port *Y* and change the destination MAC to switch burned in MAC. Or any other decision such as sending it to the switch CPU for processing (if it's a routing protocol packet, for example an OSPF LSA).

So in simple terms, in standard switches the CAM table of a switch is filled by entries that are programmed and controlled by switch CPU or switch software.

In SDN, we have a slightly different scenario, you can imagine that the SDN controller will control the CAM table of all switches. The terms are changed slightly and it is called a **flow table**. A flow table is nothing but the same CAM entries in the switch, but it's called a flow table and each entry is called a **flow entry**.

SDN controller programs each switch CAM table via a protocol that is called **southbound** protocol. There are multiple southbound protocols where the most famous and standard one is OpenFlow; however, the others such as NETCONF and OVSDB also exist in standard protocol groups. Cisco's OpFlex (`https://tools.ietf.org/html/draft-smith-opflex-03`) is also an open source protocol which is a southbound protocol between Cisco APIC controller and Cisco Nexus switches. OpFlex is also supported on OpenDaylight.

OpenFlow is a protocol that allows SDN controller to program each switch in the SDN network. Please remember that the OpenFlow is a piece of software, it's a protocol. The OpenFlow agent runs on each switch and starts communicating with the OpenFlow server piece on SDN controller.

You may have heard about overlays. Especially if you have heard about the SD-WAN, which is completely based on overlay networking. An overlay is a network built on top of an underlay network. Seems complex? Let me provide a more familiar example. An SSL VPN tunnel is an overlay on top of a IP network. In SSL VPN, the underlay is IP, and an overlay is an SSL.

The real packets are encapsulated as new payload inside the SSL packets. You can make more examples of overlays, GRE, IPSEC, and also the new overlays such as VXLAN and NVGRE:

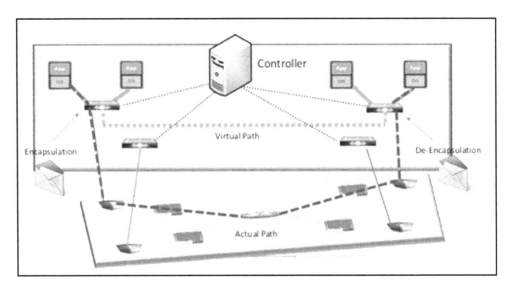

Overlays are also considered as part of the SDN family. Yes, they are software defined. They are created and managed by software. Overlays are not dependent on the underlay IP network; therefore deploying an overlay network is much easier than deploying a full SDN with SDN controller and switches. In data center overlay networks there are two main protocols used for encapsulation: VXLAN and NVGRE.

VXLAN is a UDP packet, which encapsulates the whole IP packet as a UDP payload and sends over the other end. VXLAN endpoints are called **Virtual Tunnel End Points** (**VTEP**). VTEPs create virtual tunnels between each other and transmit the UDP packets that are all having the packets encapsulated inside the UDP payload.

VXLAN uses an identification number for networks called **virtual network ID** (**VNID**), which identifies which packet belongs to which virtual network.

VXLAN is very common between most of the vendors and are very well supported.

Network Virtualization using GRE (**NVGRE**) is another protocol similar to VXLAN, but it is not very popular. Microsoft is one of the promoters of NVGRE on their SONIC switch operating system.

The most important overlay solution on the market is VMware NSX.

Now we have learned very briefly about SDN and overlays, let's have a comparison between these two technologies:

	Direct fabric programming	Overlay
Can work in co-existance with existing underlay IP network	Yes or No depending on switch type.	Yes
Requires to use an encapsulation protocol such as VXLAN, NVGRE	No	Yes
Scalable	Yes	Yes

In summary, SDN and overlays are somehow completing each other, but they are different. Some people don't consider overlays as SDN, and some do.

OpenDaylight is an SDN controller, it is not an overlay.

Futuristic view on networking and SDN

The future of SDN might be a generic platform on which the network application would be written and create a new industry of network application service. We may expect different network applications to be released, which all tend to add intelligence to the network and get integrated with other applications and software. Many services are changing to some kind of anycast that requires an intelligent network to decide which client's request must be directed to which server. Some of these services are available now, for example the new NAS servers with anycast support integration with OpenFlow to the SDN network (products from Coho Data).

Similar to a computer operating system that delivers computing resources to an application, an SDN network operating system might be able to deliver packets to the application. The application decides how they would like to use the services.

With popularity of VMware and OpenStack as well as cloud services such as Amazon AWS and Azure, we expect that the SDN platforms in the future will support such integration natively. SDN platforms will be able to extend the local networks toward the AWS cloud virtual network and provide a seamless network from user premises to the cloud. They will handle all type of API integrations and creation of the required overlay or VPNs between sites and manage the packet delivery (a.k.a. routing in the legacy world).

SDN as it stands for Software-Defined Network, will get more visibility on applications. SDN platform will be able to understand the applications by integration with other platforms. SDN will know a Hadoop HDFS replication running between servers, and knows what priority it has and how to deal with it to ensure the application performance, while at the same time deals with a telepresence call between multiple parties and manages the real-time traffic and ensures no disruption on real-time traffic.

We have been using the IP addressing schema for many years. IP subnets are always used for grouping the networks and hosts and they are the key for routing decisions. All routing protocols exchange the subnets and prefixes to perform routing and build their routing tables. In an SDN enabled network there is no routing and this may change the way we used to perform IP address assignments. In a legacy network we understand the layer 2 broadcast very well. A host with an IP address of `192.168.1.1/24` will be able to reach another host with the IP address of `192.168.1.2/24` on the same network. The host sends an ARP request, the legacy switch broadcasts the ARP and destination replied back the ARP with its MAC address and finally the communication happens as both hosts find out the MAC addresses of each other.

Our defined rules of hosts on the same subnets or in different subnets doesn't apply in an SDN network. The SDN controller is the god of the network and decides which hosts shall be able to communicate with each other, regardless of their IP address or subnet mask. For example, imagine two hosts with IP details as follows:

- Host A: `192.168.1.1/24`
- Host B: `192.168.2.2/24`

Normally if host A needs to communicate with host B, it needs to send its traffic to its default gateway and default gateways should perform a *routing* to reach the destination network.

In the SDN platform, the SDN controller knows where both host A and host B are connected. Once host A needs to send a packet to host B, it's the SDN controllers job to cheat and reply back the ARP request of host A, and enable a direct communication between host A and host B although they are not in the same subnet.

This may sound freaky as SDN can destroy all the rules and laws of networking, but remember that you should compare the SDN with a chassis-based switch. SDN has a domain and out of that domain it follows the legacy network rules and protocols. In a chassis based switch when a packet enters from port 1 on line card 3 and the destination is a host connected to port 2 on line card 2, the switch management module as well as the FIB memory on line cards has visibility on where the destination is connected, similar to SDN the switch may just forward the packet out of its port 2 on line card 2 where it is required.

It is highly likely that all of the aforementioned imaginations and scenarios will occur to some degree, but it will be mainly depending on business cases, vendors, and how customers demand such services from vendors.

BUM (broadcast, unknown, multicast)

BUM is the acronym for Broadcast, Unknown, Multicast in layer 2 frames. I know you all know about them very well, and in fact BUM is something that network engineers don't deal with on a daily basis. In traditional networking, BUM is the pure job of switch silicon.

But in an SDN world, BUM is a key element for system robustness, a very important factor. Let's look at why we need to deal with BUM carefully.

In traditional networking, a very basic layer 2 switch, regardless of its speed of 10 Mbps to 100 Gbps, has the basic capability to switch the traffic based on layer 2 information of a **frame** (frame is a layer 2 message, which holds the layer 3 packet encapsulated inside the frame's payload). When a layer 2 switch receives a frame, it builds a simple table mapping between the source MAC address and the port the frame has arrived.

Port	MAC Address
1	`00:00:11:22:33:44`
3	`0A:90:72:3A:89:01`

The preceding table is called a **TCAM** or MAC address table, or other names (by different vendors).

If a switch receives a frame destined for a MAC address that doesn't exist in its MAC address table, or it is a broadcast frame (that is ARP, destined for `FF;FF:FF:FF:FF:FF`), or a multicast frame, the layer 2 switch by default copies the frame over all of its ports, except the port the frame has arrived.

This is the way a basic layer 2 switch deals with BUM in the background where the network engineer doesn't notice.

In the SDN world, as I explained previously, we are living in a world where a single controller knows the whole network and hosts. The switches are not intelligent enough to deal with a frame that they don't know where to send it to. What will happen to a frame that enters an SDN switch with broadcast MAC or a destination MAC address unknown to the switch (not listed in its flow table)?

The SDN switch needs to send this frame to the SDN controller and ask the controller where to send this frame. This also can be a packet. SDN switch uses the southbound protocol to request the controller about how to deal with this packet or frame.

SDN controller receives the frame from the SDN switch and it needs to react and tell the switch what needs to be done for the frame. This is a very important process and if the SDN controller fails to respond to the switch within a specific time, the frames will not pass and the source will keep waiting.

An ideal SDN controller should be very proactive by filling the flow tables of the switches in such a way that the number of requests from the switch to the SDN controller for BUM is reduced.

SDN controllers

One of the key fundamentals of SDN is **disaggregation**. Disaggregation of software and hardware in a network and also disaggregation of control and forwarding planes.

The SDN controller is the main brain and controller of an SDN environment. It's a strategic control point within the network and it is responsible for communicating information to:

- Routers and switches and other network devices behind them. SDN controllers uses APIs or protocols (such as OpenFlow or NETCONF) to communicate with these devices. This communication is known as southbound.
- Upstream switches, routers or applications, and the aforementioned business logic (via APIs or protocols). This communication is known as **northbound**. An example of a northbound communication is a BGP session between a legacy router and SDN controller.

If you are familiar with chassis based switches such as Cisco Catalyst 6500 or Nexus 7k chassis, you can imagine an SDN network as a chassis, with switches and routers as its I/O line cards and SDN controller as its supervisor or management module. In fact SDN is similar to a very scalable chassis where you don't have any limitation on the number of physical slots.

SDN controller is similar to the role of the management module of a chassis-based switch and it controls all switches via its southbound protocols and APIs.

The following table compares the SDN controller and a chassis based switch:

SDN Controller	Chassis based switch
Supports any switch hardware	Supports only specific switch line cards
Can scale out, unlimited number of switches	Limited to number of physical slots in the chassis
Supports high redundancy by multiple controllers in a cluster	Supports dual management redundancy, active standby
Communicates with switches via southbound protocols such as OpenFlow, NETCONF, and BGP PCEP	Use proprietary protocols between management module and line cards
Communicates with routers, switches and applications outside of SDN via northbound protocols such as BGP, OSPF, and direct API	Communicates with other routers and switches outside of chassis via standard protocols such as BGP, OSPF or APIs

The first protocol that popularized the concept behind SDN was OpenFlow. When conceptualized by networking researchers at Stanford back in 2008, it was meant to manipulate the data plane to optimize traffic flows and make adjustments, so the network could quickly adapt to changing requirements. Version 1.0 of the OpenFlow specification was released in December of 2009; it continues to be enhanced under the management of the Open Networking Foundation, which is a user-led organization focused on advancing the development of open standards and the adoption of SDN technologies.

OpenFlow protocol was the first protocol that helped in popularizing SDN. OpenFlow is a protocol designed to update the flow tables in a switch. Allowing the SDN controller to access the forwarding table of each member switch or in other words to connect control plane and data plane in the SDN world. Back in 2008, OpenFlow was conceptualized by networking researchers at Stanford University, the initial use of OpenFlow was to alter the switch forwarding tables to optimize traffic flows and make adjustments, so the network could quickly adapt to changing requirements.

After the introduction of OpenFlow, NOX was introduced as an original OpenFlow controller (there still wasn't a concept of the SDN controller). NOX was providing a high-level API capable of managing and also developing network control applications. Separate applications were required to run on top of NOX to manage the network. NOX was initially developed by Nicira networks (which was acquired by VMware, and finally became part of VMware NSX). NOX was introduced along with OpenFlow in 2009. NOX was a closed source product, but ultimately it was donated to the SDN community, which led to multiple forks and sub projects out of original NOX. For example, POX is a sub project of NOX, which provides Python support. Both NOX and POX were early controllers. NOX appears an inactive development, however POX is still in use by the research community as it is a Python-based project and can be easily deployed.

 POX is hosted at `http://github.com/noxrepo/pox`

NOX apart from being the first OpenFlow or SDN controller also established a programming model that is inherited by other subsequent controllers. The model was based on processing of OpenFlow messages, with each incoming OpenFlow message triggering an event that had to be processed individually. This model was simple to implement, but not efficient and robust and couldn't scale.

Nicira along with NTT and Google started developing ONIX, which was meant to be more abstract and scalable for large deployments. ONIX became the base for Nicira (the core of VMware NSX or network virtualization platform) and there are rumors that it is also the base for Google WAN controller. ONIX was planned to become open source and donated to the community, but for some reasons the main contributors decided to not do it, which forced the SDN community to focus on developing other platforms.

Starting in 2010, a new controller was introduced. It was called the Beacon controller and it became one of the most popular controllers. It was born due to the contribution of developers from Stanford University. Beacon is a Java-based open source OpenFlow controller created in 2010. It has been widely used for teaching, research, and as the basis of Floodlight. Beacon had the first built-in web user-interface, which was a huge step forward in the market of SDN controllers. Also it provided an easier method to deploy and run compared to NOX. Beacon was an influence for design of later controllers after it; however, it was only supporting star topologies, which was one of the limitations of this controller.

Floodlight was a successful SDN controller that was built as a fork of Beacon. Big Switch networks are developing Floodlight along with other developers. In 2013, Beacon popularity started to shrink and Floodlight started to gain popularity. Floodlight had fixed many issues of Beacon and added lots of additional features, which made it one of the most feature rich controllers available. It also had a web interface, a Java-based GUI, and it also could get integrated with OpenStack using the quantum plugin. Integration with OpenStack was a big step forward as it could be used to provide networking to a large pool of virtual machines, compute, and storage. Floodlight adoption increased by evolution of OpenStack and OpenStack adopters. This gave Floodlight greater popularity and applicability than other controllers that came before. Most of the controllers that came after Floodlight also supported OpenStack integration.

Floodlight is still supported and developed by community and Big Switch networks, and it is a base for Big Cloud Fabric (the Big Switch's commercial SDN controller).

There are other open source SDN controllers that are introduced such as Trema (ruby-based from NEC), Ryu (supported by NTT), FlowER, LOOM, and the recent OpenMUL.

The following table shows the current open source SDN controllers:

Active open source SDN controller	Non-active open source SDN controllers
Floodlight	Beacon
OpenContrail	FlowER
OpenDaylight	NOX
LOOM	NodeFlow
OpenMUL	
ONOS	
POX	
Ryu	
Trema	

OpenDaylight

OpenDaylight started in early 2013, and it was originally led by IBM and Cisco. It was a new collaborative open source project. OpenDaylight is hosted under Linux Foundation and it draws support and interest from many developers and adopters. OpenDaylight is a platform to provide common foundations and a robust array of services for SDN environments. OpenDaylight uses a controller model that supports OpenFlow as well as other southbound protocols. It is the first open source controller capable of employing non-OpenFlow proprietary control protocols, which eventually lets OpenDaylight to integrate with modern and multi-vendor networks.

The first release of OpenDaylight was in February 2014 with the code name Hydrogen, followed by Helium in September 2014. The Helium release was significant because it marked a change in direction for the platform that has influenced the way subsequent controllers have been architected. The main change was in the service abstraction layer, which is the part of the controller platform that resides just above the southbound protocols, such as OpenFlow, isolating them from the northbound side and where the applications reside.

Hydrogen used an **API-driven Service Abstraction Layer** (**AD-SAL**), which had limitations, specifically it meant the controller needed to know about every type of device in the network AND have an inventory of drivers to support them.

Helium introduced a **Model-driven service abstraction layer** (**MD-SAL**), which meant the controller didn't have to account for all the types of equipment installed in the network, allowing it to manage a wide range of hardware and southbound protocols.

The Helium release made the framework much more agile and adaptable to changes in the applications; an application could now request changes to the model, which would be received by the abstraction layer and forwarded to the network devices.

The OpenDaylight platform built on this advancement in its third release, Lithium, was introduced in June of 2015. This release focused on broadening the programmability of the network, enabling organizations to create their own service architectures to deliver dynamic network services in a cloud environment, and craft intent-based policies.

The Lithium release was worked on by more than 400 individuals, and contributions from Big Switch Networks, Cisco, Ericsson, HP, NEC, and so on, making it one of the fastest growing open source projects ever. The fourth release, Beryllium, came out in February of 2016 and the most recent fifth release, Boron, was released in September 2016.

Many vendors have built and developed commercial SDN controller solutions based on OpenDaylight. Each product has enhanced or added features to OpenDaylight to have some differentiating factor. The use of OpenDaylight in different vendor products are:

- A base, but also sell a commercial version with additional proprietary functionality-for example: Brocade, Ericsson, Ciena, and so on
- Part of their infrastructure in their Network as a Service (or XaaS) offerings-for example: Telstra, IBM, and so on
- Elements for use in their solution-for example: ConteXtream (now part of HP)

Open Networking Operating System (**ONOS**), which was open sourced in December 2014, is focused on serving the needs of service providers. It is not as widely adopted as OpenDaylight; ONOS has been finding success and gaining momentum around WAN use cases. ONOS is backed by numerous organizations including AT&T, Cisco, Fujitsu, Ericsson, Ciena, Huawei, NTT, SK Telecom, NEC, and Intel, many of whom are also participants in and supporters of OpenDaylight.

Apart from open source SDN controllers, there are many commercial, proprietary controllers available on the market. Products such as VMware NSX, Cisco APIC, Big Switch Big Cloud Fabric, HP VAN, and NEC ProgrammableFlow are examples of commercial and proprietary products.

The following table lists the commercially available controllers and their relationship to OpenDaylight:

ODL-based	ODL-friendly	Non-ODL-based
Avaya	Cyan (acquired by Ciena)	Big Switch
Brocade	HP	Juniper
Ciena	NEC	Cisco
ConteXtream (HP)	Nuage	Plexxi
Coriant		PLUMgrid
Ericsson		Pluribus
Extreme		Sonus
Huawei (also ships non-ODL controller)		VMware NSX

Core features of SDN

Regardless of an open source or a proprietary SDN platform, there are core features and capabilities that require the SDN platform to support. These capabilities include:

- **Fabric programmability**: Providing the ability to redirect traffic, apply filters to packets (dynamically), and leverage templates to streamline the creation of custom applications. Ensuring northbound APIs allows the control information centralized in the controller available to be changed by SDN applications. This will ensure that the controller can dynamically adjust the underlying network to optimize traffic flows to use the least expensive path, take into consideration varying bandwidth constraints, and meet the **quality of service** (**QoS**) requirements.

- **Southbound protocol support**: Enabling the controller to communicate to switches and routers and manipulate and optimize how they manage the flow of traffic. Currently OpenFlow is the most standard protocol used between different networking vendors, while there are other southbound protocols that can be used. An SDN platform should support different versions of OpenFlow in order to provide compatibility with different switching equipments.

- **External API support**: Ensuring the controller can be used within the varied orchestration and cloud environments such as VMware vSphere, OpenStack, and so on. By using APIs the orchestration platform can communicate with the SDN platform in order to publish network policies. For example, VMware vSphere shall talk to the SDN platform to extend the **virtual distributed switches** (**vDS**) from virtual environment to the physical underlay network without any requirement from an network engineer to configure the network.

- **Centralized monitoring and visualization**: Since the SDN controller has a full visibility over the network, it can offer end-to-end visibility of the network and centralized management to improve overall performance, simplify the identification of issues, and accelerate troubleshooting. The SDN controller will be able to discover and present a logical abstraction of all the physical links in the network, also it can discover and present a map of connected devices (MAC addresses), which are related to virtual or physical devices connected to the network. The SDN controller support monitoring protocols, such as syslog, snmp, and APIs in order to integrate with third-party management and monitoring systems.

- **Performance**: Performance in an SDN environment mainly depends on how fast the SDN controller fills the flow tables of SDN enabled switches. Most SDN controllers pre-populate the flow tables on switches to minimize the delay. When an SDN enabled switch receives a packet that doesn't find a matching entry in its flow table, it sends the packet to the SDN controller in order to find where the packet needs to get forwarded to. A robust SDN solution should ensure that the number of requests from switches are minimum and the SDN controller doesn't become a bottleneck in the network.

- **High availability and scalability**: Controllers must support high availability clusters to ensure reliability and service continuity in case of failure of a controller. Clustering in the SDN controller expands to scalability. A modern SDN platform should support scalability in order to add more controller nodes with load balancing in order to increase the performance and availability. Modern SDN controllers support clustering across multiple different geographical locations.

- **Security**: Since all switches communicate with SDN controller, the communication channel needs to be secured to ensure unauthorized devices doesn't compromise the network. SDN controller should secure the southbound channels, use encrypted messaging, and mutual authentication to provide access control. Apart from that the SDN controller must implement preventive mechanisms to prevent from denial of services attacks. Also deployment of authorization levels and level controls for multi-tenant SDN platforms is a key requirement.

Apart from the aforementioned features SDN controllers are likely to expand their function in future. They may become a network operating system and change the way we used to build networks with hardware, switches, SFPs, and gigs of bandwidth. The future will look more software defined, as the silicon and hardware industry has already delivered their promises for high performance networking chips of 40G, 100G. The industry needs more time to digest the new hardware and silicons and refresh the equipment with new gears supporting 10 times the current performance.

SDN use cases

This topic is very crucial, as in many cases stakeholders think why do they have to invest in SDN? What can SDN provide that the legacy network cannot? That's a valid question to ask.

There are multiple good use cases where SDN can add value:

- **A network operating system**: The SDN platform can act as a network operating system, providing packet delivery to other applications. SDN is a platform and allows other applications to drive, use the network for their specific requirements. Always remember that SDN doesn't do any packet delivery on its own, but it requires SDN applications (many of them) to define how packets needs to get delivered in a network.
- **Network Access Control**: One of the SDN use cases is NAC. The SDN controller can identify the newly connected devices and checks what this new device is, and what it needs to access and push the flow settings back to the SDN enabled switches. This method eliminates the use of 802.1x and VLAN assignments.

This diagram illustrates the use of SDN to enforce **Network Admission Control (NAC)** :

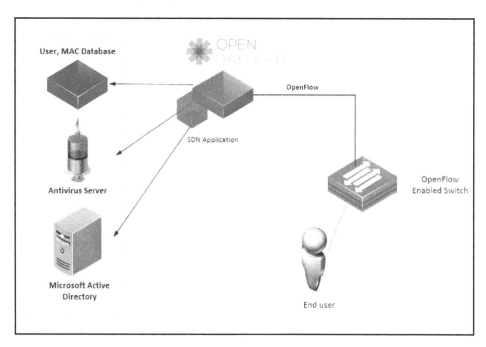

- **Anycast applications**: Anycast applications are referred to as distributed systems, which are built with multipole service nodes in a network. For example, streaming servers and file and object servers. With the change of the way application servers are built to a scale-out model, most modern service applications architecture is based on a distributed scale out model that all operates independently. An SDN platform is able to deliver the user requests to the closest, or better saying the best service node of an application. Other than being close there are other parameters such as load, bandwidth, and data availability. As an example an object storage platform might have multiple service nodes distributed in different location in the network and all working at the same time, using a single IP address. SDN networks will be able to understand where the service nodes are located (connected to which switch at what port) and will route the client requests to a particular network node that is considered as its best choice based on different parameters.
- **Integration with private cloud (VMware, OpenStack)**: With increased use of VMware vSphere and OpenStack in data centers, the need to integrate the network with cloud infrastructure is increasing. An SDN network can get integrated with cloud application and provide the ability to create virtual networks, tenant isolation, and even create overlay networks using VXLAN. Also it can support service chaining to insert L4-L7 services.

  The controller is the key component to integrate with cloud application via APIs.

- **Virtual CPE and virtual CE**: In a service provider environment, normally service providers install a dedicated *router* in each customer premises, which is always a rigid expensive box forced to clients. With the introduction of SDN, many service providers found this momentum and started using the opportunity window in order to build their SDN CPE, moving out from a dedicated router, replacing it with a commodity hardware (x86), which can run multiple virtual machines for **network functions virtualization** (**NFV**). AT&T and NTT have been successful in this area while others such as Verizon are also building their portfolio. Using SDN, the service provider will be able to use an edge SD-WAN enabled virtual machine to connect the customer to the network.

Another change in WAN and SD-WAN is the increase of reliability of consumer grade Internet connections. Many organizations prefer to use multiple cheap, high bandwidth Internet links instead of using an expensive limited bandwidth MPLS connection from their service provider. To answer this trend, which leads to popping up of SD-WAN products and vendors, service providers started to standardize a provisioning method of delivering an MPLS link and a (or more) Internet links to clients, which is called local Internet breakout. SD-WAN utilizes the local Internet breakout to build a secure tunnel to service provider networks and runs an SDN software with enough intelligence to understand what traffic should be routed via MPLS and via the Internet link.

SD-WAN is currently started to boom and there are many vendors such as Silver Peak, Riverbed, VeloCloud, Citrix, and so on, providing competitive and interesting products to enable enterprises to reduce their WAN costs and increase the quality of services.

* **Service providers**: In a service provider network where there are multiple geographical routers to provide backbone connectivity to clients, an SDN enabled network allows injecting and overriding the policies over the provider routers. In service provider networks the southbound protocols are normally BGP-PCEP, which is being promoted and used in many SP proof of concept installations. With SDN, a service provider will be able to override the MPLS or BGP decisions and route the specific traffic in a different way other than what has been determined by routing protocol. Cisco has done some progress in this area, remember that Cisco is one of the contributors to OpenDaylight and in fact the ODL web interface (Next) is donated by Cisco. You can find the Cisco service provider SDN example here:

```
https://github.com/CiscoDevNet/opendaylight-sample-apps
```

```
https://developer.cisco.com/site/opendaylight/discover/odl-at-
cisco/build-apps-on-top-of-odl/
```

Core differentiator between SDN controllers

Although the SDN concept is still young and it is still within the hype, as you realized there are multiple SDN controllers and platforms available on the market. The available solutions in the market have different features and capabilities, which you need to understand before deciding on which controller or platform to choose and build your network on it. There are also products that use the marketing buzz words of SDN and try to pitch a legacy solution, which you need to be careful while evaluating them.

I have collected some key differentiators of SDN platforms and will take you through each as follows:

- **Fabric or overlay**: This is one of the most important attributes to look at and make the decision. Overlays are also considered as key drivers for network virtualization. Overlays are not dependent on underlay networks, meaning an overlay SDN can build an overlay SDN on top of a mesh IP underlay. Looking at SDN products in the market, some of them are basically an overlay, such as VMware NSX and Juniper Contrail. On the other hand the SDN fabric products are a full SDN aware underlay, which means that the SDN controller can communicate with all SDN switches in the network and control and program their flow and CAM tables. Solutions such as Cisco ACI and OpenDaylight are examples of a full fabric SDN platform.
- **Open source versus proprietary**: This attribute should only be important if you are considering extending the controller or have proprietary modifications specific to your business. In general and based on our studies, service providers are more interested in open source solutions as they use their tools and resources to productize and provide an SDN as a service to their customers. AT&T and NTT are good examples of service providers who took OpenDaylight and build their offerings based on that.

  On the other hand, enterprises are interested in commercial and business supported products with specific SLA and support levels. Enterprises use SDN to run their business better. They are not interested to downgrade their network from a legacy L2/L3 to an SDN platform with no business case. Based on our studies, many enterprises have looked at and adopted Cisco ACI, VMWare NSX, and Big Switch Big Cloud Fabric, which are good commercial SDN platforms. When looking at commercial products, you need to always be careful about the vendor lock-in and find a solution that lets you scale and expand or even change your controller without impacting the switches in the network.

Openness in the SDN platform doesn't mean that you will be supported by the community. Commercial SDN controllers are based on OpenDaylight and are supported by companies such as Brocade and they are all open source as well as commercially supported.

- **Application ecosystem and maturity of northbound APIs**: SDN don't forget that an SDN platform doesn't work without SDN applications. SDN controller is a platform to run SDN applications. Without SDN applications the network doesn't forward any packet. A very basic SDN application is L2 switching, where you need to load and run the L2 application on a controller in order to have the very basic L2 switching (MAC learning) on your network. This may seem funny for some readers that the SDN has no built-in features; however, you should think that SDN is a methodology; it's a platform that allows you to build network applications and decide how you want the network to forward, route, or drop the packets.

   Going back to our topic, while looking for an SDN solution you should consider choosing a SDN controller that provides a rich, complete, and developer friendly application environment. Many SDN platforms support Yet Another Next Generation (YANG) language, which is used for data modeling and also it is used as payload for NETCONF protocol.

- **Where to deploy**: You should consider your main use cases and compare against the capabilities and features of the SDN controllers in the market. For example, a controller designed for a campus network is not a good fit for a data center application. Or an SDN platform that doesn't have any plugin or capability to integrate with OpenStack is not a good fit for deploying in a OpenStack environment.

   You should take into consideration your business use cases to find the best fit platform and controller for your business.

- **Compatibility, reliability, and maturity of the platform**: Although the SDN platform is a game changer in networking world, but it is still in its early stages and it's hard to find a solution that is deployed and worked for couple to years or find strong case studies. This is one of the key show stoppers for many enterprises trying to find a SDN solution that has a proven track record and has been deployed with multiple clients. CIOs and procurement look for proven solutions that have been used or certified.

Even standard protocols such as OpenFlow or OVSDB have different implementation between vendors and they might not be compatible with each other (for example, an OpenFlow switch from vendor A may not be compatible with an SDN controller from vendor B). These are challenges that require your attention prior to deciding which SDN platform you are going to live with.

- **Smoothness of integration into orchestration platforms**: Almost every commercial controller and many open source controllers provide OpenStack support in the data center. If you have a data center deployment and have picked a specific cloud management or orchestration platform (OpenStack, VMware vRealize, CloudStack, or others), check with the vendor or evaluate the open source distribution to ensure seamless integration into your orchestration environment.

- **Integration with cloud and orchestration platforms**: Nowadays almost every private cloud platform is built on VMware or some flavor of OpenStack or CloudStack. The SDN platform in data centers needs to integrate with OpenStack of VMware vSphere, and you need to check and ensure the level of integration and capabilities of the SDN solution with your choice of orchestration platform. Normally in data center environments, the SDN platforms provide direct integration with VMware vSphere and the SDN solution becomes part of the VMware virtual network and virtual distributed switches. The same applies to OpenStack and SDN solutions that will integrate with OpenStack via some kind of plugin (such as ML2 or other kinds of integrations).

    If you are planning your SDN platform for a campus topology you need to check with your orchestration and policy tool about the integration with the SDN platform. Many SDN platforms provide such orchestration and tools along with their products; however, if you are using a specific orchestration tool you need to ensure how it is going to integrate with your SDN platform.

- **Open APIs**: Regardless of being open source of a proprietary closed source solution, you need to ensure that the SDN platform provides some kind of open APIs for integration with other tools. Other tools such as monitoring, orchestration tools, billing, abstract UIs, compute and storage tools, and so on. Normally APIs are not considered as a critical factor to make decisions and normally there is no day zero requirements for APIs, however, after deployment of the SDN platform slowly you will realize the requirement for integration with other systems. A very basic example is the cloud providers, where they need to have a single web interface for customers in order to create their tenant networks, subnets, and service insertion.

- A customer should be able to use the web interface of the platform to design and build his virtual network, add virtual routers, firewalls, and load balancers in their network while it is isolated and doesn't disturb other tenants or user traffic.

You should understand that the SDN market is still in its early stages. OpenDaylight has helped to change the landscape and also other open source projects such as ONOS OpenContrail and Calico which are mainly driving use cases is service provider networks.

You need to find the real need for going the SDN way and understand the capabilities of each SDN platform to make the correct decision. Remember in order to move to SDN you don't need to migrate everything and throw away your whole legacy network, No, you can build a SDN network for a POD (in a data center) or a building (in a campus) or a path (in a service provider).

Current SDN controllers

In this section, I'm putting the different SDN controllers in a table. This will help you to understand the current market players in SDN and how OpenDaylight relates to them:

Vendors/product	Based on OpenDaylight?	Commercial/open source	Description
Brocade SDN controller	Yes	Commercial	It's a commercial version of OpenDaylight, fully supported and with extra reliable modules.
Cisco APIC	No	Commercial	Cisco **Application Policy Infrastructure Controller** (**APIC**) is the unifying automation and management point for the **Application Centric Infrastructure** (**ACI**) data center fabric. Cisco uses APIC controller and Nexus 9k switches to build the fabric. Cisco uses OpFlex as the main southbound protocol.

Ericsson SDN controller	Yes	Commercial	Ericsson's SDN controller is a commercial (hardened) version OpenDaylight SDN controller. Domain specific control applications that use the SDN controller as a platform form the basis of the three commercial products in our SDN controller portfolio.
Juniper OpenContrial /Contrail	No	Both OpenContrail is open source, and Contrail itself is a commercial product.	Juniper Contrail Networking is an open SDN solution that consists of Contrail controller, Contrail vRouter, an analytics engine, and published northbound APIs for cloud and NFV. OpenContrail is also available for free from Juniper. Contrail promotes and uses MPLS in data centers.
NEC Programmable Flow	No	Commercial	NEC provides its own SDN controller and switches. The NEC SDN platform is one of the choices of enterprises and it has lots of traction and some case studies.
Avaya SDN Fx controller	Yes	Commercial	Based on OpenDaylight, bundled as a solution package.

Big Cloud Fabric	No	Commercial	Big Switch networks solution is based on the Floodlight open source project. Big Cloud Fabric is a robust, clean SDN controller and it works with bare metal white box switches. Big Cloud Fabric includes Switch Light OS, which is a switch operating system that can be loaded on white box switches with Broadcom Trident 2 or Tomahawk silicons. The benefit of Big Cloud Fabric is that you are not bound to any hardware and you can use bare metal switches from any vendor.
Ciena's Agility	Yes	Commercial	Ciena's Agility multilayer WAN controller is built atop the open-source baseline of the OpenDaylight Project-an open, modular framework created by a vendor-neutral ecosystem (rather than a vendor-centric ego-system) that will enable network operators to source network services and applications from both Ciena's Agility and others.
HP VAN (Virtual Application Network)	No	Commercial	The building block of the HP open SDN ecosystem, the controller allows third-party developers to deliver innovative SDN solutions.
Huawei Agile controller	Yes and No (based on editions)	Commercial	Huawei's SDN controller that integrates as a solution with Huawei enterprise switches.

Nuage	No	Commercial	Nuage Networks VSP provides SDN capabilities for clouds of all sizes. It is implemented as a non-disruptive overlay for all existing virtualized and non-virtualized server and network resources.
Pluribus Netvisor	No	Commercial	Netvisor Premium and Open Netvisor Linux are distributed network operating systems. Open Netvisor integrates a traditional, interoperable networking stack (L2/L3/VXLAN) with an SDN distributed controller that runs in every switch of the fabric.
VMware NSX	No	Commercial	VMware NSX is an Overlay type of SDN, which currently works with VMware vSphere. The plan is to support OpenStack in the future. VMware NSX also has a built-in firewall, router, and L4 load balancers allowing micro segmentation.

OpenDaylight as an SDN controller

In previous sections, we went through the role of the SDN controller, and a brief history of ODL. ODL is a modular open SDN platform that allows developers to build any network or business application on top of it to drive the network in the way they want.

Currently OpenDaylight has reached its fifth release (Boron, which is the fifth element in the periodic table). ODL releases are named based on periodic table elements, started from the first release, Hydrogen. ODL has a six month release period, with many developers working on expanding the ODL, two releases per year is expected from the community.

For technical readers to understand it more clearly, the following diagram will help:

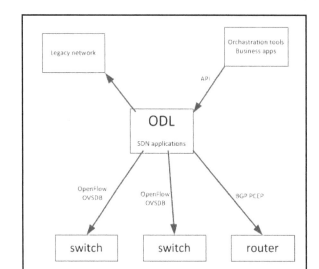

The ODL platform has a broad set of use cases for multivendor, brown field, green fields, service providers, and enterprises. ODL is a foundation for networks of the future.

Service providers are using ODL to migrate their services to a software enabled level with automatic service delivery and coming out of a *circuit-based* mindset of service delivery.

Also they work on providing a virtualized CPE with NFV support in order to provide flexible offerings.

Enterprises use ODL for many use cases, from data center networking, Cloud and NFS, network automation and resource optimization, visibility, control, to deploying a full SDN campus network.

ODL uses an MD-SAL, which makes it very scalable and lets it incorporate new applications and protocols faster. We will cover more details about MD-SAL in upcoming chapters where we will dive into ODL.

ODL supports multiple standard and proprietary southbound protocols, for example, with full support of OpenFlow and OVSDB, ODL can communicate with any standard hardware (or even the virtual switches such as **Open vSwitch** (**OVS**) supporting such protocols). With such support, ODL can be deployed and used in multivendor environments and control hardware from different vendors from a single console no matter what the vendor and what device it is, as long as they support standard southbound protocols.

ODL uses a micro service architecture model, which allows users to control applications, protocols, and plugins while deploying SDN applications. Also ODL is able to manage the connection between external consumers and providers.

The following diagram explains the ODL footprint and different components and projects within the ODL:

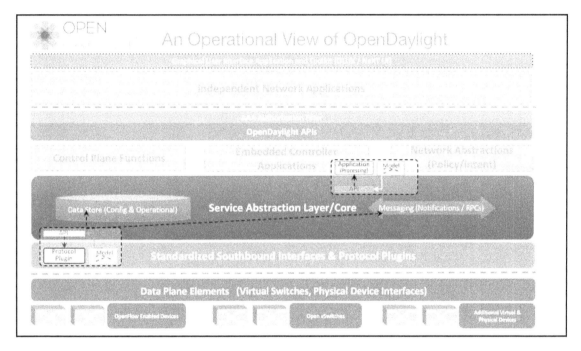

Microservices architecture

ODL stores its YANG data structure in a common data store and uses messaging infrastructure between different components to enable a model-driven approach to describe the network and functions.

In ODL MD-SAL, any SDN application can be integrated as a service and then loaded into the SDN controller. These services (apps) can be chained together in any number and ways to match the application needs.

This concept allows users to only install and enable the protocols and services they need, which makes the system light and efficient.

Also services and applications created by users can be shared among others in the ecosystem since the SDN application deployment for ODL follows a modular design.

ODL supports multiple southbound protocols. OpenFlow and OpenFlow extensions such as **Table Type Patterns** (**TTP**), as well as other protocols including NETCONF, BGP/PCEP, CAPWAP, and OVSDB. Also ODL supports the Cisco OpFlex protocol:

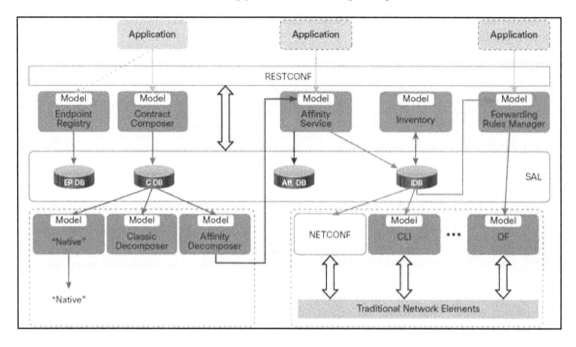

The ODL platform provides a framework for **Authentication, Authorization, and Accounting** (**AAA**), as well as automatic discovery and securing of network devices and controllers.

Another key area in security is to use encrypted and authenticated communication through southbound protocols with switches and routers within the SDN domain. Most southbound protocols support security encryption mechanisms.

Traditional networking terms and features in the world of SDN

As a network professional, you will have been involved with day to day networking tasks. Tasks such as creating and managing VLANs and ports, trunking (802.1q), managing spanning trees, link aggregation, routing, accessing lists, troubleshooting, and logging.

Let's have a look at what happens to these fundamentals in SDN:

- **Spanning tree**: Spanning tree has been always a painful protocol to manage for all network professionals. Spanning tree is a complex (when it comes to per VLAN, MSTP, RSTAP, compatibility, and so on) mechanism to create a loop-free layer 2 network. Spanning tree is not efficient as it disabled the links that may create a loop.

    > In recent years, many organizations have tried to eliminate the spanning tree by migrating to a full layer 3 routed fabric or using proprietary multi-chassis link aggregation technologies.

    > Anyhow, the good news is that in SDN, there is no need for spanning trees. The SDN controller, as the brain of the whole network knows how each switch in the network should send and receive packets in order to have a complete loop-free network.

    > Also remember that BUM is managed and handled by the SDN controller, which reduces the risk of loops.

    > The required features of spanning trees are also included in the L2 switching application of ODL.

- **VLANs**: Let's review our traditional understanding of VLANs. A **virtual LAN (VLAN)** is a method to divide a basic layer 2 switch into multiple standalone switches. Ports in different VLANs will not be able to communicate with each other. Technically the VLAN concept is implemented in the switch's silicon, and doesn't allow any entry in the TCAM table where the source and destination ports belong to different VLANs (that's a simple implementation in silicon).

    > In the world of SDN, as all forwarding is controlled by the SDN controller, the concept of VLAN is managed by the SDN controller. In ODL it is managed by the L2 application.

- **Trunking (802.1q)**: Trunking and the concept of tagged and untagged frames exists in SDN very similar to the traditional world. In traditional layer 2, a switch was able to send a packet untagged (access-port) or with a tag that can only be the VLAN ID of that frame.

In the world of SDN, a switch will send a frame with any 802.1q tag, which the SDN controller decides. For example, a switch might receive a frame with VLAN tag of 100, and then sends it out with the VLAN ID of 200. This is something that is beyond the concepts of traditional 802.1q and VLANs.

- **Link aggregation**: Link aggregation uses standard protocols such as LACP. Link aggregation exists in SDN similar to the traditional networking world. Link aggregation is supported by most SDN controllers, as well as ODL. ODL includes specific modules to support link aggregation.

  Technically, when you configure two ports as a link aggregation using the ODL interface, the ODL SDN controller sends the required configuration to the related switch using a southbound protocol (for example, NETCONF) and tells that switch hardware to configure the ports in link aggregation mode.

- **Routing**: Routing between the switches within the SDN domain is not required. It is managed by the SDN controller. However, the SDN controller supports routing protocols such as BGP and OSPF to communicate outside of the world of SDN.

Summary

In this chapter, we learned about SDN and why it is important. We reviewed the SDN controller products, the ODL history, as well as core features of SDN controllers and market leader controllers. We managed to look at aspects of SDN in detail such as BUM and flow tables and, at the end, we reviewed how the traditional concepts and protocols function in the world of SDN.

In the next chapter, we will start looking at ODL components and modules.

2
Overview of OpenDaylight

This chapter is about the OpenDaylight project and its components, history, and versions. It is a complex project based on multiple components that are tightly integrated. The aim of this chapter is to make you familiar with the architecture of OpenDaylight so you have a better understanding of how OpenDaylight works and the logic behind it.

We will learn the following topics here:

- Overview of OpenDaylight components
- OpenDaylight modules
- The NeXt UI

Overview of OpenDaylight components

As discussed in `Chapter 1`, *Introduction to SDN - Transformation from Legacy to SDN*, ODL is a modular platform for software-defined networking. It is not a single piece of software; it's a combination of all integrated projects under one umbrella.

ODL has a board and chair persons; they decide the priority of each project. This team consists of a group of developers or business leaders who sponsor projects and drive the need and motivation required to cater to specific requirements.

Each project has a project proposal; this is the first step when it comes to launching a feature in ODL.

The structure of ODL is similar to that of OpenStack. The difference is that OpenStack consists of different projects that are managed by different project groups.

The following map shows a high level view of ODL projects. We will look at each one of them so you can understand their features and functions.

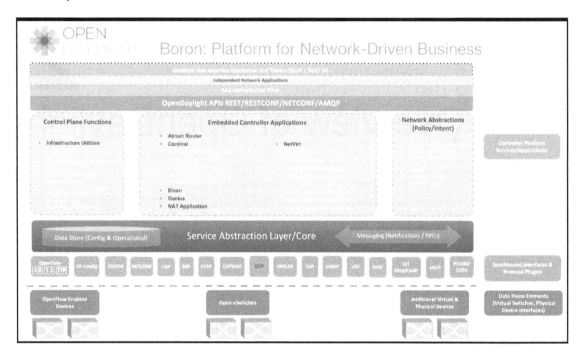

Some of the projects are called **Main**; these are projects listed as the main components of ODL. Some others are more niche projects; they are not similar to Main and are designed to deliver a specific need, probably for a specific use case.

The following table summarizes the current ODL modules and their use:

Module name	Type	Use
AAA	Security	Authentication authorization accounting module; provides AAA security service
ALTO	Networking	**Application-Layer Traffic Optimization** (**ALTO**); provides network maps and cost maps

Armoury	Core	The controller sometimes needs to request the workload manager to compute resources and/or get **Network Function** (**NF**) (physical or virtual) orchestrations to provide its services
Atrium	Core	SDN distribution packaging
BGP LS PCEP	Networking	BGP PCEP southbound module
BIER	Networking	**Bit Indexed Explicit Replication(BIER)**; BIER introduces a method for multicast flow forwarding without storing states in every node along the multicast path
CAPWAP	Networking	**Control and Provisioning of Wireless Access Points** (**CAPWAP**) is a southbound protocol for managing and provisioning of wireless access points.
Cardinal	Management	A monitoring service
Centinel	Management	A distributed, reliable framework for efficiently collecting, aggregating, and sinking streaming data across persistence DB and stream analyzers
Controller Shield	Security	The controller shield project aims at creating a repository called the **Unified Security Plugin** (**USecPlugin**); this is a general purpose plugin that provides controller security information to northbound applications. This information will be collected by the plugin and may be used to configure firewalls and create IP blacklists for the network. With information, we mean collating the source of different attacks reported in southbound plugins, suspected controller intrusions, or information about other trusted controllers in the network.

Daexim	Management	This is a target use case related to system upgrade; it enables the development of importing or exporting data administrative procedures.
DIDM	Networking	**Device Identification Driver Management (DIDM)**
DluxApps	Management	A web UI
EMAN	Management	Refers to energy management
FaaS	Networking	In general, FaaS aims to create a common abstraction layer on top of a physical network
Federation	Management	In order to allow multiple ODL clusters to cooperate (federate) for a given application, there is a need to allow state exchange between ODL clusters federation helps us do this.
Genius	Core	The genius project provides generic network interfaces, utilities, and services. Any ODL application can use it to achieve interference-free coexistence with other applications.
Group-Based Policy (**GBP**)	Management	This is an intent-based system for a network. It implements a system based on *what you want*, that is, it offers services based on user requests.
Honeycomb	Management	Honeycomb exposes bridge domain models via f YANG. The purpose of this project is to build a controller app that allows OpenDaylight to build virtual bridge domains that can then be configured across multiple honeycomb agents.
Infrastructure utilities	Core	This project offers various utilities and infrastructures for other projects to use
IoTDM	Management	The **IoT Data Management** (**IoTDM**) project is an open source implementation of one M2M running on OpenDaylight

JSON-RPC2.0	Core	JSON-RPC2.0 aims to provide binding for an ODL data store
Kafka producer	Management	The Kafka producer plugin is a northbound plugin that allows you to stream data from OpenDaylight to a Kafka endpoint on real-time basis.
L2 switch	Networking	Layer 2 switch
LACP	Networking	LACP
MD-SAL	Core	**Model Driven Service Abstraction Layer** (**MD-SAL**) is one the famous frameworks for building applications for ODL.
Messaging4Transport:	Core	Implementation of ActiveMQ for northbound APIs
NATApp Plugin	Networking	
NEMO	Management	**Northbound Interface** (**NBI**)
NETCONF	Networking	Southbound NETCONF protocol
NetIDE	Management	**Network Engine** (**NetIDE**) enables portability and cooperation inside a single network; it uses a client or server multicontroller architecture to do this
NetVirt	Networking	NetVirt is a network virtualization solution. It includes the following components among others: Open vSwitch-based virtualization for software switches, hardware VTEP for hardware switches, and service function chaining support within a virtualized environment.
Network Intent Composition:	Networking	Network Intent Composition enables the OpenDaylight controller to manage network services and resources based on describing the model and intent for network topology and policies. Intents are described to the controller through a new northbound interface.

NeutronNorthbound	Management	Northbound API for OpenStack's Neutron provides communication from the ODL drivers in OpenStack to the ODL's neutron service and saves the neutron models into ODL data store for other providers to use.
NeXt	Management	A web interface
OCP plugin	Management	Plugin for an open compute project
ODL Root Parent	Core	ODL Root Parent provides common settings for all the projects that participate in a simultaneous release
ODL-SDNi App	Core	The OpenDaylight SDN interface application project aims at enabling inter-SDN controller communication by developing SDNi
OF-CONFIG	Networking	OpenFlow
OpenDaylight Controller	Core	Refers to the controller itself. The controller also contains the MD-SAL clustering pieces which includes the clustered data store and the remote RPC broker
OpenDaylight Lisp Flow Mapping	Networking	Refers to network virtualization and overlay via LISP
OpenDaylight OFextensions Circuitsw	Networking	Using the extensions to the OpenFlow Protocol in support of circuit switching addendum to OpenFlow protocol specification (v1.0).
OpenDaylight OpenFlow Plugin:	Networking	OpenFlow southbound protocol
Openflow Protocol Library:Main	Networking	OpenFlow library
OpFlex	Networking	OpFlex southbound protocol
OVSDB Integration:Main	Networking	OVSDB southbound protocol
PacketCablePCMM:Main	Networking	Provides integration with the PCMM system

Persistence	Core	Persistence is a framework to implement application persistence logic for query-able and non-modeled data (also known as object stores)
Reservation	Networking	This project is meant to provide dynamic low level resource reservation so that users can get network as a service, connectivity, or a pool of resources (ports or bandwidth) for a specific period of time
Secure Network Bootstrapping	Networking	The **Secure Network Bootstrapping Infrastructure** (**SNBI**) project securely and automatically brings up an integrated set of network devices and controllers
Service Function Chaining	Networking	Service Function Chaining provides the ability to define an ordered list of a network service (for example, firewalls and load balancers)
SNMP Plugin	Management	The SNMP project addresses the need for a southbound plugin that allows applications and controller services to interact with devices
SNMP4SDN	Management	
Spectrometer	Management	The main purpose of Spectrometer is to deliver transparent statistics of contributions to OpenDaylight
TCPMD5	Security	The goal of this library is to provide access to the RFC-2385 TCP MD5 signature option in operating systems that support it in their TCP stack
TransportPCE	Core	TransportPCE describes an application running on top of the OpenDaylight controller

TSDR	Networking	**Time Series Data Repository** (**TSDR**) in ODL contains a time series data repository and a set of time series data services such as MD-SAL service modules; these modules collect, store, query, and maintain time series data in an OpenDaylight deployment environment
Unimgr	Networking	User Network Interface Manager is a project of OpenDaylight that provides data models and APIs that enable software applications and service orchestrators to configure and provision connectivity services. In particular, it refers to Carrier Ethernet services, as defined by MEF Forum, in both physical and virtual network elements.
USC	Security	**Unified Secure Channel** (**USC**) is a **Software-Defined Networking** (**SDN**) component that uses unified secure channels to enable communication between SDN controllers and enterprise network elements
VPNService	Networking	
VTN	Networking	VTN provides network virtualization support
YANG PUBSUB	Management	YANG PUBSUB allows subscriptions to be placed on targeted subtrees of YANG data stores that reside on remote devices
YANG Tools:Main	Management	YANG Tools is an infrastructure module of OpenDaylight that provides the necessary tooling and libraries to support NETCONF and YANG on Java-based projects and applications in OpenDaylight. **Model Driven SAL**(**MD-SAL**) for controller (which uses YANG as it's modeling language) and Netconf/OFConfig plugins are example projects that use YANG Tools.

YANG IDE	Management	The YANG IDE subproject provides an Eclipse plugin that can be used to create, edit, and view YANG model files

OpenDaylight modules

As learned earlier, OpenDaylight is a modular platform for integrating multiple plugins and modules. There are many plugins and modules built for OpenDaylight. Some are in production, while some are still under development. We have collected a list of important OpenDaylight modules here, and we will describe their functions.

Authentication, Authorization, and Accounting

Project type: Main

This is also referred to as triple A , It is an implementation of an enterprise-level identity provider for the OpenDaylight controller.

AAA projects have a larger domain that includes not only authenticating the users accessing the ODL web interface, but also acting as an identity provider for ODL. If you are familiar with OpenStack, you'd know that it is similar to what a keystone project does in an OpenStack platform, although with some different features and capabilities.

Let's go back to the basic principles in order to become familiar with AAA. It stands for authentication, authorization, and accounting. It is a mechanism for gaining access control, defining who can access the system, and what resources they can access :

- **Authentication**: This means verifying the authenticity of the identity of both human and machine users that are independent of the choice of binding.
- **Authorization**: This means authorizing the specific user who has authentication to access all resources or levels of the system, including RPCs, notification subscriptions, and subsets of the data tree.
- **Accounting**: This means recording and accessing the records of an authenticated user who has accessed and used the system. Accounting has different parameters and can be viewed in the form of time of use, resources used, or amount of traffic transferred to the authenticated user.

AAA provides a pluggable mechanism for performing authentication authorization accounting functions. You will be able to use it via APIs within your SDN application or when using other integrated SDN applications.

Application-Layer Traffic Optimization (ALTO)

Project type: Main

ALTO is a protocol defined by IETF with functions to provide network information to applications.

Specifically, ALTO defines abstractions and services to provide simplified network views and network services to guide the application usage of network resources, including cost. It includes five services:

1. **Cost map service**: ALTO's cost map provides costs between defined groupings.
2. **Network map service**: This service provides aggregate information to ALTO clients in the form of ALTO network maps.
3. **Filtered map service**: This service allows ALTO clients to send a parameter-based query to an ALTO server and request for a more specific network map and/or cost map.
4. **Endpoint property service**: This service allows ALTO clients to look up properties for each individual endpoint.
5. **Endpoint cost service**: This service allows an ALTO server to return the costs of direct endpoints.

ALTO implementation in ODL includes both MD-SAL and AD-SAL models; it also includes services. The `alto-manager` is a command-line tool to generate network maps and cost maps using ALTO.

These services, the `alto-hosttracker` service for example, rely on the L2 switch module and generate a network map, a corresponding cost map, and the endpoint cost service.

BGP LS PCEP

Project type: Main

You are all familiar with **Border Gateway Protocol** (**BGP**). BGP is known more as a networking application than a protocol . For folks who are not familiar with BGP, it is a communication protocol between Internet routers, where connected networks are exchanged and how to reach each network is decided.

In the SDN world, as we have already learned, we move in a direction that helps us come out of the limitation of using legacy protocols. We don't want to use legacy protocols between the controller and switches within networks. We would like to use a method for direct programing of the fabric between the SDN controller and switches. However, in service provider networks, where they like to integrate a distributed MPLS or private IP VPN via SDN, there is very little chance to have large routers (such as Juniper T series or TX Matrix) with OpenFlow support.

BGP **Path Computation Element Protocol** (**PCEP**) is a southbound protocol used between the SDN controller and the routers in the network in order to override routing and forwarding tables (at a higher level).

ODL can use BGP PCEP as a southbound protocol to talk to routers. BGP PCEP is an extension of BGP that has support on specific routers.

BGP **Linkstate** (**LS**) is another BGP extension that allows BGP to distribute the link state information of routing protocols.

BGP PCEP has many use cases for service providers. It brings SP networks to a mid-generation state where the SDN controller will be able to influence the networks.

Bit Indexed Explicit Replication

Project type: Main

BIER is a mechanism to provide multicast routing in an SDN network. As you may know, in a legacy network, there are multicast delivery protocols in L2 and L3, such as PIM, IGMP, DVMRP, MSDP, and so on. These protocols run in a router or switch and help the network node build a state table of multicast flows where they need to be replicated. In SDN and OpenDaylight, multicast delivery is handled by the controller. None of the transit routers and switches need to build a per flow state table, as the controller provides the function and builds a global state table for multicast flows. This simplifies the configuration state of transit switches and routers.

Multicast packets enter a BIER domain via **Bit-Forwarding Ingress Router** (**BFIR**) and leave the domain via one or more **Bit-Forwarding Egress Routers** (**BFERs**).

When the packets enter the SDN domain, the ingress BEIR router adds a BIER header to the packet. This header is a bit string, where each bit represents exactly one BFER to forward the packet to. A set of BFERs to which the multicast packet needs to be forwarded is expressed by setting the bits that correspond to the routers in the BIER header.

The following diagram explains the BIER domain:

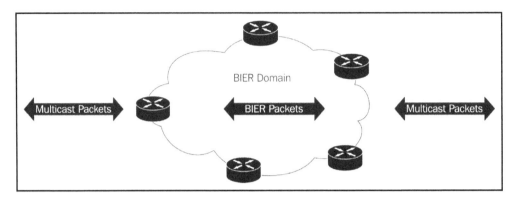

The following diagram explains the BFER header:

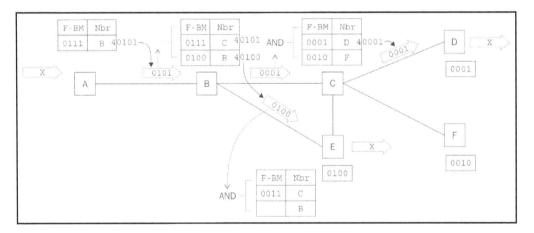

CAPWAP

Project type: Main

Yes, you got it right, CAPWAP or Control and Provisioning of Wireless Access points! It is a module to let ODL manage the Wireless network and access points. ODL uses CAPWAP as a southbound protocol to directly communicate with wireless access points.

The aim of CAPWAP is to support a basic implementation of the CAPWAP protocol. The message parser of the CAPWAP project can work with headers and message elements. It also supports DTLS encryption, but the implementation of DTLS is currently very limited.

It is one of the cool features of ODL and will be an enabler of wireless SDN in future, which will support both IOT applications and access to them.

Cardinal monitoring service

Project type: Main

Cardinal is OpenDaylight monitoring as a service component which allows ODL and software-defined network to be remotely monitored by a **Network Management System** (**NMS**). It provides a northbound REST API as well as SNMP (v2c, v3) to OpenDayLight.

Also, as a basic feature, it supports sending SNMP trap messages to trap receivers; this is similar to all other networking equipment. It also supports the basic security features of SNMP v3 with authentication and encryption and allows you to have secure communication between NMS and ODL.

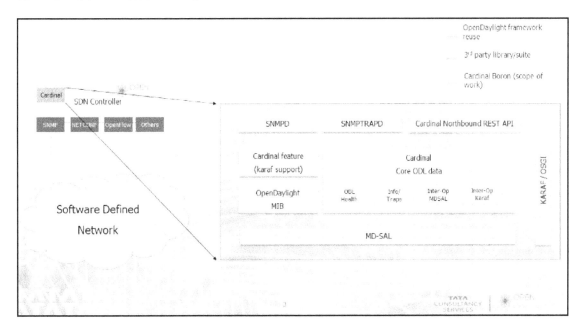

Controller shield - unified security

Project type: Main

Controller shield is a general purpose plugin that provides controller security information to northbound applications. ODL collects lots of security information from different sources, such as endpoints or flows, and reports them to a correlation system that can analyze and provide details about an attack. Such information can be used to manually or dynamically configure firewalls, IPS, and other security systems.

Unified security also deals with information about compromising the SDN controller security itself. The ODL SDN controller is the only brain behind the whole network; therefore, securing and protecting the SDN controller itself is one of the main tasks that needs to be planned in advanced, during deployment.

Controller security can be compromised via different methods, such as an SDN application, network, and peers. Controller shield can monitor and report suspicious activities and attacks to an SDN controller via east-west (another SDN controller trying to establish peering) or via a network element (attacker within the network):

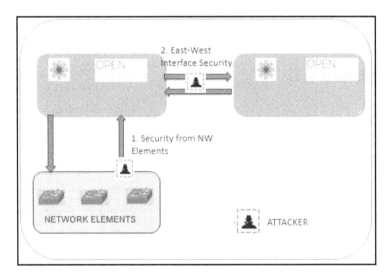

Device Identification Driver Management (DIDM)

Project type: Main

DIDM maintains a list of devices in the network and identifies what features and protocols they support. For example, it identifies all OpenFlow-enabled switches or routers that support BGP PCEP. It helps the ODL ensure that a correct southbound protocol is used to communicate with a device and that the commands and requests sent to this specific device are valid and supported by the device. Remember that ODL is a **Model-Driven SAL** (**MD-SAL**). It works with abstractions and orchestrations. An SDN application doesn't know about the underlying southbound protocol used for communicating with a specific switch, it doesn't even know whether that switch supports OpenFlow version 1.o0 or 1.3 or NETCONF.

The DIDM project creates a logical infrastructure to support the following functions:

- **Discovery**: The infrastructure helps identify that a device exists in the controller management domain, and connectivity to the device can be established. For devices that support the OpenFlow protocol, the existing discovery mechanism in OpenDaylight suffices. Devices that do not support OpenFlow will need to be discovered through manual means, such as the operator entering device information via GUI or REST API.
- **Identification**: This refers to determination of the device type.
- **Driver registration**: This refers to registration of device drivers as routed RPCs.
- **Synchronization**: This refers to collection of device information, device configuration, and link (connection) information.
- **Defining data models for common features**: Data models will be defined to perform common features, such as VLAN configuration. For example, applications can configure a VLAN by writing VLAN data to the data store as specified by the common data model.
- **Defining RPCs for common features**: Configuring VLANs and adjusting Flow mods are examples of features. RPCs will define the APIs for these tasks. Drivers implement tasks   for specific devices and support the APIs defined by the RPCs. There may be different driver implementations for different device types.

DluxApps the UI

Project type: Main

Dlux is the web user interface of ODL and is based on Angular JS. It consists of two logical parts, namely core and applications:

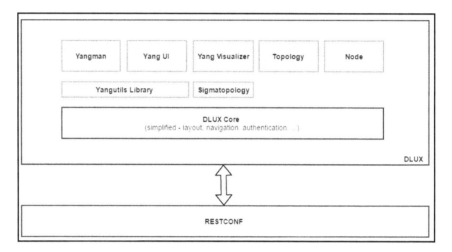

Core is a framework that provides basic functionalities, such as navigation, authentication, and so on. Applications are built on top of the core. The following applications are currently available as part of Dlux:

- **YANG UI**: This is a simple UI for interaction with the controller. It is based on Yang models, and it renders a form so that users can read or write data even if they have no knowledge of the models.
- **YANGMAN**: This is an advanced and more user-friendly YANG UI replacement.
- **YANG Visualizer**: This provides visualization of YANG models in graphical form.
- **Node**: This is a very simple inventory node manager.
- **Topology**: This is a very simple OpenFlow topology visualizer.

Energy management (EMAN)

Project type: Main

EMAN provides an energy management plugin for ODL. It's an energy management abstraction. It communicates with network switches and other equipment via southbound protocols and drives energy management parameters and protocols or standards. Remember that networking gears support energy management, fan speed, and reporting back energy utilization in different periods and intervals.

EMAN also provides a northbound interface for SDN applications and other external applications to interact with energy management of devices within the particular ODL SDN domain.

The information model is inherited from the SCTE 216 standard **Adaptive Power Systems Interface Specification** (**APSIS**), which in turn inherits definitions within the IETF EMAN document set.

Fabric As A Service

Project type: Main

FaaS is an interesting component of ODL. It creates a common abstraction layer on top of a physical network. This makes it easy for you to map the northbound API and the real physical network his mk according to their own needs even if they don't have too muc the real physical network .

SDN (**Software defined Networking**) allows users and administrators to define a logical network according to their own needs even if they don't have too much of information about the physical details or the vendor CLI commands. A network is an infrastructure that could provide network services, such as connectivity, QoS, and policy, to applications. The language used to define a networking infrastructure should be unified and simple. It should focus on networking and should only declare networking needs and nothing else.

FaaS defines the following top-level basic abstracted network primitives and presents them to users over northbound APIs:

- Logical switch
- Gateway
- Logical router
- Tunnel between the logical switch and logical router
- ACL

The common abstraction layer that FaaS provides builds a model of the physical network as a topology that consists of abstracted nodes and fabrics (physical or virtual).

Fabric is an abstraction; it is a portion of the network. Normally, it is within the same control plane and uses technologies such as VXLAN or VLAN. Every fabric offers a set of unified services as well as primitive constructs to create and manage a logical network based on user requirements.

For example, you can build an SDN application to use FaaS or create a VLAN between five racks in a data center. As a network programmer, you just need to declare how the fabric (in this example, layer 2 VLAN) should look. FaaS will do the rest. It will find out how the physical switches in the network are configured and which southbound protocols do they support (when it uses DIDM). After doing this, it will deliver an outcome which will be the VALN fabric you requested for.

Applications built on top of FaaS can use high-level primitives to build a network. For example, using FaaS to build applications is like using a C library other than an assembly to program a machine.

Currently, as you know, network applications and administrators mostly rely on low-level interfaces, such as CLI, SNMP, OVSDB, NETCONF, or OpenFlow, to directly configure individual devices for network service provisioning. As a core feature of ODL and SDN, FaaS provides an abstraction of the network topology that could work with any underlying network gear and vendor. This means that as a network programmer, you only need to learn how to build SDN applications or use the APIs; there is no need to either use or learn complex CLI commands of vendors such as IOS, Junos OS, EOS, Comware, and so on.

FaaS tries to provide fabric abstraction of the physical network. Using this abstraction, FaaS presents devices, vendors, or network details, such as control and optimization, into bigger building blocks. This is illustrated by the term fabric in the following diagram . Each fabric provides common network services; these include L2/L3 routing and switching, connectivity, **Quality of Services** (**QoS**), and security and access controls. In traditional networking we used to configure each and every network device individually, however with FaaS, you can build and an application to configure network components such as routers and switches.

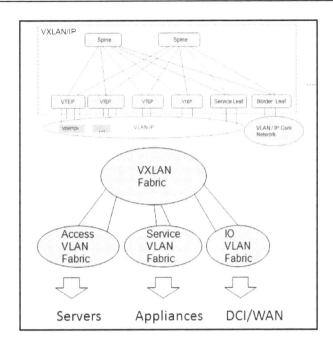

A simple network could just be a fabric, such as VXLAN. In reality though (as in the preceding diagram), a network usually consists of multiple fabrics, such as VXLAN fabric, VLAN, TRILL/SPB, and so on. Hence, FaaS not only defines services within a fabric, but also provides services across multiple heterogeneous fabrics.

Federation

Project type: Main

An application may need to communicate with different ODL clusters. This happens mostly in use cases where there are different ODL domains deployed, for example, in multiple PODs of a data center. Such deployments require that ODL clusters co-operate with other applications. The federation project helps form a group of different ODL clusters and enables communication between them. It also enables them to exchange their state if possible:

- Initial (full) synchronization between remote clusters
- Publishing state updates between clusters while preserving event ordering and possibly allowing data transformation and filtering
- Subscribing to state updates from remote clusters

The federation service is intended to complement other services such as Messaging4Transport and the conceptual data tree. So it refers to services that are focused on sharing states between ODL clusters (and potentially other systems) without the need for any transformation, filtering, or event ordering.

One of the first application use cases was NetVirt federation for the purpose of neutron network federation.

The following is a high-level diagram of the relationship between the federation service, other ODL services, MD-SAL, and state sharing mechanisms such as Messaging4Transport and the conceptual data tree:

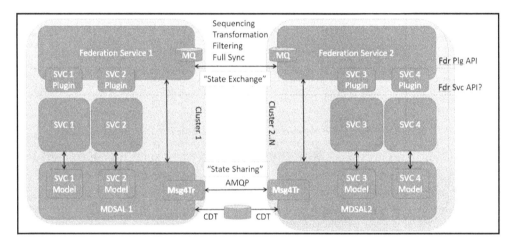

Genius generic network interfaces

Project type: Main

Genius allows any ODL application to use its services to achieve interference-free coexistence with other applications.

It provides the following:

- Modules that provide a common view of the network interfaces of different services
- Interface (logical port) manager
- Allows bindings or registration of multiple services to logical ports or interfaces
- The ability to plug in different types of southbound protocol renderers
- Overlay tunnel manager
- Creating and maintaining overlay tunnels between configured TEPs
- Modules that provide commonly used functions as shared services to avoid duplication of code and waste of resources
- Aliveness monitor
- Tunnel or nexthop aliveness monitoring services
- ID manager
- Generates persistent unique integer IDs
- MD-SAL utils
- Common generic APIs for interaction with MD-SAL

Internet of Things Data Management (IoTDM)

Project type: Main

IoTDM is an open source implementation of oneM2M running on OpenDaylight. OneM2M is a global organization that creates the requirements, architectures, and interoperability function of IoT technologies.

This module is a middleware that acts as a oneM2M-compliant IoT data broker, and it enables authorized applications to retrieve IoT data uploaded to the network by small IoT devices.

The IoTDM application (plugin) interacts with data producers (IoT devices such as sensors and IoT management systems) and data consumers (analytics engines). The interaction happens through a variety of IoT protocol plugins, such as CoAP, MQTT, HTTP, and so on:

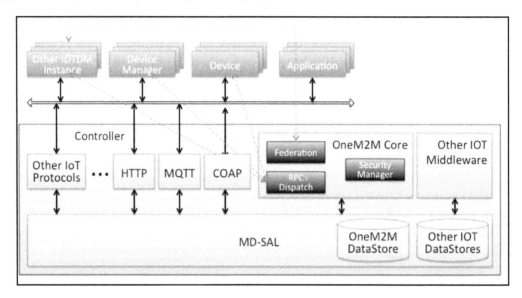

L2 switch

Project type: Main

L2 switch is an MD-SAL-based implementation of a learning switch with optimizations on how a packet should be forwarded. L2 switch is a basic layer 2 switch feature within ODL. It includes layer 2-specific handling and also provides several reusable services, as follows:

- **PacketHandler**: This provides an infrastructure in an ODL controller to process incoming packets and forward them as required. It gives a pluggable architecture for handling the life cycle of a packet (term from OpenFlow's OFPT_PACKET_IN message) in the ODL controller. This infrastructure can limit to handle only packets with reason as No matching flow (table-miss flow entry).

    Packets are decoded, modified and transmitted as part of PacketHandler.

- **AddressTracker** (**Endpoint tracker**): AddressTracker builds and maintains a mapping table that may have multiple attributes such as:
  - Host MAC address
  - Connected switch ID
  - Switch port number
  - VLAN, VNI (VXLAN),
  - MPLS tag.
- **Path Computation Service**: This provides an optimal path (route) between hosts. It can be the shortest path, lowest cost, and so on, similar to the algorithms of routing protocols. Path Communication Service leverages and modifies topology data. It can also work with multiple topologies.
- **Flow Writer Service**: This service takes care of programming all the intermediate switches with appropriate flows once an optimal path has been computed between two hosts. It keeps track of mapping, from metaflow to individual flows, such that appropriate flows can be reprogrammed when a port goes down or an entire switch goes down.
- **STP Service**: This is the spanning tree protocol service that allows ODL to participate in a spanning tree. It is useful when ODL is deployed in a hybrid network (SDN and non-SDN with layer 2 connections) and you need to let ODL participate in a spanning tree. For a spanning tree, standard protocols are available.

Additional functionality that can be implemented by the L2 switch includes MAC address aging, packet filtering, static MAC addresses, and so on:

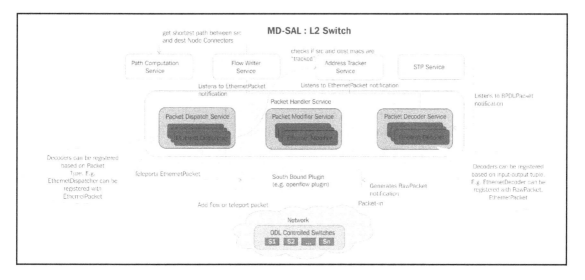

Remember that the L2 switch is a software module running on the ODL server. When one of the switches in the SDN domain receives a packet that doesn't have any entry that matches with its headers (source, destination MAC and IP, and so on), then the switch encapsulates the whole packet in an OpenFlow `PACKET_IN` message and sends it to the ODL. This packet is decapsulated and handed over to the L2 switch module to handle (find where the packet needs to be forwarded).

The L2 switch module performs MAC address learning using the `OpenFlow-PACKET_IN` messages it receives from the switches in the SDN domain. It is similar to a standard L2 switch. The following is a list of switch actions:

Source MAC	Target MAC	L2 switch action	Comments
Unknown	Unknown	Learn the source; broadcast packets on all external ports minus ingress	
Unknown	Known	Learn the source; unicast packets to the target	L2 is essentially teleporting the packet to the node where the target is attached. The attachment point refers to the target that is physically attached.
Known	Unknown	Broadcast packets on all external ports minus ingress	L2 doesn't need to learn as it already knows the source. There could be a case, however, where a host has moved from one node to another in the network. In this implementation, we don't update the attachment point.
Known	Known	Unicast the packet to the target, find the shortest path between the source and destination, and install `mac-to-mac` flows on all the nodes in this path	

The following diagram illustrates the communication between L2 switch components:

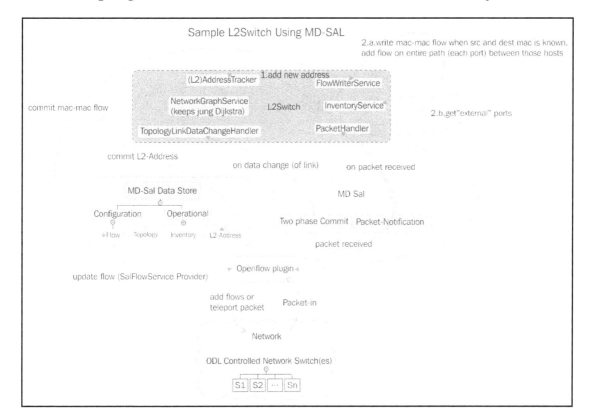

Link Aggregation Control Protocol

Project type: Main

LACP modules is a link aggregation control protocol implementation in the form of an ML-SAL service module. It is used for auto discovery and aggregation of multiple links between the ODL network (the switches or routers) and other LACP-enabled endpoints or switches and routers, firewalls, and load balancers.

The LACP protocol was initially released as the IEEE Ethernet 802.3ad specification, but it was later moved to help bridge and manage groups, as apparent in the 802.1AX specification.

LACP modules within OpenDaylight receive and process LACP control packets through the SAL packet processing service. They also send out LACP control packets through all the active switch ports using the SAL packet processing service; this is done at regular intervals, based on the timer interval configuration. Since this module is designed to aggregate only external links, it ignores the LACP packets received through internal links. It uses the SAL-FLOW service to create LAGs within the switch:

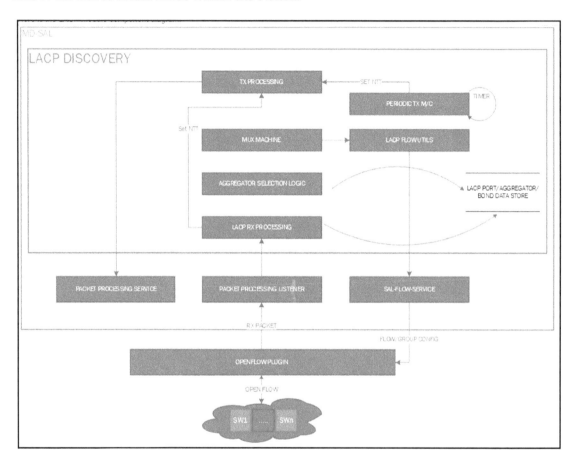

Messaging4Transport

Project type: Main

ODL is based on an MD-SAL that allows modeling of data, RPCs, notifications, and queries. Because of this model, everything that is modeled gets exposed automatically over northbound APIs.

Messaging4Transport adds ActiveMQ (AMQP-based) to be used in the case of northbound communications in addition to the current RESTCONF NB bindings. It adds AMQP bindings to the MD-SAL, which would automatically make all MD-SAL APIs available via the mechanism.

Network Address Translation (NATApp)

Project type: Main

This plugin provides network address translation service to ODL. It installs flow rules in OpenFlow switches with the respective NAT rules.

NATApp consists of various types of NAT implementations, including static NAT, dynamic NAT, and **Network Address Port Translation** (**NAPT**) or PAT. The users of this plugin can select the type of NAT implementation and subsequently feed in the floating and private IP addresses.

NAT functionality is one of the basic features available in any enterprise network. Through this, local IP addresses can be translated into global IP addresses and vice versa for Internet connectivity. This is traditionally done by the perimeter router of the firewall in the enterprise network, which is connected to the service provider. In the SDN scenario, this functionality has to be hosted (in the router) as an application on the SDN controller.

NATApp in ODL supports the following NAT scenarios:

- One-to-one NAT (static NAT)
- One-to-many NAT (dynamic NAT)
- NAPT or **Port Address Translation** (**PAT**)
- Full cone NAT
- (Address)-restricted-cone NAT
- Port-restricted cone NAT
- NAT loopback (Hair pining)
- Stateful and stateless NAT64 for **Address Family Translation** (**AFT**) with IPv6 to IPv4 conversion

The following diagram illustrates how an SDN controller running a NAT application can inject NAT policies to an OpenFlow capable router. (Remember that there are OpenFlow extensions that define any alternation in a packet. NAT is one of the use cases that tells the router how to alter and modify a packet before sending it out.)

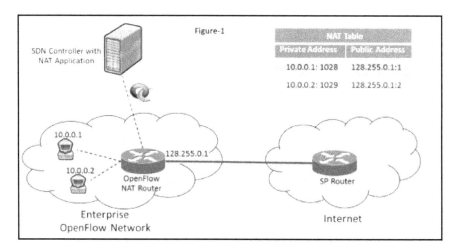

The following image illustrates how the NAT plugin communicates with applications and network elements:

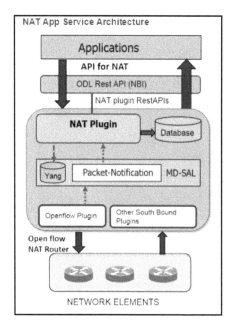

NETCONF as a southbound protocol

Project type: Main

ODL supports NETCONF as a southbound protocol; also, it can act as a NETCONF server for northbound uses and queries.

NETCONF that we are discussing here is related to the southbound NETCONF. It is a protocol that is available with vendors such as Cisco. It allows you to have a remote configuration or communication with a router or a switch supporting NETCONF. ODL uses NETCONF to communicate with physical networking devices.

NetVirt

NetVirt is a network virtualization solution. This solution comprises components, including Open vSwitch-based virtualization for software switches, hardware VTEP for hardware switches, and service function chaining support within a virtualized environment.

The NetVirt project is based on the code split from the OVSDB NetVirt. This project was composed with the help of two main pieces: an OVSDB southbound plugin and a network virtualization solution. In the Boron release, a decision was taken to split the project into two separate projects. The projects still share the same meeting, mailing list, and IRC channel.

NeutronNorthbound

Project type: Main

The neutron northbound module provides communication from the ODL to OpenStack via the ODL neutron service; also, it saves the neutron models in the ODL data store for other providers to use. It does not include direct manipulation of low-level networks or overlay elements. These are left to the providers that receive information from the project.

The ODL-SDNi SDN interface

Project type: Main

The SDN interface is a form of communication between SDN controllers. It enables them to exchange different pieces of information, such as configuration, states, and other elements, with each other. SDNi is used in SDN clustering.

The following diagram illustrates how two different ODL controllers in different domains can communicate with each other via an SDNi module:

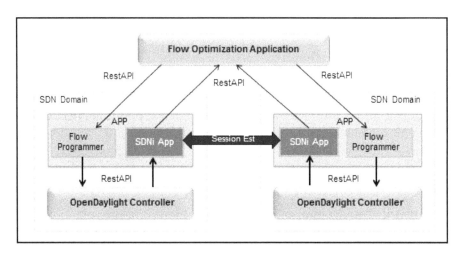

The OF-CONFIG OpenFlow configurator

Project type: Main

This module is to enable ODL to be able to configure OpenFlow data paths remotely on OpenFlow switches.

OF-CONFIG acts as an OpenFlow driver for ODL in order to configure OpenFlow-enabled switches. It even defines an abstraction called the OpenFLow logical switch that represents an OpenFLow switch. OF-CONFIG is used for carrying communication from the controller back to the SDN switch.

The OpenFlow protocol library

Project type: Main

The OpenFlow protocol library is the OpenFlow driver component in OpenDaylight. It enables communication between the controller and OpenFlow switches. It also enables a daemon on port 6653 (for secure TLS encryption) or 6633 (for non-secure encryption) to listen for OpenFlow messages coming from OpenFlow devices.

It supports multiple versions of the OpenFlow protocol (v1.1, 1.2, and 1.3), and the way it is built allows it to support future versions of OpenFlow.

The following list describes the key features of this module:

- Pipeline processing
- Input or output processing, which is done via processing pipeline (this could be modified at runtime, based on session characteristics).
- Scatter buffer
- TLS support
- Serialization (message coding or decoding) logic, which is separated from the implementation of transfer objects

OpFlex

Project type: Main

OpFlex is created by Cisco and is a southbound protocol similar to OpenFlow. However, this protocol is open source as Cisco has already submitted it to IETF. Cisco uses OpFlex in their Nexus 9,000 switches as well as on their SDN controller platform (ACI) and controller (APIC).

This module in ODL is built to implement the OpFlex southbound protocol in order to control and communicate with switches and equipment that support OpFlex.

This module currently provides support for the following key components:

The OpFlex project consists of three things:

- The OpFlex protocol
- The OpFlex southbound plugin
- The OpFlex policy agent

The following diagram shows the OpFlex policy agent working in conjunction with other elements of an OpFlex policy fabric:

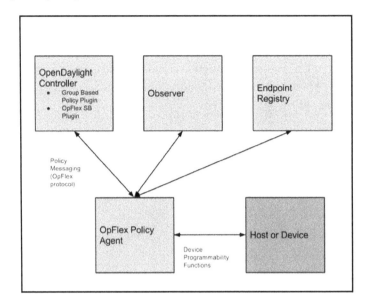

OVSDB southbound integration

Project type: Main

OVSDB is a southbound protocol for managing OVS-enabled switches and virtual switches. OVSDB is the protocol used to manage and configure OVS instances (physical or virtual). This enables OpenDaylight to view, create, modify, and delete OVS objects such as bridges and ports.

Open vSwitch (**OVS**) is an open source software project that implements virtual switching that is interoperable with almost all popular hypervisors. OVS uses OpenFlow to perform message forwarding in the control plane for both virtual and physical ports.

The OVSDB project provides two major functionalities:

- **OVSDB southbound plugin**: This plugin allows users to manage the OVS device that supports the OVSDB schema and the OVSDB management protocol.
- **OVSDB hardware vTep plugin**: This plugin handles the OVS device that supports the OVSDB hardware vTep schema and supports the OVSDB management protocol.

The following image describes OVSDB communication between the controller and switches:

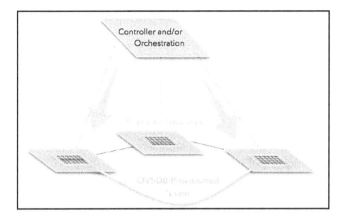

Service function chaining

Project type: Main

This module provides service chaining to ODL. Service chaining is a policy that can be defined by a user for specific traffic; it must be passed to a list of network services (for example, firewall, IPS, or load balancer).

This module manages the abstract to ensure packets are being sent to the network services in chain order.

It provides the infrastructure (chaining logic and APIs) needed for ODL to provision a service chain in the network and an end-user application for defining such chains.

SNMP4SDN - using SNMP as a southbound protocol

Project type: Main

SNMP is another protocol that is supported by ODL as a southbound protocol. This module allows ODL and SDN applications to manage and use SNMP-enabled switches. It uses an SNMP write to push a specific configuration to the switches.

In some deployments, ODL will be able to program the function of forwarding tables using SNMP. However, some other deployments only use SNMP for carrying out the initial configuration and creating a basic OpenFlow configuration on the switch to point it to the SDN controller and enable secure pairing.

In general, remember that ODL provides an abstraction of networks. You, as an SDN application programmer, don't need to worry about how ODL communicates with the switches. From your perspective, when you create a fabric, it should be up; it doesn't matter how ODL translates your abstraction parameters into a switch-understandable format and transfers it via which protocol.

The following diagram describes the communication between an SNMP southbound plugin and other components of ODL:

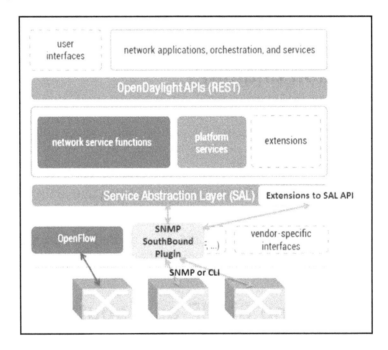

VPNService

Project type: Main

This module is mainly designated for using SDN to provide VPN services in service provider network. We mainly target the MPLS type of private IP circuits. (Don't get confused with IPsec or SSL VPN.)

Providing a virtual IP network is one of the main services of service providers. Service providers have a network of routers located in different locations (countries or cities). They use these routers to provide a virtual network to their customers using technologies such as MPLS, VRF (virtual routing forwarding), and BGP-MPLS; these technologies help exchange the MPLS label and IP prefixes between routers.

Architectures such as L2/L3 BGP-MPLS VPNs (RFC 4364 or EVPN) are also gaining good traction in data center network virtualizations (for tenant network isolation) as well as orchestration systems, such as OpenStack.

This module provides layer 3 VPN services using L3VPN based on BGP-MPLS (RFC 4364). The layer 2 VPN service based on EVPN (draft-ietf-l2vpn-evpn) is planned for a future ODL release.

The layer 3 VPN service of the module includes the following components:

- **L3 VPN manager**: This provides a VRF infrastructure in the controller for BGP MPLS L3 VPN.
- **MP-BGP routing stack**: This runs an instance of MP-BGP to provide the L3 VPN service.
- **MPLS label manager**: This is a service to allocate labels to each VPN. These labels are distributed to remote sites using BGP; therefore, they are expected to be unique, within a tenant's L3 domain.
- **Nexthop manager**: The FIB maintains a mapping of route prefixes to nexthop.
- **FIB service**: This module supports the **Forwarding Information Base** (**FIB**) service, which maintains the forwarding state that is, association of route with nexthop for each VRF and push it to vSwitch using rules.
- **OpenStack neutron service**: L3 services in OpenStack are implemented as service plugins that run in the context of a neutron server.

Virtual Tenant Network (VTN)

Project type: Main

The VTN module provides network virtualization support for multitenant virtual networks on the ODL SDN controller.

VTN is one of the very interesting and key components of ODL. It allows you to create virtual tenants where each tenant can have its own fabric, virtual routers, namespaces, and so on. The main application for VTN is private clouds orchestration platforms such as OpenStack or VMware vSphere.

VTN provides a full logical abstraction to the user. When multiple networks and virtual routers are created in a tenant, VTN itself takes care of all of the underlying communication. It communicates with NFV and creates virtual routers, assigns IP addresses, or programs the flow tables of physical or virtual switches.

VTN is a logical abstraction plane. This enables you to completely separate the logical plane from physical and data planes. Users can leverage this abstraction, build a design, and deploy any desired network without being aware of the physical network topology or bandwidth restrictions.

Defining the virtual networks and components in VTM makes it more manageable; it also hides the complexity and probably tons of configuration lines that VTN applies to the underlying network components.

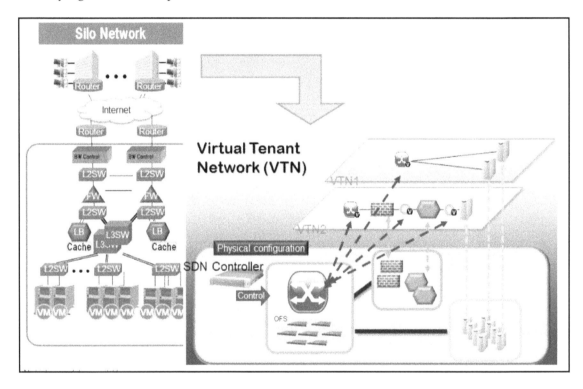

The NeXt UI

NeXt is an ODL web interface for visualizing a network and the communication within this network. It's an open graphical tool that can show physical or virtual network elements, such as traffic, tunnel path, and groups and their attributes. Also, it can build a layered topology, for example, to show the overlay network over the underlay. It can work together with Dlux to build ODL apps.

NeXt is highly contributed by Cisco and you can find many enhancements of NeXt in Cisco DevNet.

The following image illustrates NeXt:

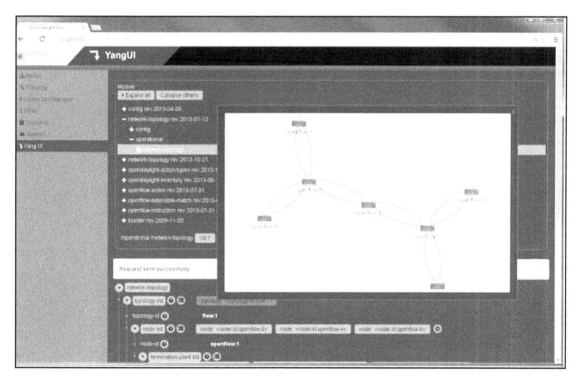

Summary

In this chapter, we learned about the details of components and modules of ODL. We learned that ODL has multiple modules where they are categorized into different verticals, such as management, networking, core, and security. I hope this chapter has given you an overview of what's going on under the hood of ODL. We haven't dived too deeply into modules yet; however, in the next chapter, we will learn how to use them and build our SDN application.

Also, in the next chapter, we will get our hands dirty by installing and deploying ODL; we will learn how to successfully install ODL Boron.

3
OpenDaylight Installation and Deployment

This chapter will provide step-by-step instructions on how to install OpenDaylight in a virtual environment and from scratch. You will also learn how to prepare a virtual machine for ODL installation and cover the basic steps required to have your first instance of ODL running. For your convenience, we have covered the process of installation over both Oracle VirtualBox and VMware workstation.

We'll explore the following topics:

- Plan to deploy OpenDaylight
- Stepwise installation of OpenDaylight - standalone
- Stepwise installation of OpenDaylight - distributed
- Basic operation of OpenDaylight to verify the installation
- OpenDaylight in a Docker container

Plan to deploy OpenDaylight

Let's get our hands dirty and build our first ODL installation. We will start by preparing a virtual environment and creating an ODL controller. We will use the basis of this deployed controller in later parts of this book.

Also, we will look at the highly available distributed deployment model as a pilot, but we will not use it in future chapters.

Let's have a look at ODL deployment models. First, let's discuss the standalone model:

- In this model, the ODL controller will be deployed as a standalone server. All components of ODL will be installed and enabled on the same instance.
- This type of deployment will be enough for small to medium installations or lab environments.
- Remember that standalone installation doesn't mean that you will not have redundancy or any level of high availability. Thanks to the available enterprise virtual environment features-such as vMotion or HA, which are available in most virtual environments (VMware vSphere, OpenStack, Xen, Proxmox, and oVirt)-the basic level of redundancy and high availability will be provided by the virtual environment. This means that if the host server running the ODL instance fails for some reason, the ODL virtual machine will be moved and started on a separate host.

Now let's move on to the distributed (highly available) deployment model:

In distributed deployment, there will be a cluster of ODL servers sharing some sort of common database and running as a group; they will share responsibilities and functions. Distributed deployment is popular in an enterprise environment where business cannot tolerate downtime (still, if you use virtual environment redundancy and high availability features, there will be some amount of downtime when the virtual machine is being migrated to or booted on a different host).

ODL supports both standalone and distributed deployments, and we will go through both of them in more detail.

ODL basics

ODL is based on Java, which means that you should be able to run it over any platform that supports Java. Most ODL installations are based on Linux; however, you can run it on Windows as well.

ODL uses the following tools and components to run:

- **Maven**: Apache Maven is a build and automation tool for Java projects. It can manage dependencies very well. OpenDaylight uses Apache Maven for easier build automation.

Maven uses Project Object Model to script the dependencies between bundles and to describe the order of loading and starting the bundles and modules.

- **Open Service Gateway Initiative** (**OSGi**): OSGi is the backend framework of OpenDaylight. It allows you to dynamically load JAR files of bundles and packages and bind bundles together for exchanging information.
- **Java interfaces**: Java interfaces are used for event listening, specifications, and forming patterns.
- **REST APIs**: These are northbound APIs that are provided to the users. The REST API server of ODL interfaces between the user and the application. It is REST that calls ODL modules.

For user and application access to ODL, the ODL controller provides the OSGi framework and bidirectional REST as northbound APIs. Both these methods can be used by SDN applications.

OSGi applications should be written in Java and must run in the same address space as the ODL controller so they can have direct access to ODL modules.

If an application is out of the ODL address space, written in any other language, or placed in a different server, it would need to use web-based REST API calls to communicate and talk to ODL.

ODL supports different southbound protocols, such as OpenFlow, BGP PCEP, OVSDB, and so on. These modules and plugins link dynamically to the **Service Abstraction Layer** (**SAL**) of ODL. SAL exposes these plugins to SDN applications or northbound APIs. It is responsible for managing the requested network services received from SDN applications or northbound API calls. It communicates with the underlying network device (switch or router) via the southbound protocol, which the device supports. This communication is transparent to the SDN application, and SAL manages this communication.

ODL needs to be aware of all the devices in its domain along with their features and capabilities. This information is stored and managed by a topology manager module in ODL.

Topology manager gathers topology information from various modules and protocols, such as ARP, host tracker, device manager, switch manager, and OpenFlow.

Prerequisites

To start ODL deployment, we need to host virtual machines. In this book, I have used VMware Workstation 12. However, you can use any hypervisor of your choice, such as Oracle VirtualBox (free), OpenStack, or VMware ESXi.

On the host PC (Windows or Mac), we will need the following:

1. Hypervisor (if you are using VMware Workstation or Oracle VirtualBox).
2. An SCP client (WinSCP on Windows).
3. Web browser (we use Chrome).
4. Postman (for calling REST API queries to ODL).

Virtual machine size

For our first ODL virtual machine, we will use the following configuration:

- vCPU: 4
- RAM: 8 GB
- Storage: 60 GB

Operating system

ODL is based on Java and Apache Maven. Therefore, you can use almost any Linux-based operating system to host and run ODL. Also, you can test it by running it on BSD-based systems, such as FreeBSD or OpenBSD.

The operating system and Linux flavour comes to your taste, and I leave it to you to choose. In this book, I have used Ubuntu Server 16.04 LTS as the base operating system for running ODL.

Java

Java Runtime Environment (JRE) needs to be installed on the virtual machine in order to run ODL.

Note that the Boron release (version 0.5) requires Java version 1.8 (minimum).

For Java, I recommend that you install OpenJDK version 1.8, which will be enough to run ODL.

ODL distribution

I have used the latest version of ODL, which is the Boron version. You can download the Boron distribution from `https://www.opendaylight.org/downloads`:

You can use either a ZIP or TAR file.

VTN is a separate component that can be downloaded separately. As we learned in `Chapter 2`, *Overview of OpenDaylight*, VTN is a module of ODL.

The NeXt UI toolkit is an additional feature; you can use it to customize the NeXt UI.

OpFlex is a southbound protocol implementation that comprises libraries and binary files that can get plugged in to ODL so it could communicate with OpFlex-based switches (such as Cisco Nexus 9000 series).

Standalone installation

OK! Let's start with our first standalone installation of ODL. I have discussed most of the basic Linux commands as many of you with networking background might not have experience in using them.

Also, I have created a virtual machine and have installed Ubuntu Server 16.04 LTS. I have enabled SSH as well:

```
    sudo apt-get update
  sudo apt-get upgrade
  sudo service ssh start
```

The following screenshot illustrates the virtual machine I used for installing ODL:

```
learningodl@ODL01:/$ cat /etc/issue
Ubuntu 16.04.1 LTS \n \l

learningodl@ODL01:/$
```

We have a user created, named learningodl:

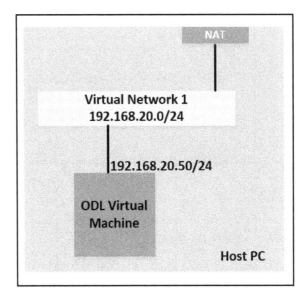

To create the user and add it to the sudo group, run the following commands:

```
    sudo adduser learningodl
  sudo usermod -aG sudo learningodl
  su - learningodl
```

IP address settings

I have allocated the following IP address schema for the virtual machine:

IP Address: `192.168.20.51`

Subnet mask: `255.255.255.0`

To set the IP address on Ubuntu, you need to modify the `interfaces` file under `/etc/network/`.

Use the following command to edit the `interfaces` file:

```
sudo nano /etc/network/interfaces
```

The following image illustrates the IP address settings in our ODL virtual machine:

```
# This file describes the network interfaces available on your system
# and how to activate them. For more information, see interfaces(5).

source /etc/network/interfaces.d/*

# The loopback network interface
auto lo
iface lo inet loopback

# The primary network interface
auto ens33
iface ens33 inet static
        address 192.168.20.51
        netmask 255.255.255.0
        gateway 192.168.20.2
        dns-nameservers 4.2.2.4 8.8.8.8
```

In newer versions of Ubuntu, the concept of using the naming convention `eth` is deprecated. You need a prefix `ens` with the interface name.

Using the preceding example, you can change your network settings and assign the correct IP address to your virtual machine. After editing the file and saving it, restart the networking service in order to activate the changes. Use the following command to restart the service:

```
sudo service networking restart
```

Java installation

The next step is installation of Java. To install Java, run the following commands, which will install **Java Development Kit** (**JDK**) version 1.8:

```
apt-get install openjdk-8-jdk
```

To verify the Java installation after you install JDK, run `java -version`; it should give you the following output:

```
learningodl@ODL01: ~
learningodl@ODL01:~$ java -version
openjdk version "1.8.0_111"
OpenJDK Runtime Environment (build 1.8.0_111-8u111-b14-2ubuntu0.16.04.2-b14)
OpenJDK 64-Bit Server VM (build 25.111-b14, mixed mode)
learningodl@ODL01:~$
```

 Note that Java used to have an environment variable called `JAVA_HOME`, which normally is set to the home location of the Java installation. `JAVA_HOME` is deprecated now, and most Java applications are not dependent on this environment variable.

ODL doesn't need the `JAVA_HOME` environment variable; however, having it set up is considered a best practice:

```
sudo update-alternatives --config java
```

The following screenshot illustrates the output of the preceding command. It shows the JRE path and where to find Java binaries inside the JRE:

```
learningodl@ODL01:~$ sudo update-alternatives --config java
There is only one alternative in link group java (providing /usr/bin/java):
/usr/lib/jvm/java-8-openjdk-amd64/jre/bin/java
Nothing to configure.
learningodl@ODL01:~$
```

The preceding command provides the full path to the Java executable file. We don't need the section highlighted in yellow but the one in red.

Copy the path from your preferred installation, then edit `/etc/environment` using the nano text editor:

```
sudo nano /etc/environment
```

At the end of this file, add the following line, making sure you replace the highlighted path with your own copied path:

```
  GNU nano 2.5.3                                    File: /etc/environment

PATH="/usr/local/sbin:/usr/local/bin:/usr/sbin:/usr/bin:/sbin:/bin:/usr
JAVA_HOME="/usr/lib/jvm/java-8-openjdk-amd64/jre"
```

Enter the following command to reload the environment file:

```
source /etc/environment
```

You can now test whether the environment variable has been set by executing the following command:

```
echo $JAVA_HOME
```

This should return the path you have already configured in the environment file.

Downloading and installing ODL

Now that we have prepared our environment, we need to download ODL to the virtual machine. If your virtual machine is connected to the Internet via a host (NAT or direct), you can use the following wget command to directly download the Boron version of ODL to your new virtual machine.

To download it directly to your ODL virtual machine, use the wget command:

```
Wget
```

Alternatively, visit https://nexus.opendaylight.org/content/repositories/opendayl ight.release/org/opendaylight/integration/distribution-karaf/0.5.1-Boron-SR 1/distribution-karaf-0.5.1-Boron-SR1.tar.gz.

You can also download the files from `https://www.opendaylight.org/downloads` and then copy them to the virtual machine using an SCP client. I use this method for copying files.

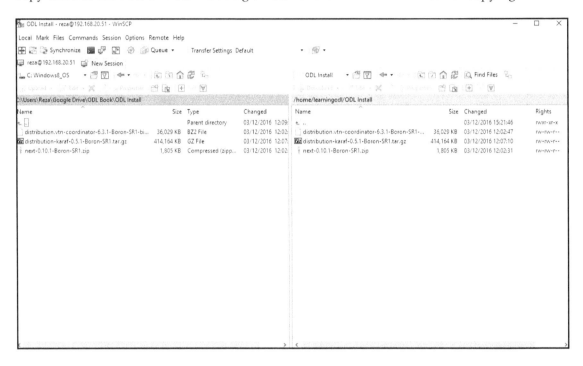

We will create and use `/opt/odl` as our main directory for the ODL installation:

```
sudo mkdir /opt/odl
sudo mv distribution-karaf-0.5.1-Boron-SR1.tar.gz /opt/odl/
cd /opt/odl/
sudo tar -xzf distribution-karaf-0.5.1-Boron-SR1.tar.gz
```

The preceding commands unzip the ODL instance in `/opt/odl/ distribution-karaf-0.5.1-Boron-SR1/`. To make our operation easier, let's create a symbolic link to this directory:

```
sudo ln -s distribution-karaf-0.5.1-Boron-SR1 boron
```

The following screenshot illustrates the output of the preceding command:

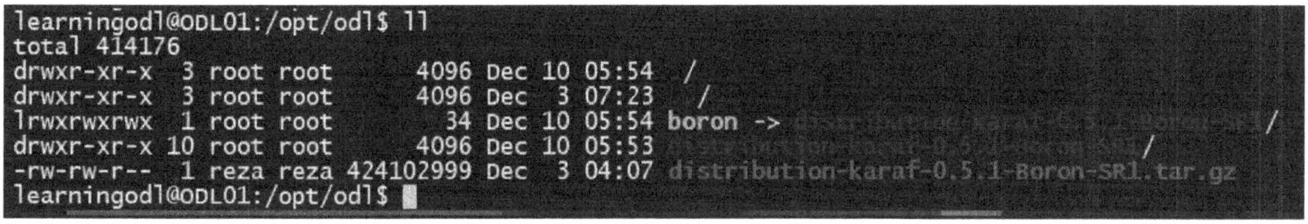

learningodl@ODL01:/opt/odl$ ll
total 414176
drwxr-xr-x 3 root root 4096 Dec 10 05:54 /
drwxr-xr-x 3 root root 4096 Dec 3 07:23 /
lrwxrwxrwx 1 root root 34 Dec 10 05:54 boron ->
drwxr-xr-x 10 root root 4096 Dec 10 05:53
-rw-rw-r-- 1 reza reza 424102999 Dec 3 04:07 distribution-karaf-0.5.1-Boron-SR1.tar.gz
learningodl@ODL01:/opt/odl$

The symbolic link I mentioned is similar to a shortcut in Windows. From now on, we can use `/opt/old/boron` to access our ODL instance.

First run with ODL

To start ODL, we need to run `karaf`. Apache Karaf is a small OSGi-based runtime that provides a lightweight container on which various components and applications can be deployed:

```
sudo /opt/odl/boron/bin/karaf
```

Running the preceding command will provide you with a result similar to the following screenshot:

karaf: JAVA_HOME not set; results may vary
Hit '<tab>' for a list of available commands
and '[cmd] --help' for help on a specific command.
Hit '<ctrl-d>' or type 'system:shutdown' or 'logout' to shutdown OpenDaylight.
opendaylight-user@ >

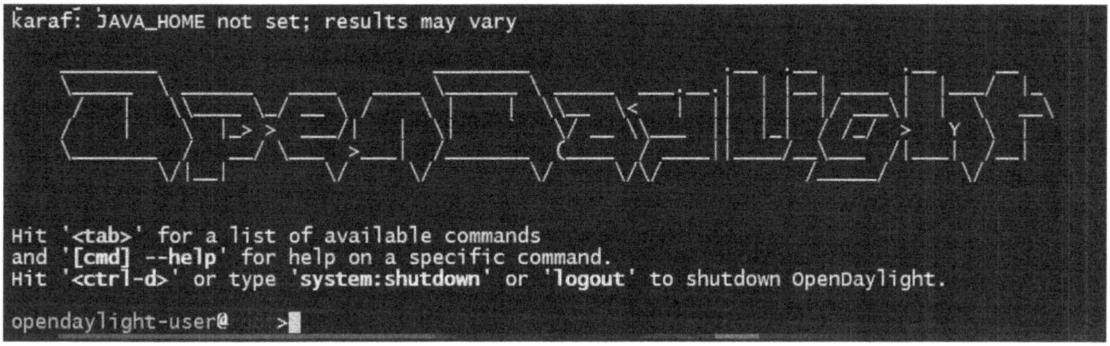

This is the ODL Command Prompt that allows you to deploy ODL to the machine. This screen is also referred to as the ODL console, which is the landing space of ODL.

Once you launch `karaf`, the virtual machine will start binding to a couple of TCP ports, as follows:

- `44444`: Java RMI
- `8101`: Karaf SSH shell port
- `1099`: Java RMI

You will get the main ODL command interface, but we have not enabled the web GUI yet. Dlux is the web interface of ODL, and we need to enable this plugin in order to access the web interface.

Karaf Command Prompt is similar to the industry standard Command Prompt. You can use the Tab button to complete the command or a question mark to find specific commands.

You can use the grep filter in Karaf to filter and find specific commands that you are looking for.

Enter the following command:

```
feature:list | grep dlux
```

The `feature:list` command lists all the available features in ODL that are either installed or available for installation. We covered most of these features and modules in `Chapter 2`, *Overview of OpenDaylight*.

To start the Dlux web interface, issue the following command on Karaf:

```
feature:install odl-dlux-all
```

Once you run the previous command, Dlux will be enabled and you will find that the virtual machine has started listening on additional ports, such as the following:

- `8181`: Web UI and MD-SAL RESTCONF
- `8185`: **Authentication Authorization Accounting (AAA)**
- `8080`: Web UI and MD-SAL RESTCONF

You can get the ODL port list from `https://wiki.opendaylight.org/view/Ports`.

Distributed installation

Distributed deployment requires a minimum of three nodes. You can build a cluster with two nodes, but if one of the nodes fails, the cluster will not be operational (ODL doesn't allow you to build a cluster with two nodes). The ODL clustering mechanism checks whether the majority of the servers in a cluster are up; if yes, it allows you to switch over to the next active node. Another example: if you have four servers in a cluster and lose two, the cluster will not be operational.

As a rule of thumb, always try to design your cluster with odd number of member servers:

Cluster size	Maximum number of servers can be down
2	0
3	1
4	1
5	2
6	2
7	3

Each node in a cluster must have a unique identifier. ODL uses the role of each node for this purpose. Node roles are defined in the `akka.conf` file.

ODL's MD-SAL datastore uses the concept of shards. Shard is a partition or part of the whole data that can be stored on one or multiple servers. Data shards in ODL are used to store the MD-SAL database; this database contains the data of ODL modules, for example, topology data, inventory data, counter data, and so on. Each of these data shards can be stored on different servers or on the default datastore server.

If you specify a module in the ODL module configuration file but do not specify its shard in the module-shard configuration. In this scenario, by default, ODL will transfer all of the data of the module to the default shard, which is configured in the module-shard configuration.

In a three-node cluster, you need to ensure that each shard is available on each and every server in the cluster. This means that for a particular shard, you need to verify that member-1 is hosting it (lead node) and the replica of this shard is stored on both member-2 and member-3 servers (seed nodes).

As per ODL documentation, it is recommended that you have multiple seed nodes configured in the cluster. When a cluster member is started, it sends a message to all its seed nodes. Once the seed node (any of them) responds, the cluster member sends a join command to the first seed node that initiated the response. If none of the seed nodes respond, the cluster member repeats the process until it successfully establishes a connection with one of the seed nodes; else, it remains shutdown.

If a node fails for any reason, it needs to be restarted so it could rejoin the ODL cluster. Once restarted, it will find the lead member, start synchronizing the data, and join the cluster.

Distributed installation is a bit different than the standard standalone installation. The first thing that we need to consider is using the cluster-ready version of the MD-SAL datastore.

Now let's discuss how to set up a three-node cluster:

To start with, use the standalone installation as a source and clone two more virtual machines from the ODL virtual machine we created in the standalone installation section. Rename the virtual machines once you clone them to avoid confusion.

The following table illustrates our multiserver lab setup:

	Server 1	Server 2	Server 3
Hostname	ODL01	ODL02	ODL03
IP address	192.168.20.51	192.168.20.52	192.168.20.53
RAM	4 GB	4 GB	4 GB

Start the three virtual machines and ensure that they follow the preceding configuration. Now let's move on to the modifications we need to make:

- First, change the hostname using this command:

```
sudo nano /etc/hostname
```

- Change the hosts using this command:

```
sudo nano /etc/hosts
```

- Change the IP address using this command:

```
sudo nano /etc/network/interfaces
```

- The following command deletes the ODL instance

```
sudo rm /opt/odl/distribution-karaf-0.5.1-Boron-SR1 -dr
```

- We need a fresh installation now. Clustering needs to be enabled prior to the installation of any other modules. Use the following to do this:

```
sudo tar xz -C /opt/odl -f /opt/odl/distribution-karaf-0.5.1-Boron-
SR1.tar.gz
```

- The preceding command extracts a fresh copy of ODL in /opt/odl/ for each server
- Reboot the virtual machine to have the changes applied.

```
Sudo reboot
```

Once the virtual machine is booted up, establish an ssh connection to each host to ensure you have access to the new IP addresses you configured on hosts. Also verify the hostnames, ensure the new host names are in place in each host.

We will follow the steps discussed in the next section to set up clustering in our virtual nodes.

Step 1 - Editing the Akka configuration file

Edit the Akka configuration file on each of the three virtual machines:

```
sudo nano /opt/odl/boron/configuration/initial/akka.conf
```

In this file, you need to make the following three changes:

1. Find the following string:

```
netty.tcp {
        hostname = "127.0.0.1"
```

2. Replace 127.0.0.1 with the IP address of the virtual machine. For example, change the existing string to 192.168.20.51 in ODL01, 192.168.20.52 in ODL02, and so on.

3. Find the following string:

```
cluster {seed-nodes = ["akka.tcp://opendaylight-cluster-
data@127.0.0.1:2550"]
```

4. Replace `127.0.0.1` with the IP address of the virtual machine. For example, change the IP address to `192.168.20.51` in ODL01, `192.168.20.52` in ODL02, and so on.

5. Find the following string:

```
roles = [
    "member-1"
  ]
```

6. Change the member number to the server number as per the following table:

Server name	Role
ODL01	member-1
ODL02	member-2
ODL03	member-3

Step 2 - Editing the module-shard configuration file

Edit the module-shard configuration file on each server using this command:

```
sudo nano /opt/odl/boron/configuration/initial/module-shards.conf
```

In this file, you will need to make the following change:

1. Find the following string:

```
replicas = [
        "member-1"
    ]
```

2. Replace it with the following:

```
replicas = [
        "member-1",
        "member-2",
        "member-3"
]
```

3. This commands tells ODL to replicate each shard to all the three servers.

Step 3 - Starting the ODL

Now on each server, run the ODL instance as per the following commands:

```
cd /opt/odl/boron/bin/
sudo JAVA_MAX_MEM=4G JAVA_MAX_PERM_MEM=512m ./karaf
```

Step 4 - Enabling MD-SAL clustering in ODL

The MD-SAL clustering feature has special compatibility criteria. It must be installed before other features are installed.

1. In ODL Command Prompt, enter the following command on each server:

```
feature:install odl-mdsal-clustering
```

2. This may take between 5 to 10 minutes, so be patient.

This will enable the cluster-ready version of the MD-SAL datastore, but it will not actually create a cluster of multiple instances. The result is data persistence without scaling or high availability advantages.

Verifying the installation and accessing the web interface

Port 8181 is used for the Dlux web interface, and you can access it through your browser by entering `http://192.168.20.51:8181/index.html` (specifying `index.html` is important):

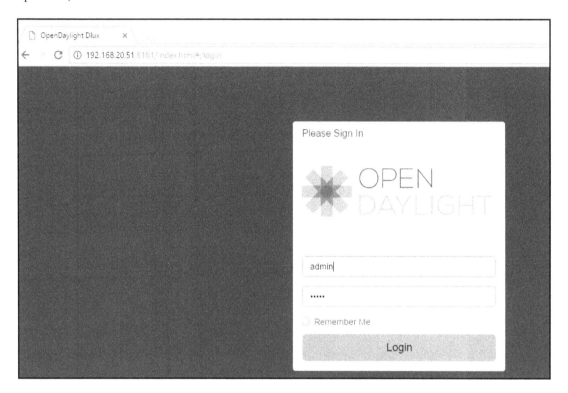

You can log in to Dlux using the following default credentials:

Username	admin
Password	admin

Once you log in, you will find the basic ODL web interface:

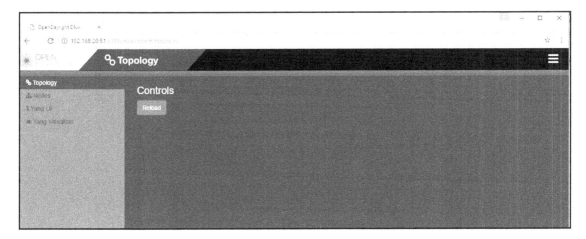

The UI has four options on the left-hand side of the screen. These options will change based on the module and features that are installed in ODL.

Topology

The topology section visualizes network topology. It creates a visual graph of the network, showing all the managed switches and routers and how they are connected together. Once we add the new switches to be managed by ODL, they will get listed in this section along with their connectivity details. Remember that ODL, as an SDN controller, has full visibility and knowledge of the network that can be used to draw a real-time diagram of the SDN network.

Node

The node section shows the list of devices managed by the ODL controller. In subsequent chapters, you will be able to see the new nodes that would be added to this section.

YANG UI

YANG UI has multiple sections, such as **API**, **HISTORY**, **COLLECTION**, and **PARAMETERS**.

The **API** section is a REST API caller that you can use to call ODL northbound APIs and manage the results, as illustrated in the following screenshot:

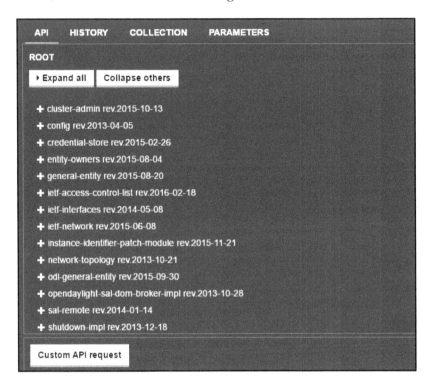

We will start working on ODL from the next chapter.

Running ODL on a Docker container

Have you heard about Docker? It is a great tool for shipping and managing Linux containers.

You can run ODL on a Docker container. You just need to have Docker installed on your host PC (Linux, Windows, or Mac) and let it download and run the ODL instance.

I have prepared an ODL container and published it to Docker. You can use this container for practice. You can use Docker on Mac, Linux, or Windows. Docker on Windows requires Windows 10, and it uses Hyper-V as its hypervisor.

To download the Docker container, use the following command:

```
docker pull learningopendaylight/boron
```

In this example, we will use Docker on Windows 10 to build our ODL instance:

1. Ensure you have Windows 10 64-bit Pro, Enterprise, or Education (1511 November update with build 10586 or later)

   Download and install Docker on Windows from
   https://docs.docker.com/docker-for-windows/install/

2. After the installation is complete, you may get a message as illustrated in the following screenshot:

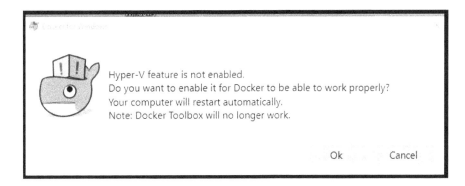

3. Once you click on **OK**, Docker will enable the Hyper-V feature on your Windows machine and restart the PC.

   Caution!
   Note that installing Docker enables the Hyper-V feature on your Microsoft Windows 10 machine. Hyper-V is not compatible with either VMware Workstation or Oracle VirtualBox. Therefore, you will not be able to use your virtual machines in either VMware workstation or Oracle VirtualBox when Hyper-V is enabled. Starting a VirtualBox VM when Hyper-V is installed might cause your Windows application to crash and show a blue screen of death.

Once you restart your PC, open a Windows PowerShell command link (you can find it by typing PowerShell in the task bar):

1. Enter the following command in PowerShell to ensure your Docker instance is up and running:

   ```
   docker version
   ```

2. You should get an output similar to the following screenshot:

```
PS C:\Users\Reza> docker version
Client:
 Version:      17.03.0-ce
 API version:  1.26
 Go version:   go1.7.5
 Git commit:   60ccb22
 Built:        Thu Feb 23 10:40:59 2017
 OS/Arch:      windows/amd64

Server:
 Version:      17.03.0-ce
 API version:  1.26 (minimum version 1.12)
 Go version:   go1.7.5
 Git commit:   3a232c8
 Built:        Tue Feb 28 07:52:04 2017
 OS/Arch:      linux/amd64
 Experimental: true
```

Now let's download the OpenDaylight container we have built for this book:

1. In this step, we will download the OpenDaylight container, which we have built for this book.
2. Enter the following command in your PowerShell session:

   ```
   docker pull learningopendaylight/boron
   ```

3. It will take some time for the downloading to complete. Once done, you should have a result similar to the following screenshot:

```
PS C:\Users\Reza> docker pull learningopendaylight/boron
Using default tag: latest
latest: Pulling from learningopendaylight/boron
d54efb8db41d: Pull complete
f8b845f45a87: Pull complete
e8db7bf7c39f: Pull complete
9654c40e9079: Pull complete
6d9ef359eaaa: Pull complete
62effac8c946: Pull complete
71278939a794: Pull complete
6cd3d1c61611: Pull complete
4ca4da3f9e8b: Pull complete
58939183c122: Pull complete
Digest: sha256:f704534b8a5cb203bf0786037f02af66314a022e7c5ad8a48455ed9e62cfd3bb
Status: Downloaded newer image for learningopendaylight/boron:latest
PS C:\Users\Reza>
```

The next task is to check the downloaded image. Follow these steps to do this:

1. To check whether the image has been properly downloaded, enter the following command in your PowerShell session:

   ```
   docker images
   ```

2. You should have a result similar to the following screenshot:

```
PS C:\Users\Reza> docker images
REPOSITORY                       TAG         IMAGE ID         CREATED          SIZE
learningopendaylight/boron       latest      08a356afd986     3 hours ago      1.88 GB
PS C:\Users\Reza>
```

Now let's start the ODL container:

1. To do this, run the following command in your PowerShell session:

   ```
   docker run -it -p 8181:8181 learningopendaylight/boron
   ```

2. This command tells Docker to run the newly downloaded container named `learningopendaylight/boron:latest`. (The latest is the default tag that is used to specify the latest version of the file).

Other arguments that are used are as follows:

1. `-it`: This argument tells Docker to keep the session interactive and allocate a `psudo tty` command. The argument `tn` is the default in most cases when you use Docker.
2. `-p 8181:8181`: This is an important argument. Here we are telling Docker to forward the port `TCP 8181` on the host machine to the container port `8181`. Remember that the container is sitting in a virtual network between the host and container and does not have access to the outside world unless we define it so.
3. The port `8181` is the default Dlux (web interface) port that we are going to use.
4. Once you run the preceding command, the container will start. It starts ODL Karaf by default, so you do not need to worry about running the ODL instance manually.

5. You should have a window similar to the following after executing the Docker run command:

```
PS C:\Users\Reza> docker run -it -p 8181:8181 learningopendaylight/boron
karaf: JAVA_HOME not set; results may vary
Apache Karaf starting up. Press Enter to open the shell now...
100% [========================================================================]

Karaf started in 3s. Bundle stats: 64 active, 64 total
```

```
Hit '<tab>' for a list of available commands
and '[cmd] --help' for help on a specific command.
Hit '<ctrl-d>' or type 'system:shutdown' or 'logout' to shutdown OpenDaylight.

opendaylight-user@root>
```

6. As you can see, you have already landed in the Karaf CLI.
7. Now enable the ODL features, such as Dlux, to access the web interface.

The following list explains how to enable the web interface:

1. In Karaf, enter the following command to install the Dlux package and enable the web interface:

   `feature:install odl-dlux-all`

2. You should get a result similar to the following screenshot:

```
opendaylight-user@root>feature:install odl-dlux-all
opendaylight-user@root>
```

We move on to the next step, that is, accessing the web interface:

1. To access the web interface of ODL from the same Windows 10 PC, which is running Docker, open a browser and try to access the loopback IP on port 8181.

   Remember that we told Docker to forward port 8181 of the host PC to the container.

2. Enter the URL `http://127.0.0.1:8181/index.html` in your browser.

3. You should get a result similar to the following screenshot:

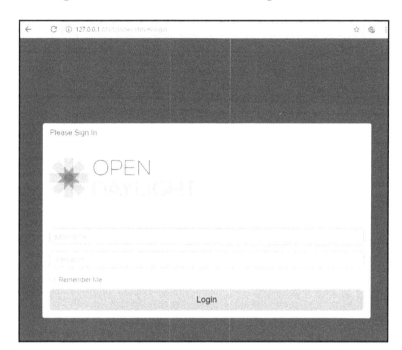

4. You can log in to your ODL instance using the default ODL credentials, which is `admin`, both username and password.

5. To exit the container, enter the `shutdown` command:

The container is a read-only filesystem and your changes are not persistent. Once you exit the container, all your changes will be lost. So every time you run the container, you need to enable the ODL modules you need.

What's going on behind the scenes of Docker on Windows?

You may ask what is Docker doing to run a Linux container? It is actually running a Linux virtual machine inside your Hyper-V hypervisor.

Once you run your Docker, open the Hyper-V manager application to find out the virtual machines that are running inside your Hyper-V. You will find a screen similar to the following:

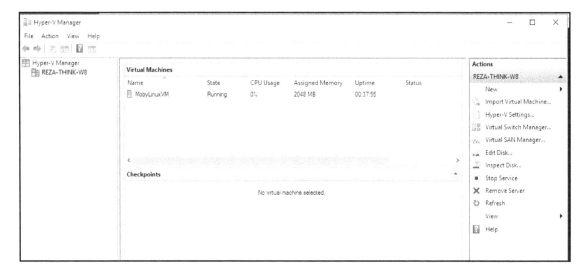

As you can see, there is a virtual machine called **MobyLinuxVM**, which is created by Docker and is running. This virtual machine is the Docker engine that is creating and running the containers.

The Docker service running on your Windows system is an interface between PowerShell and the Docker engineer to interface and translate the user commands in Windows PowerShell to the Docker Linux Virtual machine running inside Hyper-V.

How did we create the ODL container image for Docker?

Creating a Docker container requires a script file. We used the following script to build the container:

Line	Command
1	`FROM ubuntu:16.04`
2	`RUN apt-get -y update && apt-get install -y openjdk-8-jre wget`
3	`RUN mkdir /opt/odl`
4	`RUN wget -O /opt/odl/odl.tar.gz https://nexus.opendaylight.org/content/repositories/opendaylight.release/org/opendaylight/integration/distribution-karaf/0.5.2-Boron-SR2/distribution-karaf-0.5.2-Boron-SR2.tar.gz`
5	`RUN tar -xzf /opt/odl/odl.tar.gz -C /opt/odl/`
6	`RUN mv /opt/odl/dist* /opt/odl/boron`
7	`CMD /opt/odl/boron/bin/karaf`

Let's understand what each line in this Docker file does:

- **Line 1**: This line tells the Docker file that we need an Ubuntu 16.04 OS. Docker on its own will prepare an Ubuntu 16.04 OS for us to use.
- **Line 2**: Once Ubuntu 16.04 is booted up, it runs a full update and then installs Java and Wget.
- **Line 3**: This line creates the ODL directory in `/opt`.
- **Line 4**: This is for downloading the ODL Boron from the OpenDaylight website.
- **Line 5**: This is for extracting the ODL instance inside `/opt/odl`.
- **Line 6**: This is for renaming the folder name to `boron` in order to build `/opt/odl/boron`.
- **Line 7**: This is to start ODL Karaf. This command runs every time the container is started.

Summary

In this chapter, we learned how to install ODL and also went through a basic installation process of ODL in a distributed environment. You can practice doing this on other operating systems, such as FreeBSD and Windows, as it is a cross-platform software application based on Java.

In the next chapter, we'll build a virtual OpenFlow-switching lab using ODL and Mininet. You will see how ODL utilizes the OpenFlow protocol to populate the flow tables of OpenFlow-enabled switches.

4
Building a Virtual SDN Test Lab with Virtual Switches

In the previous chapters, we learned about software-defined networking, the OpenDaylight controller, and the basic installation of OpenDaylight in both standalone and distributed modes. In this chapter, we will build a virtual SDN lab. You may think that having OpenDaylight in a virtual environment means actually having a lab, but we need other elements for our SDN lab, which are switches.

As you already know, switches are physical devices with multiple Ethernet ports, from 10 MBps to 100 GBps. Remember that a software-defined network is a combination of an SDN controller and underlay switches and routers managed by the controller. We need switches to build our OpenDaylight lab and test our YANG applications. Plus, we need to build them in our virtual environment to ensure they are easy to manage and integrate with OpenDaylight and the SDN environment.

If you are a Cisco guru, you may know how to virtualize Cisco switches. Just use the Dynamips hypervisor and virtualize a Cisco 3600 series router with a virtual 16 Ethernet module. (Dynamips is now the core of GNS3, which is a great network lab virtualization platform).

Dynamips was created back in 2006 (or earlier), when there was no concept of network virtualization. Slowly, virtual switches came into production, starting with VMware virtual switches in ESX, then ESXi platforms, followed by the birth of Cisco Nexus 1000V, which was the first real production virtual switch.

After this, many virtual switches were introduced, such as **Open vSwitch** (**OVS**) and VMware VDS.

OVS is a very interesting virtual switch, and it is used in many open source and commercial networks and virtualization platforms. It was created by *Nicira*, which was acquired by VMware. OVS is a virtual switch that can be loaded on a Linux kernel and is used mainly with Linux hypervisors, such as KVM and XEN. Apart from the basic layer 2 switching capabilities, OVS also has SDN capabilities, such as supporting OVSDB and OpenFlow protocols. This means that an SDN controller can manage an OVS switch via OVSDB or OpenFlow southbound protocols. In this chapter, we will cover the following topics:

- What is Mininet?
- How to stepwise build a Mininet-enabled virtual switch
- Integration of a Mininet virtual switch with OpenDaylight
- Mininet commands
- Viewing flow mappings
- Using OVS as an SDN-capable virtual switch

What is Mininet?

Mininet creates a realistic virtual network that runs a real kernel, a switch, and application code on a single machine (VM, cloud, or native), in seconds, with a single command. It normally is in the form of a virtual machine that can be loaded on your hypervisor, and it has its own tiny operating system with a single CLI command. It is a tool to create OpenFlow virtual switches and hosts. With Mininet, you can also create virtual hosts that could be connected to the virtual ports of virtual switches; once it connects them, it assigns them with IP addresses as well. It's a complete all-in-one test tool to use with OpenDaylight.

For those of you familiar with Dynamips, Mininet is a tool that is similar to the command tool of Dynamips. In this chapter, we will explore Mininet and learn how to use its features to test our SDN platform. Mininet requires only 1 GB of RAM, but you can assign more memory when building complex topologies.

After downloading Mininet, you need to import it to your hypervisor (VMware or Oracle VirtualBox). After importing Mininet to your virtual environment and booting it up, you can log in to it via the following default credentials:

Username	mininet
Password	mininet

The Mininet command base is very simple to remember because it just has a single command:

```
sudo mn
```

Remember that Mininet is a tool, not a virtual switch or a virtual host. It is a tool to create one or more virtual switches with virtual hosts connected to them. Also, it enables its vertical switches to communicate and register with the SDN controller via OpenFlow.

The following diagram shows how Mininet operates and communicates with OpenDaylight:

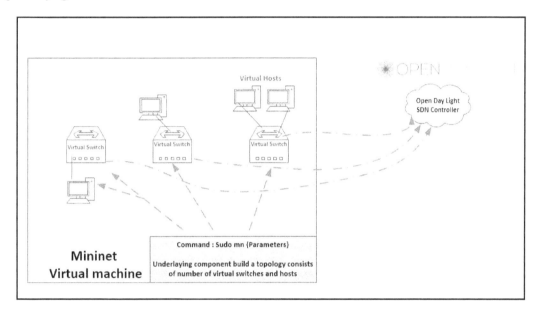

Once you run the mn command, Mininet starts, builds a topology (creates virtual switches and virtual hosts), and lands in Mininet Command Prompt.

Running sudo mn -help provides information about the command arguments you supply to Mininet:

- mininet@mininet-vm:/$ sudo mn --help
- Usage: mn [options]
- (type mn -h for details)

The mn utility creates a Mininet network from the command line. This network can create parameterized topologies, invoke the Mininet CLI, and run tests:

```
 -h, --help              show this help message and exit
 --switch=SWITCH
default|ivs|lxbr|ovs|ovsbr|ovsk|user[,param=value...]
                        ovs=OVSSwitch default=OVSSwitch
ovsk=OVSSwitch
                        lxbr=LinuxBridge user=UserSwitch ivs=IVSSwitch
                        ovsbr=OVSBridge
 --host=HOST             cfs|proc|rt[,param=value...]
                        rt=CPULimitedHost{'sched': 'rt'} proc=Host
                        cfs=CPULimitedHost{'sched': 'cfs'}
 --controller=CONTROLLER

default|none|nox|ovsc|ref|remote|ryu[,param=value...]
                        ovsc=OVSController none=NullController
                        remote=RemoteController
default=DefaultController
                        nox=NOX ryu=Ryu ref=Controller
 --link=LINK             default|ovs|tc[,param=value...]
default=Link
                        ovs=OVSLink tc=TCLink
 --topo=TOPO
linear|minimal|reversed|single|torus|tree[,param=value
                        ...] linear=LinearTopo torus=TorusTopo
tree=TreeTopo
                        single=SingleSwitchTopo
                        reversed=SingleSwitchReversedTopo
minimal=MinimalTopo
 -c, --clean            clean and exit
 --custom=CUSTOM        read custom classes or params from .py
file(s)
 --test=TEST
cli|build|pingall|pingpair|iperf|all|iperfudp|none
 -x, --xterms           spawn xterms for each node
 -i IPBASE, --ipbase=IPBASE
                        base IP address for hosts
 --mac                  automatically set host MACs
 --arp                  set all-pairs ARP entries
  -v VERBOSITY, --verbosity=VERBOSITY
                        info|warning|critical|error|debug|output
 --innamespace         sw and ctrl in namespace?
 --listenport=LISTENPORT
                        base port for passive switch listening
 --nolistenport        don't use passive listening port
 --pre=PRE             CLI script to run before tests
 --post=POST           CLI script to run after tests
```

```
    --pin                      pin hosts to CPU cores (requires --host cfs
or --host
                           rt)
    --nat                      adds a NAT to the topology that connects
Mininet hosts
    route any                  to the physical network. Warning: This may
                               traffic on the machine that uses Mininet's IP
subnet
                               into the Mininet network. If you need to change
                               Mininet's IP subnet, see the --ipbase option.
    --version                  prints the version and exits
    --cluster=server1,server2...
                               run on multiple servers (experimental!)
    --placement=block|random
                               node placement for --cluster (experimental!)
```

As you can see, the `--switch` option allows you to choose the type of virtual switch you are expecting Mininet to build and use. Mininet can use OVS, IVS, lxbr (Linux bridge), or OVS bridge.

Another important parameter that you need to know is the `controller` parameter. Controller parameters let Mininet connect its virtual switches to an external SDN controller. As you can see from command line help section, Mininet supports different SDN controllers such as NOX, Ryu, ODL supported.

Using the `controller` parameter, we will tell Mininet to connect our virtual switches to the OpenDaylight server that we built in the previous chapter:

```
sudo mn -controller=remote, ip=192.168.20.51
```

Running Mininet with no parameter results to the creation of a default topology. This topology consists of a single virtual switch and two virtual hosts connected to the virtual switch:

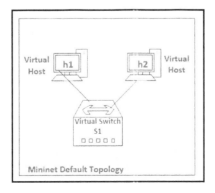

As you can see in the following screenshot, once you run the mn command, you land in the Mininet Command Prompt shell:

```
mininet@mininet-vm:/$ sudo mn
*** Creating network
*** Adding controller
*** Adding hosts:
h1 h2
*** Adding switches:
s1
*** Adding links:
(h1, s1) (h2, s1)
*** Configuring hosts
h1 h2
*** Starting controller
c0
*** Starting 1 switches
s1 ...
*** Starting CLI:
mininet>
mininet>
```

When you are in the Mininet shell, you can use Mininet commands to do the following:

- Tell hosts to ping each other
- Run a specific command on a host (example, ifconfig)
- Change the topology
- Run commands on virtual switches to dump or modify the flows
- Run commands on virtual hosts

The net command in Mininet provides the current topology and details on the hosts and switches are connected to each other:

```
mininet> net
h1 h1-eth0:s1-eth1
h2 h2-eth0:s1-eth2
s1 lo:  s1-eth1:h1-eth0 s1-eth2:h2-eth0
c0
mininet>
```

The preceding screenshot demonstrated the host `h1` and `h2` port connectivity as:

Source device	Source interface	Destination device	Destination port
h1	eth0	s1 (Switch 1)	eth1
h2	eth0	s1 (Switch 1)	eth2
s1	eth1	h1	eth0
s1	eth2	h2	eth0

To check the IP addresses of hosts `1` and `2`, you can run the `ifconfig` command on each host using the Mininet shell. The command is `h1 ifconfig`:

```
mininet> h1 ifconfig
h1-eth0   Link encap:Ethernet  HWaddr aa:58:44:58:97:74
          inet addr:10.0.0.1  Bcast:10.255.255.255  Mask:255.0.0.0
          UP BROADCAST RUNNING MULTICAST  MTU:1500  Metric:1
          RX packets:0 errors:0 dropped:0 overruns:0 frame:0
          TX packets:0 errors:0 dropped:0 overruns:0 carrier:0
          collisions:0 txqueuelen:1000
          RX bytes:0 (0.0 B)  TX bytes:0 (0.0 B)

lo        Link encap:Local Loopback
          inet addr:127.0.0.1  Mask:255.0.0.0
          UP LOOPBACK RUNNING  MTU:65536  Metric:1
          RX packets:0 errors:0 dropped:0 overruns:0 frame:0
          TX packets:0 errors:0 dropped:0 overruns:0 carrier:0
          collisions:0 txqueuelen:0
          RX bytes:0 (0.0 B)  TX bytes:0 (0.0 B)

mininet> h2 ifconfig
h2-eth0   Link encap:Ethernet  HWaddr 5e:80:93:72:8b:d2
          inet addr:10.0.0.2  Bcast:10.255.255.255  Mask:255.0.0.0
          UP BROADCAST RUNNING MULTICAST  MTU:1500  Metric:1
          RX packets:0 errors:0 dropped:0 overruns:0 frame:0
          TX packets:0 errors:0 dropped:0 overruns:0 carrier:0
          collisions:0 txqueuelen:1000
          RX bytes:0 (0.0 B)  TX bytes:0 (0.0 B)

lo        Link encap:Local Loopback
          inet addr:127.0.0.1  Mask:255.0.0.0
          UP LOOPBACK RUNNING  MTU:65536  Metric:1
          RX packets:0 errors:0 dropped:0 overruns:0 frame:0
          TX packets:0 errors:0 dropped:0 overruns:0 carrier:0
          collisions:0 txqueuelen:0
          RX bytes:0 (0.0 B)  TX bytes:0 (0.0 B)

mininet>
```

The preceding screenshot shows how to get the IP address of hosts 1 and 2 from Mininet. Mininet is the wrapper on top of its virtual switches and hosts; therefore, it has the ability to communicate with them and run specific commands on them.

Even you can check the version of the hosts:

```
mininet> h2 cat /etc/issue
Ubuntu 14.04 LTS \n \l

mininet>
```

Alternatively, you can even jump into the bash of the host:

```
mininet> h1 bash
root@mininet-vm:~#
root@mininet-vm:~#
root@mininet-vm:~#
root@mininet-vm:~# ls /
                                                              tmp
          initrd.img                                              vmlinuz
root@mininet-vm:~#
```

How to stepwise build a Mininet-enabled virtual switch

In this section, we will follow a basic stepwise procedure to build our first Mininet virtual lab.

Step 1 - Downloading

Download Mininet from `http://mininet.org/download/`.

To start your journey with Mininet, download the Mininet virtual machine files from `http://mininet.org/download/`.

There are three ways to build Mininet, as follows:

1. Using the prebuilt virtual machine, download Mininet from the mininet.org website.

   This is the easiest option; the prepackaged virtual machine includes a fully tested Mininet application running on a light Ubuntu server.

2. Download and compile Mininet from the source.

> This option would be good if you don't have resources to load a virtual machine. Say you want to use Mininet on Amazon AWS. To download the Mininet source code, follow the steps provided in GitHub and use the installer script to install and build it.

3. Build it using the Mininet packages on Ubuntu.

> This option works only on Ubuntu. Depending on the version of Ubuntu, you can use `apt-get install mininet` to install Mininet.

In general, 90 percent of Mininet deployment is based on a virtual machine; in our case, we will use this virtual machine option to build our OpenDaylight virtual lab:

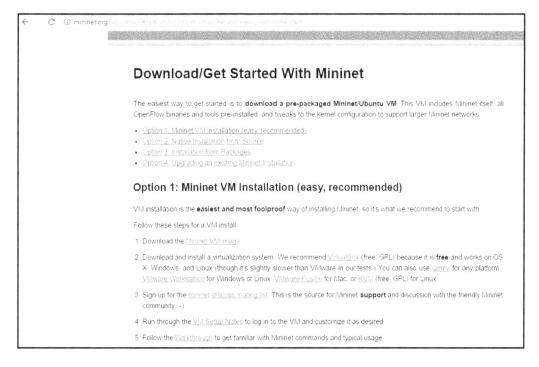

The file will be something similar to `mininet-2.2.1-150420-ubuntu-14.04-server-amd64.ovf` and placed in your default download directory. It is an **Open Virtualization Format (OVF)** that can be imported on different hypervisors, such as VMware, KVM, or Oracle VirtualBox.

Step 2 - Importing the Mininet OVF file to a hypervisor

The following demonstration shows how to import the OVF file to VMware Workstation and Oracle VirtualBox:

1. In Oracle VirtualBox, select **Import Virtual Appliance** from the **File** menu and use the browsing tool to point to the location where you have saved the Mininet virtual machine downloaded from the Mininet website earlier:

2. Choose the `Mininet.ovf` file and click on **Next**. You will be presented with a window similar to the following screenshot; it demonstrates the virtual appliance configuration. Normally, you don't need to change anything here, but pay attention to the network adapter; make sure it is in the same virtual network where your OpenDaylight virtual machine resides. This is important as we are going to run all our SDN lab virtual devices in the same network. Also, for troubleshooting, we use Wireshark on the same virtual interface that resides in the host PC; this allows us to capture and see full communication between ODL and Mininet.

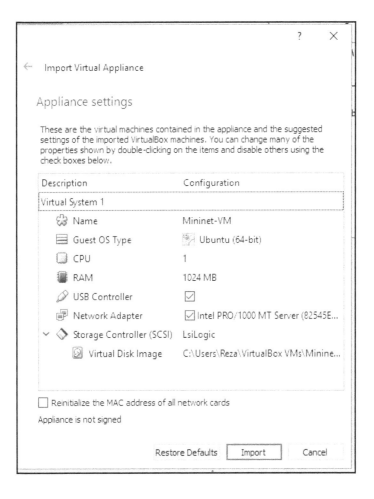

3. If you are using **VMware Workstation** as your hypervisor, go to **File** | **Open** and point to the location of the OVA file to import:

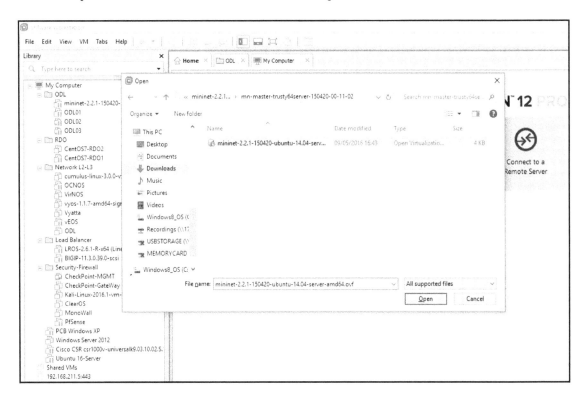

4. Select a name for the new Mininet virtual machine, such as `MiniNET`, and choose where you want to save the virtual machine files (you can skip this step):

Step 3 - Powering on

1. After successfully importing the virtual machine to your hypervisor, you can power on the Mininet virtual machine.
2. Once you power on the virtual machine, it starts booting and you will receive a login prompt (an Ubuntu login prompt). So this is a successful boot of the Mininet virtual machine.
3. Since we haven't set the IP address of our Mininet virtual appliance yet, use the hypervisor console (virtual KVM) to access the virtual appliance.

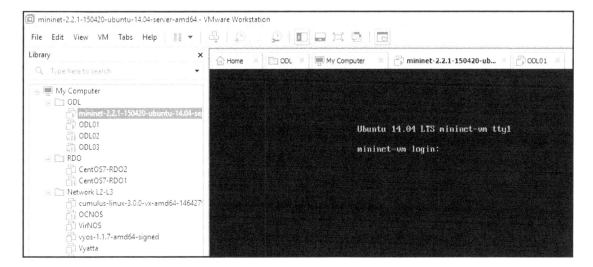

4. Use the default username and password (both Mininet) to log in. Ensure you are logged in.

Step 4 - Setting the IP address

1. We will set the IP address of the Mininet virtual machine to `192.168.20.55/24`. This is in the same subnet of our first instance of OpenDaylight, which we built in the previous chapter with this IP: `192.168.20.51`.
2. To set the IP address, edit the `/etc/network/interfaces` file, using your favorite text editor (I use nano as my text editor):

```
Sudo nano /etc/network/interfaces
```

3. Modify the section for `eth0` as follows:

```
        auto eth0
iface eth0 inet static
address 192.168.20.55
netmask 255.255.255.0
gateway 192.168.20.1
dns-nameservers 8.8.8.8
```

4. Use *Ctrl + X* to save the file.
5. To make the new IP address effective, restart the networking service using the following command:

```
sudo service networking restart
```

6. Alternatively, use the following command to restart the networking service:

```
sudo /etc/init.d/networking restart
```

Step 5 - Basic connectivity testing

Now you should be able to use your PuTTY application to establish an SSH connection to the Mininet virtual appliance:

1. Open PuTTY and enter `192.168.20.55` as the target address and connect. If you are unable to establish `ssh`, check the virtual network adapter on the Mininet VM. Ensure you have used the correct virtual NIC, the one on the `192.168.20.0/24` network.
2. After you successfully connect SSH to Mininet, check basic connectivity between Mininet VM and the OpenDaylight VM. Ensure the OpenDaylight virtual machine is also powered on and running:

```
mininet@mininet-vm:/$ ping 192.168.20.51 -c 5
PING 192.168.20.51 (192.168.20.51) 56(84) bytes of data.
64 bytes from 192.168.20.51: icmp_seq=1 ttl=64 time=0.443 ms
64 bytes from 192.168.20.51: icmp_seq=2 ttl=64 time=0.442 ms
64 bytes from 192.168.20.51: icmp_seq=3 ttl=64 time=0.372 ms
64 bytes from 192.168.20.51: icmp_seq=4 ttl=64 time=0.385 ms
64 bytes from 192.168.20.51: icmp_seq=5 ttl=64 time=0.358 ms

--- 192.168.20.51 ping statistics ---
5 packets transmitted, 5 received, 0% packet loss, time 4000ms
rtt min/avg/max/mdev = 0.358/0.400/0.443/0.035 ms
```

3. At this stage, we have our Mininet and OpenDaylight virtual appliances running and connected.

Integrating a Mininet virtual switch with OpenDaylight

Let's start building a Mininet topology with one switch and two hosts. Before we start, ensure your OpenDaylight instance is up and running and you can access it via the web interface; verify that you can successfully log in as well.

If for any reason you are unable to log in to your OpenDaylight web interface, go back to your installation steps and review the configuration or perform a fresh installation.

Now a quick flashback to Chapter 3, *OpenDaylight Installation and Deployment*. If you are reinstalling OpenDaylight, ensure you are extracting the OpenDaylight instance from the original TAR file. Run `/opt/OpenDayLight/boron/bin/karaf` for the first time. After landing on Karaf (OpenDaylight) Command Prompt, run the following command:

```
>feature:install odl-dlux-all odl-restconf odl-l2switch-switch odl-
mdsal-apidocs
```

This command will install all the required modules to enable OpenDaylight to work as a basic SDN controller. The `OpenDaylight-l2switch-switch` is a very important module.

Once you install the `OpenDaylight-l2-switch` module, OpenDaylight will start listening at TCP `6633` port, which is related to the OpenFlow service. All communication between the Mininet switch and OpenDaylight via OpenFlow happens over TCP `6633` port. So if you don't have the `OpenDaylight-l2switch-switch` feature installed, Mininet will not be able to communicate with OpenDaylight.

```
192.168.20.55      192.168.20.51      TCP      74 37654→6633 [SYN] Seq=0 Win=29200 Len=0 MSS=1460
192.168.20.55      192.168.20.51      TCP      74 37655→6633 [SYN] Seq=0 Win=29200 Len=0 MSS=1460
192.168.20.51      192.168.20.55      TCP      60 6633→37654 [RST, ACK] Seq=1 Ack=1 Win=0 Len=0
192.168.20.51      192.168.20.55      TCP      60 6633→37655 [RST, ACK] Seq=1 Ack=1 Win=0 Len=0
```

Without old-l2switch-switch modules installed

This will install and enable the Dlux web user interface. You should be able to access and log in to the web interface of OpenDaylight via `http://192.168.20.51:8181/index.html`.

OK! Assuming we have both OpenDaylight and Mininet running, let's start with a simple lab of a switch and two hosts:

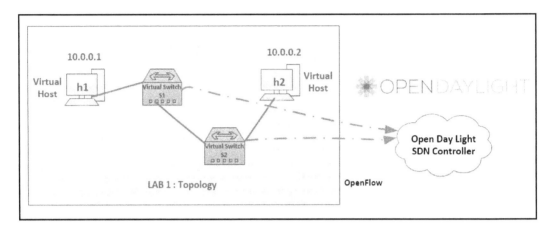

In this lab, we will create a virtual switch and two hosts in Mininet and connect the virtual switch to OpenDaylight.

Once we connect the virtual switch to OpenDaylight, it will become an SDN-enabled switch, and OpenDaylight will manage and update the forwarding tables of the virtual switch. It will not make any decision on its own.

To start, run the following command in Mininet:

```
sudo mn -controller=remote, ip=192.168.20.51 -topo=linear,2 --mac
```

Running this command will result in the creation of the topology of our lab.

The --mac option will generate a simple MAC address for the hosts. For example, the MAC address of host 1 will become 00:00:00:00:00:01 if the --mac option is used in Mininet.

If you run the preceding Mininet command, you will get a result similar to the following screenshot:

```
mininet@mininet-vm:/$ sudo mn --controller=remote,ip=192.168.20.51 --topo=linear,2 --mac
*** Creating network
*** Adding controller
*** Adding hosts:
h1 h2
*** Adding switches:
s1 s2
*** Adding links:
(h1, s1) (h2, s2) (s2, s1)
*** Configuring hosts
h1 h2
*** Starting controller
c0
*** Starting 2 switches
s1 s2 ...
*** Starting CLI:
mininet>
```

Now, log in to the OpenDaylight web interface. You should see two new switches in the topology:

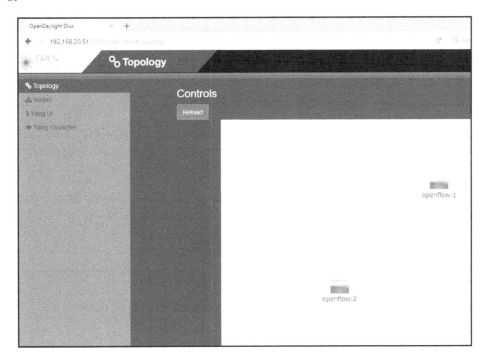

This is because of the OpenFlow communication between the Mininet OpenFlow switch and OpenDaylight.

Let's have a closer look at what happens in terms of packets after running that Mininet command.

I ran Wireshark on a host interface where the virtual machines were connected. Filtering openfLow_v1 will help you find what communication is happening between Mininet and the OpenDaylight host.

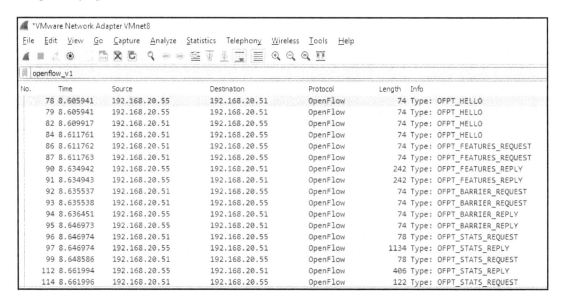

The first two packets are OpenFlow HELLO. There are two packets because we specified we wanted two virtual switches in our Mininet topology. These packets are sourced from Mininet (192.168.20.55) and moved toward OpenDaylight (192.168.20.51).

Once the HELLO packets switch (Mininet) to OpenDaylight, there are two HELLO packets that move OpenDaylight toward Mininet, which is the response received by HELLO.

Let's have a closer look at the OpenFlow HELLO packet:

```
Wireshark · Packet 78 · wireshark_28B0CB8F-F843-4526-953D-49773024E253_20170107163529_a64456      —   □

  Frame 78: 74 bytes on wire (592 bits), 74 bytes captured (592 bits) on interface 0
  Ethernet II, Src: Vmware_69:36:bc (00:0c:29:69:36:bc), Dst: Vmware_44:f0:0c (00:0c:29:44:f0:0c)
  Internet Protocol Version 4, Src: 192.168.20.55, Dst: 192.168.20.51
  Transmission Control Protocol, Src Port: 37568, Dst Port: 6633, Seq: 1, Ack: 1, Len: 8
∨ OpenFlow 1.0
     .000 0001 = Version: 1.0 (0x01)
     Type: OFPT_HELLO (0)
     Length: 8
     Transaction ID: 63
```

The `HELLO` packet is very simple and includes a few attributes: version, type, length, and `Transaction ID`. `Transaction ID` is incremented every time an OpenFlow-speaking device sends a message.

The reply to the `HELLO` packet is also very similar to the initial `HELLO` packets:

```
Wireshark · Packet 84 · wireshark_28B0CB8F-F843-4526-953D-49773024E253_20170107163529_a64456         —    □

  Frame 84: 74 bytes on wire (592 bits), 74 bytes captured (592 bits) on interface 0
  Ethernet II, Src: Vmware_44:f0:0c (00:0c:29:44:f0:0c), Dst: Vmware_69:36:bc (00:0c:29:69:36:bc)
  Internet Protocol Version 4, Src: 192.168.20.51, Dst: 192.168.20.55
  Transmission Control Protocol, Src Port: 6633, Dst Port: 37569, Seq: 1, Ack: 9, Len: 8
∨ OpenFlow 1.0
     .000 0001 = Version: 1.0 (0x01)
     Type: OFPT_HELLO (0)
     Length: 8
     Transaction ID: 65
```

This packet is sent from OpenDaylight toward the Mininet virtual switch 2 (you can identify this as the destination TCP port is different).

Now in Mininet, ping `h2` from `h1` for testing:

```
mininet> h1 ping h2
PING 10.0.0.2 (10.0.0.2) 56(84) bytes of data.
64 bytes from 10.0.0.2: icmp_seq=1 ttl=64 time=0.280 ms
64 bytes from 10.0.0.2: icmp_seq=2 ttl=64 time=0.168 ms
64 bytes from 10.0.0.2: icmp_seq=3 ttl=64 time=0.178 ms
64 bytes from 10.0.0.2: icmp_seq=4 ttl=64 time=0.197 ms
64 bytes from 10.0.0.2: icmp_seq=5 ttl=64 time=0.159 ms
64 bytes from 10.0.0.2: icmp_seq=6 ttl=64 time=0.161 ms
64 bytes from 10.0.0.2: icmp_seq=7 ttl=64 time=0.148 ms
^C
--- 10.0.0.2 ping statistics ---
7 packets transmitted, 7 received, 0% packet loss, time 6001ms
rtt min/avg/max/mdev = 0.148/0.184/0.280/0.043 ms
mininet>
```

This ping shows that `h1` is able to reach `h2` although the switches are not L2-enabled and all of the flow configuration was injected by OpenDaylight to the Mininet virtual switches.

Have a look at the OpenDaylight web interface's topology:

Check out the hosts in the screenshot. Topology drawing is based on a very fancy UI that allows you to drag switches or hosts anywhere on your screen.

Did you realize that initially we didn't have any hosts showing up in the topology? This started happening after we ran a ping from h1 to h2.

The reason for this is that initially OpenDaylight didn't have any knowledge about the hosts in the network. Once h1 requested to ping h2, OpenDaylight realized that there is a host called h1 with MAC address 00:00:00:00:00:001 and IP address 10.0.0.1 that wants to send an ICMP echo request to host h2 with the IP address 10.0.0.2.

Host h1, by default, sends an ARP request, searching for the MAC address of h2 with the IP address 10.0.0.2.

The ARP request is sent to the virtual switch 1. This request has a broadcast destination address (00:00:00:00:00:00). The virtual switch 1 doesn't know what to do with the frame received from h1. Remember, an SDN OpenFlow switch has no understanding of basic layer 2 learning and forwarding; therefore, it forwards the packet to an SDN controller asking the controller what to do.

It encapsulates the ARP request inside an OpenFlow packet-in message and sends it to OpenDaylight:

```
Ethernet II, Src: Vmware_69:36:bc (00:0c:29:69:36:bc), Dst: Vmware_44:f0:0c (00:0c:29:44:f0:0c)
Internet Protocol Version 4, Src: 192.168.20.55, Dst: 192.168.20.51
Transmission Control Protocol, Src Port: 38116, Dst Port: 6633, Seq: 34999, Ack: 1192, Len: 60
v OpenFlow 1.0
    .000 0001 = Version: 1.0 (0x01)
    Type: OFPT_PACKET_IN (10)
    Length: 60
    Transaction ID: 0
    Buffer Id: 0xffffffff
    Total length: 42
    In port: 1
    Reason: Action explicitly output to controller (1)
    Pad: 00
    Ethernet II, Src: 00:00:00_00:00:01 (00:00:00:00:00:01), Dst: Broadcast (ff:ff:ff:ff:ff:ff)
  v Address Resolution Protocol (request)
        Hardware type: Ethernet (1)
        Protocol type: IPv4 (0x0800)
        Hardware size: 6
        Protocol size: 4
        Opcode: request (1)
        Sender MAC address: 00:00:00_00:00:01 (00:00:00:00:00:01)
        Sender IP address: 10.0.0.1
        Target MAC address: 00:00:00_00:00:00 (00:00:00:00:00:00)
        Target IP address: 10.0.0.2
```

OpenDaylight receives the packets, and these packets are handled by the L2 switch module inside OpenDaylight. The L2 switch module decapsulates the ARP request from the preceding OpenFlow message and realizes that the destination address is 10.0.0.2. However, OpenDaylight and the L2 switch module have no prior information about where 10.0.0.2 is located; it doesn't exist in any table. Therefore, the OpenDaylight L2 switch module needs to tell the switches how to handle the broadcast frame. This is because virtual switches, by default, don't have any logic to forward the broadcast to all the ports as there is no flow installed inside their flow tables.

OpenDaylight tells about switches with an Flow-MOD message. An MOD message is used to modify the flow tables in switches. Using this message, OpenDaylight programs the flow table of virtual switches to forward the broadcast to their active ports.

Let's have a closer look at our Wireshark packet capture to see the Flow-MOD messages:

```
245 7.031988    192.168.20.51    192.168.20.55    OpenFlow     74 Type: OFPT_BARRIER_REQUEST
246 7.032310    192.168.20.55    192.168.20.51    OpenFlow     74 Type: OFPT_BARRIER_REPLY
251 7.521639    192.168.20.51    192.168.20.55    OpenFlow    146 Type: OFPT_FLOW_MOD
252 7.521659    192.168.20.51    192.168.20.55    OpenFlow    154 Type: OFPT_FLOW_MOD
254 7.522124    192.168.20.51    192.168.20.55    OpenFlow    154 Type: OFPT_FLOW_MOD
255 7.522342    192.168.20.51    192.168.20.55    OpenFlow    146 Type: OFPT_FLOW_MOD
257 7.532086    192.168.20.51    192.168.20.55    OpenFlow     74 Type: OFPT_BARRIER_REQUEST
258 7.532302    192.168.20.55    192.168.20.51    OpenFlow     74 Type: OFPT_BARRIER_REPLY
```

As you can see in the preceding illustration, packets 251, 252, 253, and 254 are Flow-MOD messages from OpenDaylight (192.168.20.51) to Mininet (192.168.20.55).

Now the question that arises is why there are four packets? The reason for this is twofold. First, we have two virtual switches; therefore, OpenDaylight is sending two packets to each switch. Second, remember that each switch has two active ports in our linear topology:

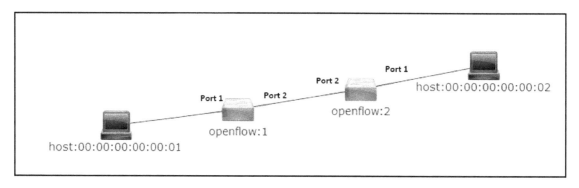

OpenDaylight needs to tell each switch to forward the broadcast message to both **Port 1** and **Port 2** on each switch; therefore, OpenDaylight generates four OpenFlow MOD packets.

Taking a closer look at the MOD packet will tell you that it simply specifies a flow to a switch. A flow has source and destination MAC addresses and source and destination ports:

Input port	Source MAC	Destination MAC	Destination IP	Output port

The following illustration shows all the four packets, and you can see the differences:

1. Packet one, to switch one (TCP destination port 38116), tells us whether there is a frame coming in from port 2, destined to 00:00:00:00:00:00; if yes, it sends it to all the ports (Out port: 65535):

```
Ethernet II, Src: Vmware_44:f0:0c (00:0c:29:44:f0:0c), Dst: Vmware_69:36:bc (00:0c:29:69:36:bc)
Internet Protocol Version 4, Src: 192.168.20.51, Dst: 192.168.20.55
Transmission Control Protocol, Src Port: 6633, Dst Port: 38116, Seq: 1016, Ack: 34991, Len: 80
OpenFlow 1.0
    .000 0001 = Version: 1.0 (0x01)
    Type: OFPT_FLOW_MOD (14)
    Length: 80
    Transaction ID: 20
    Wildcards: 3678462
    In port: 2
    Ethernet source address: 00:00:00_00:00:00 (00:00:00:00:00:00)
    Ethernet destination address: 00:00:00_00:00:00 (00:00:00:00:00:00)
    Input VLAN id: 65535
    Input VLAN priority: 0
    Pad: 00
    Dl type: 0
    IP ToS: 0
    IP protocol: 0
    Pad: 0000
    Source Address: 0.0.0.0
    Destination Address: 0.0.0.0
    Source Port: 0
    Destination Port: 0
    Cookie: 0x2b00000000000010
    Command: New flow (0)
    Idle time-out: 0
    hard time-out: 0
    Priority: 2
    Buffer Id: 0xffffffff
    Out port: 65535
    Flags: 0
```

2. Packet two, to switch two (TCP destination port 38116), tells us whether there is a frame coming in from port 1, destined to 00:00:00:00:00:00; if yes, it sends it to all the ports (Out port: 65535):

```
> Ethernet II, Src: Vmware_44:f0:0c (00:0c:29:44:f0:0c), Dst: Vmware_69:36:bc (00:0c:29:69:36:bc)
> Internet Protocol Version 4, Src: 192.168.20.51, Dst: 192.168.20.55
> Transmission Control Protocol, Src Port: 6633, Dst Port: 38116, Seq: 1096, Ack: 34991, Len: 88
v OpenFlow 1.0
    .000 0001 = Version: 1.0 (0x01)
    Type: OFPT_FLOW_MOD (14)
    Length: 88
    Transaction ID: 21
    Wildcards: 3678462
    In port: 1
    Ethernet source address: 00:00:00_00:00:00 (00:00:00:00:00:00)
    Ethernet destination address: 00:00:00_00:00:00 (00:00:00:00:00:00)
    Input VLAN id: 65535
    Input VLAN priority: 0
    Pad: 00
    Dl type: 0
    IP ToS: 0
    IP protocol: 0
    Pad: 0000
    Source Address: 0.0.0.0
    Destination Address: 0.0.0.0
    Source Port: 0
    Destination Port: 0
    Cookie: 0x2b00000000000011
    Command: New flow (0)
    Idle time-out: 0
    hard time-out: 0
    Priority: 2
    Buffer Id: 0xffffffff
    Out port: 65535
    Flags: 0
```

3. Packet three, to switch two (TCP destination port 38115), tells us whether there is a frame coming in from port 1, destined to 00:00:00:00:00:00; if yes, it sends it to all the ports (Out port: 65535):

```
Ethernet II, Src: Vmware_44:f0:0c (00:0c:29:44:f0:0c), Dst: Vmware_69:36:bc (00:0c:29:69:36:bc)
Internet Protocol Version 4, Src: 192.168.20.51, Dst: 192.168.20.55
Transmission Control Protocol, Src Port: 6633, Dst Port: 38115, Seq: 1101, Ack: 34899, Len: 88
OpenFlow 1.0
    .000 0001 = Version: 1.0 (0x01)
    Type: OFPT_FLOW_MOD (14)
    Length: 88
    Transaction ID: 20
    Wildcards: 3678462
    In port: 1
    Ethernet source address: 00:00:00_00:00:00 (00:00:00:00:00:00)
    Ethernet destination address: 00:00:00_00:00:00 (00:00:00:00:00:00)
    Input VLAN id: 65535
    Input VLAN priority: 0
    Pad: 00
    Dl type: 0
    IP ToS: 0
    IP protocol: 0
    Pad: 0000
    Source Address: 0.0.0.0
    Destination Address: 0.0.0.0
    Source Port: 0
    Destination Port: 0
    Cookie: 0x2b00000000000012
    Command: New flow (0)
    Idle time-out: 0
    hard time-out: 0
    Priority: 2
    Buffer Id: 0xffffffff
    Out port: 65535
    Flags: 0
```

4. Packet four, to switch two (TCP destination port `38115`), tells us whether there is a frame coming in from port `2`, destined to `00:00:00:00:00:00`; if yes, it sends it to all the ports (`Out port: 65535`):

```
Ethernet II, Src: Vmware_44:f0:0c (00:0c:29:44:f0:0c), Dst: Vmware_69:36:bc (00:0c:29:69:36:bc)
Internet Protocol Version 4, Src: 192.168.20.51, Dst: 192.168.20.55
Transmission Control Protocol, Src Port: 6633, Dst Port: 38115, Seq: 1189, Ack: 34899, Len: 80
OpenFlow 1.0
    .000 0001 = Version: 1.0 (0x01)
    Type: OFPT_FLOW_MOD (14)
    Length: 80
    Transaction ID: 21
    Wildcards: 3678462
    In port: 2
    Ethernet source address: 00:00:00_00:00:00 (00:00:00:00:00:00)
    Ethernet destination address: 00:00:00_00:00:00 (00:00:00:00:00:00)
    Input VLAN id: 65535
    Input VLAN priority: 0
    Pad: 00
    Dl type: 0
    IP ToS: 0
    IP protocol: 0
    Pad: 0000
    Source Address: 0.0.0.0
    Destination Address: 0.0.0.0
    Source Port: 0
    Destination Port: 0
    Cookie: 0x2b00000000000013
    Command: New flow (0)
    Idle time-out: 0
    hard time-out: 0
    Priority: 2
    Buffer Id: 0xffffffff
    Out port: 65535
    Flags: 0
```

```
>feature:install odl-dlux-all odl-restconf odl-l2switch-switch
odl-mdsal-apidocs
```

With this method, OpenDaylight installs the flows inside OpenFlow switches, and hosts will now be able to communicate with each other.

Let's have a summary of steps for a successful ping between host **H1** to **H2** in our linear topology:

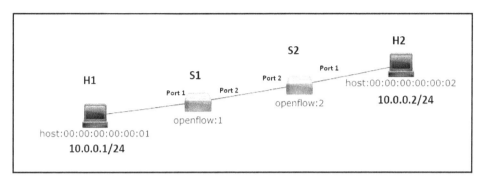

The following shows the steps for a successful ping between host **H1** to **H2** in our linear topology:

1. **H1** executes ping **H2** at the 10.0.0.2 command.
2. **H1** realizes that its NIC IP address (10.0.0.1/24) and destination IP address (10.0.0.2/24) are both in the same layer 2 subnet. Therefore, it needs to send an ARP request to find the destination MAC address of 10.0.0.2.
3. The **H1** OS generates an ARP request to find the MAC address of **H2**. The ARP request is sent out from **Port 1** to **S1** with destination MAC of 00:00:00:00:00:00 (broadcast).
4. Switch **S1** receives the frame with the source of **H1** MAC address, destined broadcast; it has no entry in its flow table to forward the frame. Therefore, **S1** needs to ask the SDN controller about how to deal with this packet.
5. Switch **S1** encapsulates the ARP request packet in an OpenFlow IN packet and sends it to OpenDaylight. The OpenFlow packet goes from 192.168.20.55 (Mininet) to 192.168.20.51 (OpenDaylight) over TCP 6633 (OpenFlow)
6. OpenDaylight receives the OpenFlow packets and passes them to the L2 switch module for processing. OpenDaylight realizes that the frame needs to be forwarded to all the ports as it is a broadcast frame.
7. OpenDaylight sends a flow configuration message to **S1** telling that if a frame is received on **Port 1**, destined broadcast, you need to send it out to all the ports.
8. **S1** installs the flow and forwards the packet to all the ports, which is only **Port 2** at this stage.
9. **S2** receives a frame on **Port 2**, destined for broadcast. It has no flow installed in its table to match; therefore, it encapsulates the packets and forwards them to OpenDaylight.

Note that OpenDaylight is smart enough to avoid this by sending an OpenFlow MOD message to **S2** prior to receiving such a message.

10. **S2** gets the OpenFlow MOD message from OpenDaylight to forward a broadcast message to all the ports. Therefore, it forwards to **Port 1**, which is connected to **H2**.
11. **H2** receives the ARP request packet and sends a reply.
12. **H2** replies to ARP and the same process will happen again.

Mininet commands

Mininet is a great tool for virtualizing the OpenFlow lab. As discussed before, Mininet is a wrapper over multiple tools, such as OVS, and Linux containers. It allows you to create different configurations and labs using virtual switches.

Mininet has lots of commands and CLI arguments; we will cover only the relevant ones here:

- Arguments
- --Topo

    Topo is used to tell Mininet what kind of topology to build. There are predefined topologies in Mininet, such as linear, tree, and minimal; also, you can create and define your own topology using a script.

    Linear and tree topologies are good topologies to use when running Mininet labs.

- --mac

    This argument generates the host's MAC addresses based on the host ID; it is very useful for debugging and testing.

- -v debug

    This argument is used for debugging the output of Mininet. If you start Mininet with this option, it starts generating lots of debug output to help you understand what's going on behind the Mininet wrapper.

- `--arp`

  This argument tells Mininet to populate the ARP table of hosts with the ARP entries of each other. For example, in a two host (`h1`- `h2`) configuration, using `-arp` will result in having the `h2` MAC address inside the ARP table of `h1` and vice versa.

  If you use this option without any flow entries, the switches and OpenDaylight will not know how to forward between your two hosts, and your hosts will not be able to ping each other.

- `--test ipref` or `--test pingall`

  This argument will tell Mininet to run a `pingall` or `ipref` test after the creation of the topology to ensure all hosts can reach each other. The `iperf` command creates an UDP sender and receiver on two hosts and sends packets between both.

- Mini command line

  Inside the Mininet shell, there are multiple commands that can be used. Important ones are as follows:

- `Net`

  This command shows the topology and connectivity of the hosts and switches in Mininet:

```
mininet> net
h1 h1-eth0:s1-eth1
h2 h2-eth0:s2-eth1
s1 lo:   s1-eth1:h1-eth0 s1-eth2:s2-eth2
s2 lo:   s2-eth1:h2-eth0 s2-eth2:s1-eth2
c0
mininet>
```

- `links`

  This shows the existing links between hosts and switches and tests them:

  ```
  mininet> links
  h1-eth0<->s1-eth1 (OK OK)
  h2-eth0<->s2-eth1 (OK OK)
  s2-eth2<->s1-eth2 (OK OK)
  mininet>
  ```

- `nodes`

  This displays the list of nodes in the topology, either switches or hosts:

  ```
  mininet> nodes
  available nodes are:
  c0 h1 h2 s1 s2
  mininet>
  ```

- `dump`

  This dumps information about all the nodes:

```
mininet> dump
<Host h1: h1-eth0:10.0.0.1 pid=19436>
<Host h2: h2-eth0:10.0.0.2 pid=19439>
<OVSSwitch s1: lo:127.0.0.1,s1-eth1:None,s1-eth2:None pid=19444>
<OVSSwitch s2: lo:127.0.0.1,s2-eth1:None,s2-eth2:None pid=19447>
<RemoteController{'ip': '192.168.20.51'} c0: 192.168.20.51:6633 pid=19430>
mininet>
```

- Run a command on a host or switch:
  - Host: the `h[x]` command
  - Switch: the `s[x]` command
  - Example: `h1 ifconfig`

```
mininet> h1 ifconfig
*** errRun: ['stty', '-icanon', 'min', '1']
  0h1-eth0   Link encap:Ethernet  HWaddr 00:00:00:00:00:01
           inet addr:10.0.0.1  Bcast:10.255.255.255  Mask:255.0.0.0
           UP BROADCAST RUNNING MULTICAST  MTU:1500  Metric:1
           RX packets:0 errors:0 dropped:0 overruns:0 frame:0
           TX packets:0 errors:0 dropped:0 overruns:0 carrier:0
           collisions:0 txqueuelen:1000
           RX bytes:0 (0.0 B)  TX bytes:0 (0.0 B)

  lo       Link encap:Local Loopback
           inet addr:127.0.0.1  Mask:255.0.0.0
           UP LOOPBACK RUNNING  MTU:65536  Metric:1
           RX packets:0 errors:0 dropped:0 overruns:0 frame:0
           TX packets:0 errors:0 dropped:0 overruns:0 carrier:0
           collisions:0 txqueuelen:0
           RX bytes:0 (0.0 B)  TX bytes:0 (0.0 B)

mininet>
```

- The following are the commands used to test the connectivity between hosts:
    - h1 ping h2

```
mininet> h1 ping h2
*** errRun: ['stty', '-icanon', 'min', '1']
  0PING 10.0.0.2 (10.0.0.2) 56(84) bytes of data.
64 bytes from 10.0.0.2: icmp_seq=1 ttl=64 time=0.169 ms
64 bytes from 10.0.0.2: icmp_seq=2 ttl=64 time=0.155 ms
^CsendInt: writing chr(3)

--- 10.0.0.2 ping statistics ---
2 packets transmitted, 2 received, 0% packet loss, time 1001ms
rtt min/avg/max/mdev = 0.155/0.162/0.169/0.007 ms
mininet>
```

- `pingall`

```
  Omininet> pingall
*** Ping: testing ping reachability
h1 -> *** h1 : ('ping -c1  10.0.0.2',)
PING 10.0.0.2 (10.0.0.2) 56(84) bytes of data.
64 bytes from 10.0.0.2: icmp_seq=1 ttl=64 time=0.268 ms

--- 10.0.0.2 ping statistics ---
1 packets transmitted, 1 received, 0% packet loss, time 0ms
rtt min/avg/max/mdev = 0.268/0.268/0.268/0.000 ms
h2
h2 -> *** h2 : ('ping -c1  10.0.0.1',)
PING 10.0.0.1 (10.0.0.1) 56(84) bytes of data.
64 bytes from 10.0.0.1: icmp_seq=1 ttl=64 time=0.144 ms

--- 10.0.0.1 ping statistics ---
1 packets transmitted, 1 received, 0% packet loss, time 0ms
rtt min/avg/max/mdev = 0.144/0.144/0.144/0.000 ms
h1
*** Results: 0% dropped (2/2 received)
mininet> 
```

- `pingpair`

```
mininet> pingpair
h1 -> *** h1 : ('ping -c1  10.0.0.2',)
PING 10.0.0.2 (10.0.0.2) 56(84) bytes of data.
64 bytes from 10.0.0.2: icmp_seq=1 ttl=64 time=0.383 ms

--- 10.0.0.2 ping statistics ---
1 packets transmitted, 1 received, 0% packet loss, time 0ms
rtt min/avg/max/mdev = 0.383/0.383/0.383/0.000 ms
h2
h2 -> *** h2 : ('ping -c1  10.0.0.1',)
PING 10.0.0.1 (10.0.0.1) 56(84) bytes of data.
64 bytes from 10.0.0.1: icmp_seq=1 ttl=64 time=0.127 ms

--- 10.0.0.1 ping statistics ---
1 packets transmitted, 1 received, 0% packet loss, time 0ms
rtt min/avg/max/mdev = 0.127/0.127/0.127/0.000 ms
h1
*** Results: 0% dropped (2/2 received)
mininet> 
```

- These commands are used to ping between hosts
    - `iperf`

```
mininet> iperf
*** Iperf: testing TCP bandwidth between h1 and h2
*** Results: ['333 Mbits/sec', '337 Mbits/sec']
mininet> 
```

- The following is used to run a simple web server on `h1` and a client on `h2`:

```
mininet> h1 python -m SimpleHTTPServer 80 &
mininet> h2 wget -O - h1
mininet> h1 kill %python
```

```
mininet> h1 python -m SimpleHTTPServer 80 &
mininet> h2 wget -O - h1
--2016-12-19 19:23:46--  http://10.0.0.1/
Connecting to 10.0.0.1:80... connected.
HTTP request sent, awaiting response... 200 OK
Length: 802 [text/html]
Saving to: 'STDOUT'

 0% [                                    ] 0          --.-K/s
<title>Directory listing for /</title>
<body>
<h2>Directory listing for /</h2>
<hr>
<ul>
<li><a href=".bash_history">.bash_history</a>
<li><a href=".bash_logout">.bash_logout</a>
<li><a href=".bashrc">.bashrc</a>
<li><a href=".cache/">.cache/</a>
<li><a href=".gitconfig">.gitconfig</a>
<li><a href=".mininet_history">.mininet_history</a>
<li><a href=".profile">.profile</a>
<li><a href=".rnd">.rnd</a>
<li><a href=".wireshark/">.wireshark/</a>
<li><a href="install-mininet-vm.sh">install-mininet-vm.sh</a>
<li><a href="loxigen/">loxigen/</a>
<li><a href="mininet/">mininet/</a>
<li><a href="oflops/">oflops/</a>
<li><a href="oftest/">oftest/</a>
<li><a href="openflow/">openflow/</a>
<li><a href="pox/">pox/</a>
</ul>
<hr>
</body>
</html>
100%[===========================================>] 802          --.-K/s    in 0s

2016-12-19 19:23:46 (171 MB/s) - written to stdout [802/802]

mininet> ▮
```

Viewing the flow mappings

Mininet allows you to use the `dpctl` command to communicate with the virtual switch and get the status of the flows.

The basic command to check the flows is `dpctl dump-flows`:

```
mininet> dpctl dump-flows
*** s1 ------------------------------------------------------------
*** s1 : ('ovs-ofctl', 'dump-flows', <OVSSwitch s1: lo:127.0.0.1,s1-eth1:None,s1-eth2:None pid=20685> )
NXST_FLOW reply (xid=0x4):
 cookie=0x2b0000000000000b, duration=927.436s, table=0, n_packets=4, n_bytes=280, idle_age=920, priority=2,in_port=1 actions=output:2,CONTROLLE
R:65535
 cookie=0x2b0000000000000a, duration=927.436s, table=0, n_packets=4, n_bytes=280, idle_age=920, priority=2,in_port=2 actions=output:1
 cookie=0x2b00000000000006, duration=930.441s, table=0, n_packets=186, n_bytes=15810, idle_age=1, priority=100,dl_type=0x88cc actions=CONTROLLE
R:65535
 cookie=0x2b00000000000006, duration=930.441s, table=0, n_packets=0, n_bytes=0, idle_age=930, priority=0 actions=drop
NXST_FLOW reply (xid=0x4):
 cookie=0x2b0000000000000b, duration=927.436s, table=0, n_packets=4, n_bytes=280, idle_age=920, priority=2,in_port=1 actions=output:2,CONTROLLE
R:65535
 cookie=0x2b0000000000000a, duration=927.436s, table=0, n_packets=4, n_bytes=280, idle_age=920, priority=2,in_port=2 actions=output:1
 cookie=0x2b00000000000006, duration=930.441s, table=0, n_packets=186, n_bytes=15810, idle_age=1, priority=100,dl_type=0x88cc actions=CONTROLLE
R:65535
 cookie=0x2b00000000000006, duration=930.441s, table=0, n_packets=0, n_bytes=0, idle_age=930, priority=0 actions=drop
*** s2 ------------------------------------------------------------
*** s2 : ('ovs-ofctl', 'dump-flows', <OVSSwitch s2: lo:127.0.0.1,s2-eth1:None,s2-eth2:None pid=20688> )
NXST_FLOW reply (xid=0x4):
 cookie=0x2b0000000000000c, duration=927.439s, table=0, n_packets=4, n_bytes=280, idle_age=920, priority=2,in_port=1 actions=output:2,CONTROLLE
R:65535
 cookie=0x2b0000000000000d, duration=927.439s, table=0, n_packets=4, n_bytes=280, idle_age=920, priority=2,in_port=2 actions=output:1
 cookie=0x2b00000000000005, duration=933.378s, table=0, n_packets=187, n_bytes=15895, idle_age=1, priority=100,dl_type=0x88cc actions=CONTROLLE
R:65535
 cookie=0x2b00000000000005, duration=933.376s, table=0, n_packets=0, n_bytes=0, idle_age=933, priority=0 actions=drop
NXST_FLOW reply (xid=0x4):
 cookie=0x2b0000000000000c, duration=927.439s, table=0, n_packets=4, n_bytes=280, idle_age=920, priority=2,in_port=1 actions=output:2,CONTROLLE
R:65535
 cookie=0x2b0000000000000d, duration=927.439s, table=0, n_packets=4, n_bytes=280, idle_age=920, priority=2,in_port=2 actions=output:1
 cookie=0x2b00000000000005, duration=933.378s, table=0, n_packets=187, n_bytes=15895, idle_age=1, priority=100,dl_type=0x88cc actions=CONTROLLE
R:65535
 cookie=0x2b00000000000005, duration=933.376s, table=0, n_packets=0, n_bytes=0, idle_age=933, priority=0 actions=drop
mininet>
```

The preceding output shows the current flow table in both `s1` and `s2` virtual switches.

Are you looking for the MAC addresses or IP addresses of the source and destination in the preceding screenshot? For sure, you are! But remember that this is the output you receive after running the `pingall` example. In the `pingall` example, OpenDaylight has created a flow entry in switches to simply send all packets from port 1 to port 2 on each switch and vice versa.

If OpenDaylight configures a specific flow with an IP address or MAC address, then you will be able to see more details in your flow table.

Try running Mininet with more hosts and different topologies for practice; capture the packets and check the flow table of the switches. This will help you get friendlier with OpenDaylight and OpenFlow.

Using OVS as an SDN-capable virtual switch

OVS is a production quality multilayer virtual switch created back in 2009. It is the same as OpenDaylight; it is also provided by *Linux Foundation*.

Open vSwitch was created by a company called **Nicira**, which was later acquired by VMware and became a core part of the current VMware NSX network virtualization platform.

OVS quickly became the favorite virtual switch for virtual environments, and it is now playing a large part in other open source projects, such as OpenStack, oVirt, and Proxmox.

OVS is layer 2 switch and it supports different technologies and protocols, such as 802.1Q, BFD, NetFlow, sFlow, port mirroring, VLANs, LACP, VXLAN, GENEVE GRE Overlays, STP, and IPv6.

From a control and management perspective, Open vSwitch supports both OpenFlow and the OVSDB management protocol, which means it can operate both as a soft switch running within the hypervisor and also as the control stack for the switch silicon. You can leverage OVS on a bare metal switch by running it on **Open Network Linux** (**ONL**) and using the OpenFlow drivers to communicate with the switch silicon.

OVS can work either as a standalone L2 switch within a hypervisor host, or it can be managed and programmed via an SDN controller, such as ODL.

The following diagram illustrates the OVS structure:

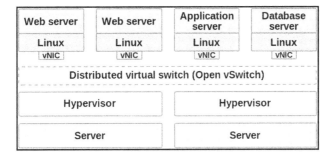

OVS supports OpenFlow protocol support (including many extensions for virtualization). This makes it a preferred testing and production virtual switch in SDN OpenFlow environments. OVS is the virtual switch used in Mininet.

Summary

In this chapter, we learned how to build a virtual SDN lab using OpenDaylight and Mininet. We found Mininet to be neat tool for virtualizing OVS-based virtual switches and Linux container hosts. We saw how OpenDaylight and Mininet communicate with each other and how hosts in a virtual lab can ping each other by leveraging the SDN controller to program the flows inside the switches.

In the next chapter, we go deeper into the networking capabilities of OpenDaylight to see how it communicates with the outside world.

5
Basic Networking with OpenDaylight

In this chapter, we will take a step further toward understanding what happens inside OpenDaylight. It is a continuation of Chapter 4, *Building a Virtual SDN Test Lab with Virtual Switches*, where we learned about OpenDaylight's networking behaviors and basic communication between hosts in a Mininet environment.

We will continue with our OpenDaylight and Mininet virtual environments. However, we will go deeper into layer 2 switching and the **Virtual Tenant Network** (**VTN**) module of OpenDaylight; we'll go through this module in detail to understand how it works as it is a fundamental part of SDN networking.

We will use VTN to create VLANs and have a lab for isolating host traffic between different VLANs. VTN is one of the key modules of OpenDaylight. It has many features, such as virtual routers and bridges; we will cover them in more detail in Chapter 9, *Building a Software-Driven Data Center with OpenDaylight*.

We will build a small virtual network inside OpenDaylight with our virtual hosts and connect it with the outside world by peering to a BGP router. We will explore another awesome open source virtual router called **VyOS** (successor of *Vyatta*, which was acquired by *Brocade*, and recently, Brocade was acquired by *Broadcom*). We will explore how OpenDaylight handles **Border Gateway Protocol** (**BGP**) with an outside router and exchanges the IP prefixes and routes.

We'll explore the following topics:

- Layer 2 switching in OpenDaylight
- How to allow hosts or virtual machines to communicate with each other
- Peering with the outside world using BGP
- Security and flow management
- Link aggregation in theory

Layer 2 switching in OpenDaylight

In the previous chapter, we learned about basic L2 switching in OpenDaylight. This was our basic topology:

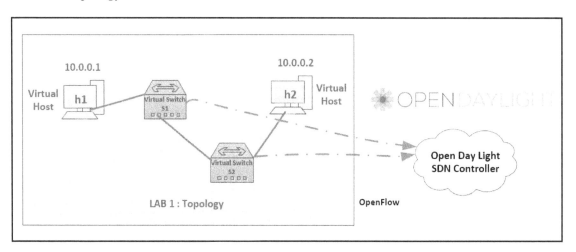

We learned that Layer 2 switching is a feature or module of OpenDaylight and needs to be enabled prior to using it. To enable L2 switching in OpenDaylight, you need to run the following command in the OpenDaylight shell:

```
feature:install OpenDaylight-l2switch-switch
```

After installing the L2 switch module, OpenDaylight enables the OpenFlow protocol and starts listening on TCP port 6633, which is the OpenFlow server port:

```
learningod1@ODL01:~$ netstat -ln
Active Internet connections (only servers)
Proto Recv-Q Send-Q Local Address           Foreign Address         State
tcp        0      0 0.0.0.0:22              0.0.0.0:*               LISTEN
tcp6       0      0 :::8080                 :::*                    LISTEN
tcp6       0      0 :::8181                 :::*                    LISTEN
tcp6       0      0 :::22                   :::*                    LISTEN
tcp6       0      0 127.0.0.1:2550          :::*                    LISTEN
tcp6       0      0 :::8185                 :::*                    LISTEN
tcp6       0      0 :::44378                :::*                    LISTEN
tcp6       0      0 :::44444                :::*                    LISTEN
tcp6       0      0 :::6653                 :::*                    LISTEN
tcp6       0      0 :::42719                :::*                    LISTEN
tcp6       0      0 127.0.0.1:42655         :::*                    LISTEN
tcp6       0      0 :::8101                 :::*                    LISTEN
tcp6       0      0 :::6633                 :::*                    LISTEN
tcp6       0      0 :::1099                 :::*                    LISTEN
Active UNIX domain sockets (only servers)
Proto RefCnt Flags       Type       State         I-Node   Path
unix  2      [ ACC ]     STREAM     LISTENING     14323    /run/user/1001/systemd/private
unix  2      [ ACC ]     SEQPACKET  LISTENING     11180    /run/udev/control
unix  2      [ ACC ]     STREAM     LISTENING     11174    /run/systemd/private
unix  2      [ ACC ]     STREAM     LISTENING     11191    /run/systemd/journal/stdout
unix  2      [ ACC ]     STREAM     LISTENING     11204    /run/systemd/fsck.progress
unix  2      [ ACC ]     STREAM     LISTENING     13768    /run/uuidd/request
unix  2      [ ACC ]     STREAM     LISTENING     16563    /var/run/dbus/system_bus_socket
unix  2      [ ACC ]     STREAM     LISTENING     13767    /var/lib/lxd/unix.socket
learningod1@ODL01:~$
```

Every physical or virtual OpenFlow-enabled switch in the SDN domain needs to first register with the OpenFlow controller (OpenDaylight). Our Mininet switches, which are actually OVS switches, will then be registered with OpenDaylight and will pop up in the OpenDaylight topology view instantly.

The registration process is completed via an OpenFlow HELLO packet originating from the OpenFlow switch sent, to the SDN controller. This controller (OpenDaylight) can authenticate the request and check whether the switch is allowed to be part of OpenDaylight's SDN domain.

The following image demonstrates basic communication between an SDN switch and SDN controller:

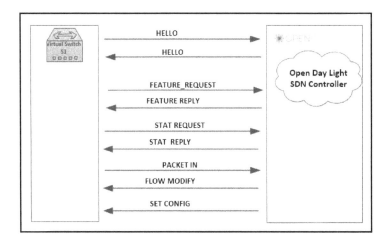

Handling the flows

Let's make the topology more complex and let OpenDaylight handle the flows. We will build a topology that is slightly more complex than the process of using a tree:

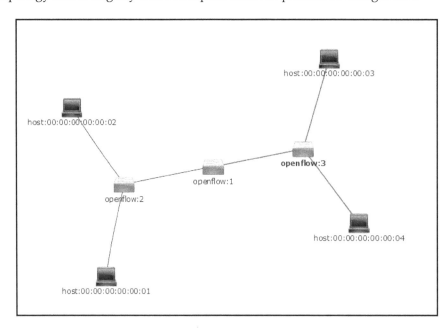

This is a tree topology built in Mininet using the following command:

```
sudo mn --controller=remote,ip=192.168.20.51 --topo=tree,2 --mac
```

In this topology, hosts 1 and 2 are connected to the virtual switch 2, hosts 3 and 4 are connected to virtual switch 3, and virtual switch 1 is connected to virtual switches 2 and 3.

Building the topology

Once you launch the mn command, Mininet starts building the topology by creating the OVS switch instances and host containers and connecting all to each other using virtual links. You can always check what is going on in the Mininet machine by establishing a second ssh session for the Mininet virtual machine and checking the processes or interfaces.

After building the topology, run a pingall command on Mininet to ensure all hosts could ping each other:

```
mininet> pingall
*** Ping: testing ping reachability
h1 -> h2 h3 h4
h2 -> h1 h3 h4
h3 -> h1 h2 h4
h4 -> h1 h2 h3
*** Results: 0% dropped (12/12 received)
mininet>
```

Once the pingall command is initiated, each host will start pinging other hosts. Since the host doesn't know the MAC address of the other host, it will send an ARP request to find the IP address of the host it is trying to ping. Say host 1 tries to ping host 2 and both are connected to the same virtual switch 2. In this case, once the virtual switch 2 receives the ARP packet (frame)-which is a layer 2 packet (no IP source and destination, just a broadcast frame) it checks in its forwarding tables whether it has a matching entry for a flow with its broadcast destined. In this case, it doesn't have it, as we just turned on the switches.

The OVS switch encapsulates the whole packet in an OpenFlow `PACKET_IN` packet and sends it to OpenDaylight.

OpenDaylight receives the packet and uses the ARP handler module to process the request. Remember, for each OpenFlow `PACKET_IN` message that is sent to OpenDaylight, the controller needs to send a reply back to the switch to state what to do with that packet.

Once the ARP packet is forwarded to all the switch ports and the ARP reply is forwarded back to host 1, which was the main ARP queried, host 1 starts sending layer 3 ICMP packets to host 2. The packets have a source and destination IP address as well as a MAC address. Again, the OVS switch does not know how to forward the packet as it does not have any flow entry for host 1 and host 2 MAC addresses yet.

The virtual switch 1 sends an OpenFlow `PACKET_IN` message back to the OpenDaylight controller and encapsulates the ICMP packet inside the frame. OpenDaylight receives the packet and runs its internal searches on its database to find out where are hosts 1 and 2, where they are connected to.

Remember that OpenDaylight does know where the hosts are connected as it receives and processes the `PACKET_IN` messages.

OpenDaylight also uses **Link Layer Discovery Protocol** (**LLDP**) to identify the hosts connected to an SDN network. For sending out LLDP packets, OpenDaylight uses OpenFlow's `PACKET_OUT` message. `PACKET_OUT` is similar to `PACKET_IN` with the difference that it is generated from OpenDaylight instead of a virtual switch.

Once the virtual switch receives an OpenFlow `PACKET_OUT` message, it decapsulates the original packet and processes it.

Up to now, the OVS virtual switch 1 received flow information from OpenDaylight on how to forward the packets from host 1 to host 2.

If you run a packet capture, you will be able to see the OFPT_FLOW_MOD messages sent from OpenDaylight to virtual switch 1, instructing it on how to handle the packets from host 1 to host 2:

```
Ethernet II, Src: Vmware_44:f0:0c (00:0c:29:44:f0:0c), Dst: Vmware_69:36:bc (00:0c:29:69:36:bc)
Internet Protocol Version 4, Src: 192.168.20.51, Dst: 192.168.20.55
Transmission Control Protocol, Src Port: 6633, Dst Port: 36652, Seq: 1399, Ack: 19955, Len: 160
OpenFlow 1.0
    .000 0001 = Version: 1.0 (0x01)
    Type: OFPT_FLOW_MOD (14)
    Length: 80
    Transaction ID: 21
    Wildcards: 3678451
    In port: 0
    Ethernet source address: 00:00:00_00:00:03 (00:00:00:00:00:03)
    Ethernet destination address: 00:00:00_00:00:04 (00:00:00:00:00:04)
    Input VLAN id: 65535
    Input VLAN priority: 0
    Pad: 00
    Dl type: 0
    IP ToS: 0
    IP protocol: 0
    Pad: 0000
    Source Address: 0.0.0.0
    Destination Address: 0.0.0.0
    Source Port: 0
    Destination Port: 0
    Cookie: 0x2a000000000000c8
    Command: New flow (0)
    Idle time-out: 1800
    hard time-out: 3600
    Priority: 10
    Buffer Id: 0xffffffff
    Out port: 65535
    Flags: 0
```

With Mininet, you can build very complex scenarios to include hundreds of hosts and switches. Try the following command on your Mininet application and see the results:

```
sudo mn --controller=remote,ip=192.168.20.51 --topo=tree,8 --mac
```

You will get a complex topology, similar to what is shown here:

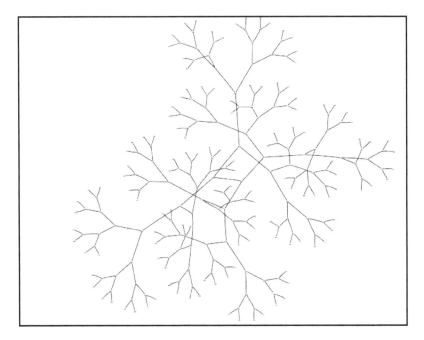

Try the `pingall` command and you will be able to see how fast OpenDaylight populates the follow table of the OVS switches in Mininet. This complex scenario not only proves the scalability and power of OpenDaylight, but also the complete creditability of SDN and OpenFlow-based solutions.

Implementing VLANs and host isolation in OpenDaylight

In this section, we will explore the most well-known L2 feature, which is VLAN. VLAN or L2 isolation, is one of the most basic features of every Ethernet switch. For those of you who are not familiar with the VLAN concept, in simple terms, it means dividing an Ethernet switch into smaller isolated switches that do not communicate with each other. This is mostly done in the switch ASIC (main switch hardware chipset), and it does not require the processing power of a switch CPU (Switch CPU is where the switch operating system runs). Normally, ASIC partitions the internal CAM table and assigns specific ports to the partitions; this results in full isolation of the ports assigned to different VLANs in a switch.

In a pure SDN world, as we have learned, we only have flow tables and the OpenFlow agent. Switch doesn't have the feature to create VLANs; therefore, it is the SDN controller's job to translate the VLAN function into a flow table.

> In hybrid SDN solutions, where switches run their own software along with an OpenFlow agent, switches can still use VLAN and other software features. In this context, we are talking about pure Openflow-based switches without running any other switch software.

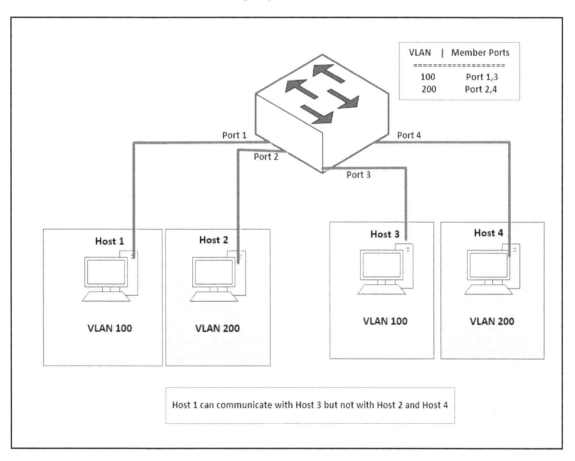

The same implementation in SDN is as follows:

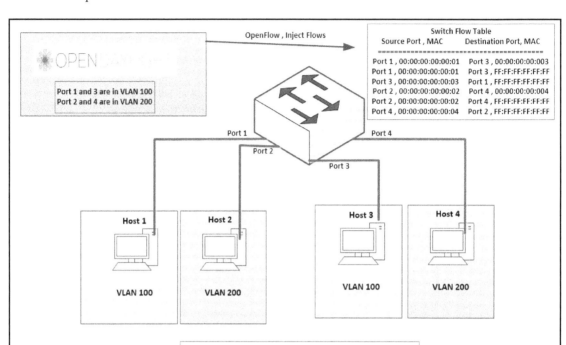

VLANs in SDN and OpenDaylight will be implemented in the SDN controller (OpenDaylight). Once it is defined which switch port is assigned to which VLAN, OpenDaylight will populate the flow tables of that particular switch with the relevant flows; this only allows communication between the hosts in the same VLAN.

Even the broadcasts in each VLAN is programmed to traverse only to the ports within that particular VLAN, without any leak to ports in other VLANs.

Virtual Tenant Network (VTN)

As you already know, OpenDaylight is a modular-based platform. The module that we will explore to implement VLAN is called VTN. It is one of the big modules of OpenDaylight with lots of features, such as virtual bridges and routers. In this chapter, we will look at only the VLAN feature of VTN and will continue to explore the other features of VTN in Chapter 9, *Building a Software-Driven Data Center with OpenDaylight*.

OpenDaylight VTN is an application that provides a multitenant virtual network on an SDN VTN is a plugin which can create isolated network resources. Similar to VLANs, where we use them to isolated L2 networks, VTN also can create isolated infrastructure but not only limited to VLAN or L2.

VTN works well when integrated with OpenStack. Any newly created tenant (project) in OpenStack will be reflected in OpenDaylight via VTN. VTN tracks the resources of each tenant including the networks, ports, switches. VTN then injects the required policies to the switches in order to isolate the traffic between tenants. VTN is a MD-SAL based plugin and its not bound to use OpenFlow. It relies on MD-SAL to decide what technology or south bound protocol needs to be used to implement, apply the isolation when using different switches.

VTN has two major components in OpenDaylight:

VTN Manager

VTN Manager is the core component of VTN and is an OpenDaylight module. It has a REST interface, which is designed to be used by a VTN coordinator; however, you can communicate with VTN Manager directly via a REST API.

VTN coordinator

VTN coordinator is an external application that can be downloaded from the OpenDaylight website. It provides a REST API for users to use VTN Manager. It translates the REST calls from the user into REST API calls to VTN Manager. VTN Manager is a module in OpenDaylight that communicates with other components of OpenDaylight to build the VTN's components.

The following table shows the elements that make up the VTN. In the VTN, a virtual network is constructed using virtual nodes (vBridge and vRouter) and virtual interfaces and links. It is possible to configure a network, which has the L2 and L3 transfer function, by connecting the virtual interfaces made on virtual nodes via virtual links.

Name of element		Description
Virtual node	vBridge	Logical representation of an L2 switch function
	vRouter	Logical representation of a router function
	vTep	Logical representation of **Tunnel End Point (TEP)**
	vTunnel	Logical representation of Tunnel
	vBypass	Logical representation of the connectivity between controlled networks
Virtual interface	interface	Representation of an endpoint on the virtual node
Virtual link	vLink	Logical representation of L1 connectivity between virtual interfaces

Implementing VLAN in SDN

Let's get back to our topic of this section, which is about creating VLAN in SDN and OpenDaylight. We need to understand how to create isolated L2 domains in OpenDaylight, distribute them between switches, and manage the communication. From the VTN component table that was just demonstrated, use the vBridges (virtual bridges) feature to implement VLANs in OpenDaylight.

For those of you who might not be familiar with the term bridge, it defines an L2 domain, mostly limited to a single VLAN. It is the same as a switch or VLAN in the traditional networking world. Bridge is mostly a Linux term, and it refers to the creation of virtual switches in Linux, which are called bridges.

To implement VLANs in OpenDaylight, we will use VTN, create a virtual tenant, and create multiple vBridges and assign different VLAN IDs to them:

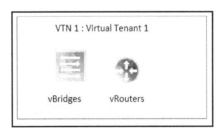

OpenDaylight VLAN LAB

In this lab, we will build a network with three switches and six hosts. We will create two VLANs (VLAN 100 and VLAN 200) and assign hosts 1, 3, and 5 to VLAN 100 and hosts 2, 4, and 6 to VLAN 200. This is an interesting and important lab. I highly recommend you have this lab as it may lead you from traditional networking to the SDN world.

Let's have a look at our VLAN lab topology:

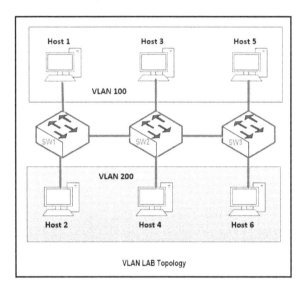

The topology is very simple: two VLANs, three switches, and six hosts. Host are assigned to different VLANs. Our objective is to use OpenDaylight and VTN to deploy VLAN (or better put, the layer 2 isolation) between the hosts. Switches are the OVS-enabled switches based on Mininet.

Here are the steps you need to follow in this lab:

1. Setting up the environment in Mininet
2. Setting up the VTN modules in OpenDaylight
3. Setting up and building your REST client
4. Using the Rest API to create a virtual tenant and virtual bridges in OpenDaylight
5. Testing

Let's start with having some fun with Mininet.

Step 1 - Setting up the environment in Mininet

As we have learned until now, in Mininet, we can use predefined topologies, such as tree and linear, to build a topology. However, in this lab, we need to tell Mininet that we need three switches and six hosts and how they are going to be connected to each other.

Mininet supports Python-based coding, and we will build a topology using Python to tell Mininet what to build.

I have put the following Python code for creating the Mininet topology:

```python
#!/usr/bin/python

from mininet.node import Host, RemoteController
from mininet.topo import Topo
import apt

#Note Vlan package check only work with ubuntu
#Please comment the package check if your running the script other
than ubuntu

#package check Start
cache = apt.Cache()
if cache['vlan'].is_installed:
    print "Vlan installed"
else:
    print "ERROR:VLAN package not  installed please run sudo apt-
get install vlan"
    exit(1)
#package check End

class VLANHost( Host ):
        def config( self, vlan=1, **params ):
                """Configure VLANHost according to (optional)
parameters:

                        vlan: VLAN ID for default interface"""
                r = super( Host, self ).config( **params )
                intf = self.defaultIntf()
# remove IP from default, "physical" interface
                self.cmd( 'ifconfig %s inet 0' % intf )
# create VLAN interface
                self.cmd( 'vconfig add %s %d' % ( intf, vlan ) )
# assign the host's IP to the VLAN interface
                self.cmd( 'ifconfig %s.%d inet %s' % ( intf, vlan,
params['ip'] ) )
# update the intf name and host's intf map
                newName = '%s.%d' % ( intf, vlan )
```

```
        # update the (Mininet) interface to refer to VLAN interface name
                    intf.name = newName
        # add VLAN interface to host's name to intf map
                    self.nameToIntf[ newName ] = intf
                    return r

class MyTopo( Topo ):
    "Simple topology example."

    def __init__( self ):
        "Create custom topo."

        # Initialize topology
        Topo.__init__( self )

        # Add hosts and switches
        host1=self.addHost( 'h1', cls=VLANHost, vlan=100)
        host2=self.addHost( 'h2', cls=VLANHost, vlan=200)
        host3=self.addHost( 'h3', cls=VLANHost, vlan=100)
        host4=self.addHost( 'h4', cls=VLANHost, vlan=200)
        host5=self.addHost( 'h5', cls=VLANHost, vlan=100)
        host6=self.addHost( 'h6', cls=VLANHost, vlan=200)

        s1 = self.addSwitch( 's1' )
        s2 = self.addSwitch( 's2' )
        s3 = self.addSwitch( 's3' )

        self.addLink(s1,host1)
        self.addLink(s1,host2)
        self.addLink(s1,s2)
        self.addLink(s2,host3)
        self.addLink(s2,host4)
        self.addLink(s2,s3)
        self.addLink(s3,host5)
        self.addLink(s3,host6)
topos = { 'simplevlan': ( lambda: MyTopo() ) }
```

This simple Python code will generate the topology we need in this lab, inside the Mininet. Mininet provides Python classes, and in this example, we used the topo class and created multiple hosts, switches, and links between them.

If you look deeper into the preceding Python code, you would see that we are creating VLAN virtual interfaces on the hosts and telling them to use the 802.1q tagging on the frames they will send out over their interface.

This means that every packet that the host is sending has a `802.1q` tag with the VLAN ID of that host. For example, all packets generated by host 1 will have the `802.1q` tag with `VLAN-ID = 100`.

To build this topology in Mininet, establish `ssh` connection to your Mininet machine (`192.168.20.55` in our lab environment) and use your favorite editor to copy and paste the code and save it as `vlan.py`.

After you save it, use the following command to tell Mininet that we need to build the topology:

```
sudo mn --controller=remote,ip=192.168.20.51 --custom vlan.py --topo
simplevlan --mac
```

After running the preceding command you should get a output similar to shown here:

```
mininet@mininet-vm:~$ sudo mn --controller=remote,ip=192.168.20.51 --
custom vlan.py --topo simplevlan --mac
*** Creating network
*** Adding controller
*** Adding hosts:
h1 h2 h3 h4 h5 h6
*** Adding switches:
s1 s2 s3
*** Adding links:
(s1, h1) (s1, h2) (s1, s2) (s2, h3) (s2, h4) (s2, s3) (s3, h5) (s3, h6)
*** Configuring hosts
h1 h2 h3 h4 h5 h6
*** Starting controller
c0
*** Starting 3 switches
s1 s2 s3 ...
```

Log in to the web interface of OpenDaylight and have a look at the topology. The URL to access our lab is `http://192.168.20.51:8181/index.html#/topology`.

As you can see, OpenDaylight has build and shown the same topology we were expecting:

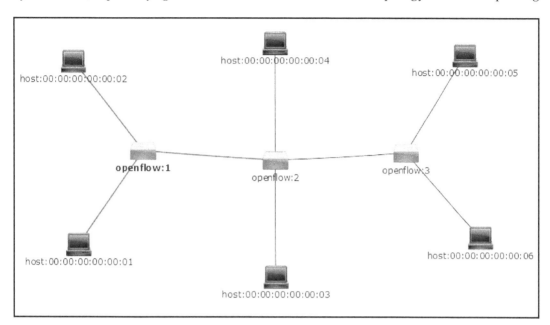

Let's proceed with the VTN configuration.

Step 2 - VTN configuration on OpenDaylight

To install VTN, use the following command on the OpenDaylight Karaf command line:

```
feature:install OpenDaylight-vtn-manager OpenDaylight-vtn-manager-rest
```

After installing the module, you can start using the REST API of VTN Manager to ask VTN to create virtual bridges (VLANs).

Step 3 - Setting up and building our REST client

Most of you are using either a Windows or Mac machine and have your OpenDaylight and Mininet virtualized in a hypervisor.

In order to communicate with OpenDaylight via REST API calls, you can either use the `curl` program on Linux (the same host as in OpenDaylight) or a GUI-based REST client, such as postman.

Postman is an extension of Google Chrome and provides a very structured management interface for calling REST API calls to any system. You need to get familiar with the postman, as mobbing forward, we need to use lots of REST API calls to different OpenDaylight modules. REST calls are based on HTTP-standard HTTP methods, such as GET, POST, and PUT-to either get information from OpenDaylight and the modules or inject a configuration to OpenDaylight.

The GET method is mainly used for reading or getting information from OpenDaylight, such as reading a configuration of the status of OpenDaylight. The results are received from IDL.

The PUT and POST methods are used for injecting a configuration to OpenDaylight:

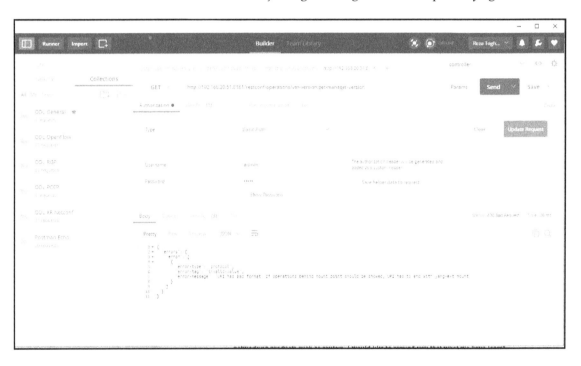

To continue and access the VTN Manager REST API interface, we will use the curl command on the OpenDaylight host, which is easier and quicker for this example. You can use curl when there is some data being sent and received to and from OpenDaylight. There is no limitation with curl, but from considering human readability and managing a text-based interface for sending lots of XML stream, curl may become challenging.

Step 4 - Using a REST API to create the virtual tenant and virtual bridges in OpenDaylight

Let's continue with our VTN configuration via a REST API.

Open an SSH connection to OpenDaylight (another one, as your current SSH is landed in OpenDaylight's Karaf CLI).

Creating a VTN

The first step is to create a VTN, namely `Tenant1`:

```
curl -v --user "admin":"admin" -H "Accept: application/json" -H
"Content-type: application/json" -X POST
http://localhost:8181/controller/nb/v2/vtn/default/vtns/Tenant1 -d
'{"description": "Virtual Tenant 1"}'
```

Creating the first virtual bridge (vbr1)

After the creation of our first virtual tenant, create a virtual bridge:

```
curl -v --user "admin":"admin" -H "Accept: application/json" -H
"Content-type: application/json" -X POST
http://localhost:8181/controller/nb/v2/vtn/default/vtns/Tenant1/vbridges/vb
r1 -d '{}'
```

Assigning VLAN 100 to virtual bridge 1 (vbr1)

And we assign the virtual bridge 1 (vbr1) to VLAN 100.

```
curl -v --user "admin":"admin" -H "Accept: application/json" -H "Content-
type: application/json" -X POST
http://localhost:8181/controller/nb/v2/vtn/default/vtns/Tenant1/vbridges/vb
r1/vlanmaps -d '{"vlan": 100 }'
```

Creating the second virtual bridge (vbr2)

This virtual bridge will be used for VLAN 200:

```
      curl -v --user "admin":"admin" -H "Accept: application/json" -H
"Content-type: application/json" -X POST
http://localhost:8181/controller/nb/v2/vtn/default/vtns/Tenant1/vbridges/vb
r2 -d '{}'
```

Assigning VLAN 200 to vbr2

And we assign the virtual bridge 2 (vbr2) to VLAN 200:

```
      curl -v --user "admin":"admin" -H "Accept: application/json" -H
"Content-type: application/json" -X POST
http://localhost:8181/controller/nb/v2/vtn/default/vtns/Tenant1/vbridges/vb
r2/vlanmaps -d '{"vlan": 200 }'
```

Step 5 - Testing

Please add some content at this stage:

```
      mininet> pingall
Ping: testing ping reachability
h1 -> X h3 X h5 X
h2 -> X X h4 X h6
h3 -> h1 X X h5 X
h4 -> X h2 X X h6
h5 -> h1 X h3 X X
h6 -> X h2 X h4 X
```

The output of the `pingall` command matches with our topology and what we were expecting. The hosts in VLAN 100 can communicate with each other; however, they cannot communicate with the hosts in VLAN 200. Note that we are using the `802.1q` tagging on all the hosts in this lab. This means that even host `h1` is not able to ping host `h2` as they put different VLAN ID numbers embedded in their `802.1q` headers.

Peering with the outside world using BGP

In this section, we will start looking at how OpenDaylight communicates with other legacy networking products, such as routers. I would like to remind you that what we have learned until now about SDN and OpenDaylight was through a standalone, isolated SDN domain, meaning that the hosts and switches in the SDN domain were able to communicate with each other. We learned that the SDN domain is similar to a very large chassis-based switch with many line cards to connect to servers.

Now let's connect our SDN domain, which consists of many hosts and servers, to the outside world. For this, we need to first learn how to communicate with the outside world and then program the fabric in such a way that it would allow real traffic to transit from the SDN domain to the outside.

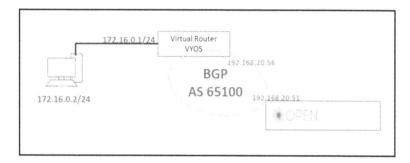

For communication with the outside world, we need to run a legacy routing protocol with legacy external routers. This is the role of OpenDaylight: to run routing protocols and establish communication with external routers.

OpenDaylight supports **Border Gateway Protocol** (**BGP**). It is a well-known, industry standard routing protocol to exchange routes. BGP is the primary routing protocol used to form the Internet, and in recent years, it is becoming a protocol of choice to run inside data centers as well.

Enabling BGP

To enable BGP in OpenDaylight, run the following command on OpenDaylight Command Prompt:

```
Feature:install OpenDaylight-bgpcep-bgp-all
```

This feature will install everything needed for BGP: from establishing the connection and storing the data in **Route Information Base** (**RIB**) to displaying data in a network topology overview.

The BGP feature consists of multiple modules and features that communicate with each other to provide its service to OpenDaylight. The following diagram shows the relation between the BGP modules in OpenDaylight:

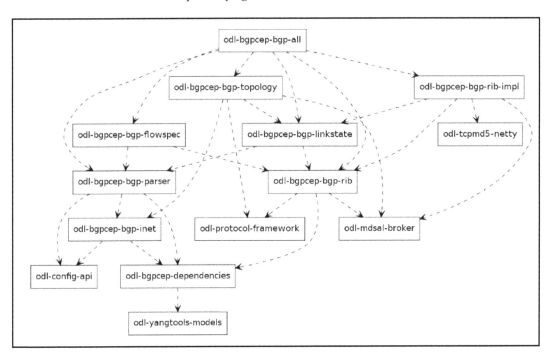

If you are familiar with BGP, you know that many extensions, options, and standards are built for BGP. For those not familiar, note that there are many features and extensions in BGP that can carry IPv4, IPv6, and MPLS labels; MAC addresses and external tags BGP. The BGP, in its basic sense, is a protocol for exchanging prefixes between BGP peers; it runs a standard calculation method to select potential routes inside a routing table.

The BGP implementation in OpenDaylight supports RFC4271, RFC 4760, RFC4456, RFC1997, and RFC4360.

OpenDaylight's BGP parser includes messages and attributes from RFC4271, RFC4760, RFC1997, and RFC4360.

There is an API module that defines BGP messages in YANG.

After the installation of the BGP feature set in OpenDaylight, its configuration files will be generated and placed in `/opt/OpenDaylight/boron/etc/OpenDaylight/karaf`:

- `31-bgp.xml` (defines the basic parser and RIB support)
- `40-bgp-openconfig.xml`
- `41-bgp-example.xml` (contains a sample configuration)

BGP lab

In this section, we will build a lab to test the OpenDaylight BGP practically. We will follow a simple lab and use BGP to exchange routes between our SDN domain and an external network with a BGP router. We will use VyOS, which is a free open source virtual router, as a legacy BGP router and will peer it with OpenDaylight.

Upon the successful establishment of BGP session, external hosts must be able to access the hosts inside an SDN domain:

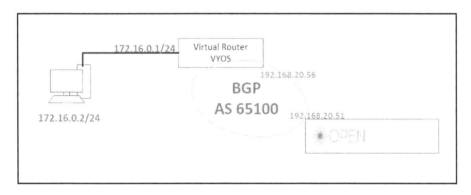

We will configure the VyOS router and OpenDaylight to establish BGP peering and exchange their prefixes. VyOS advertizes the `172.16.0.0/24` network to OpenDaylight. After the successful prefix exchange, OpenDaylight will perform the necessary flow changes inside the SDN domain to enable the SDn domain to communicate with the `172.16.0.0/24` network, which is received from VyOS.over BGP

We will try to make the configuration very simple as this is a very important lab and I would like you to lab this up and test it.

Configuration of OpenDaylight

As discussed, we have already enabled the BGP feature on OpenDaylight using this command:

```
Feature:install OpenDaylight-bgpcep-bgp-all
```

Once the feature is enabled, OpenDaylight puts the BGP configuration files in the following folder:

`/opt/OpenDaylight/boron/etc/OpenDaylight/karaf.`

We need to apply the configuration in the `41-bgp-example.xml` file.

Prior to jumping into changing the file, let's have a look at the structure of this configuration file. This XML configuration file is a modular approach to what the basic configuration of BGP resists. The first section of the file that starts with `<snapshot>` and `<required-capabilities>` are related to the general behavior of the BGP process and module inside OpenDaylight. After this, for each module, there is a `<module>` tag; this tag includes the configuration of each module.

You will find multiple module configurations in the form of this:

```
<module>
<type> .......</type>
<name>.........</name>
Parameters
</module>
```

We will modify the configuration for a couple of modules, that is, we'll change the parameters. Before we proceed with this stepwise configuration, open the configuration file in you favorite editor. Just remember that we need to perform a search in the file to find the sections that we need to modify. Ensure your favorite text editor supports searching and you know how to use it. (For network engineers, who are not too familiar with Linux, I suggest you use the nano text editor; remember to use *Ctrl + W* to perform the search inside nano.)

Step 1 - Changing the RIB configuration

In the `41-bgp-example.xml` file, search for `rub-id`. You will find it in a module named `<name>example-bgp-rib</name>`.

The RIB module includes configuration for local BGP settings, such as the local AS number, router ID, and `rid-id` (the most important one).

For my network engineer friends, `rid-id` is the same as the BGP process ID in a legacy router. This means you can run multiple BGP instances on OpenDaylight.

The important parameters in this module are as follows:

- `rib-id`: This is also known as BGP RIB Identifier. In this configuration file, you can specify more BGP RIBs by copy and pasting the preceding module. These RIBs must have a unique `rib-id` and name.
- `local-as`: This refers to our local AS number (where OpenDaylight is deployed); we use this in best path selection.
- `bgp-id`: This is our local BGP identifier (the IP of the VM where OpenDaylight is deployed); we use this in best path selection.

You need to change the parameters as per the following code:

```
<rib-id>example-bgp-rib</rib-id>
<local-as>65100</local-as>
<bgp-rib-id>192.168.20.51</bgp-rib-id>
```

We have set `local-as` as `65100`, which is our BGP AS number for this lab. The router ID is set to the IP address of the OpenDaylight instance that is peering with VyOS.

Step 2 - Configuring VyOS

Now we need to configure the VyOS to enable BGP and establish a session with our OpenDaylight BGP module. Run the following command inside the VyoS Command Prompt.

```
    set protocols bgp 65100 neighbor 192.168.20.51 remote-as 65100.
  set protocols bgp 65536 network 172.16.0.0/24.
  set protocols bgp 65536 parameters router-id 192.168.20.56.
  set protocols bgp 65536 parameters hold time 180
   end
    commit
```

To verify the established session between OpenDaylight and VyOS, issue the show IP BGP neighbors on the VyOS router:

```
    vyos@vyos:~$ show ip bgp neighbors
BGP neighbor is 192.168.20.51, remote AS 65100, local AS 65100, internal
link
  BGP version 4, remote router ID 192.168.20.51
  BGP state = Established, up for 00:01:47
  Last read 07:27:00, hold time is 180, keepalive interval is 60 seconds
  Neighbor capabilities:
    4 Byte AS: advertised and received
    Route refresh: advertised and received(new)
    Address family IPv4 Unicast: advertised and received
  Message statistics:
    Inq depth is 0
    Outq depth is 0
                      Sent          Rcvd
    Opens:             42            41
    Notifications:      1             1
    Updates:            2             0
    Keepalives:        45             1
    Route Refresh:      0             0
    Capability:         0             0
    Total:             90            43
  Minimum time between advertisement runs is 5 seconds

 For address family: IPv4 Unicast
  Community attribute sent to this neighbor(both)
  0 accepted prefixes

  Connections established 2; dropped 1
  Last reset 00:01:58, due to User reset
Local host: 192.168.20.56, Local port: 47609
Foreign host: 192.168.20.51, Foreign port: 179
Nexthop: 192.168.20.56
Nexthop global: fe80::20c:29ff:fe54:dbde
Nexthop local: ::
BGP connection: non shared network
Read thread: on  Write thread: off
vyos@vyos:~$
```

To check the status in OpenDaylight, we can use the REST client and postman to send a `GET` request to check the status of BGP:

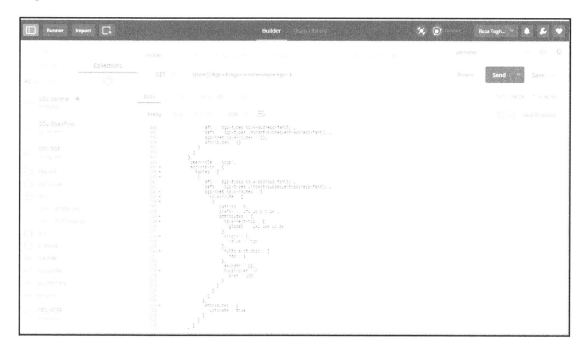

Send the following REST call to OpenDaylight usnig postman:

```
http://192.168.20.51:8181/operational/bgp-rib:bgp-rib/rib/example-bgp-r
ib
```

This REST call will provide complete details of the BGP RIB, which we created in this example.

As you can see in the results, it shows `192.168.20.56`, which is our VyOS virtual router as a peer, and `172.16.0.0/24` as a received prefix:

```
{
   "rib": [
      {
         "id": "example-bgp-rib",
          "peer": [
             {
                "peer-id": "bgp://192.168.20.51",
                "peer-role": "internal",
                "adj-rib-in": {
                   "tables": [
```

```
              {
                "afi": "bgp-types:ipv4-address-family",
                "safi": "bgp-labeled-unicast:labeled-unicast-
subsequent-address-family",
                "bgp-labeled-unicast:labeled-unicast-routes": {},
                "attributes": {
                  "uptodate": false
                }
              },
              {
                "afi": "bgp-types:ipv6-address-family",
                "safi": "bgp-flowspec:flowspec-l3vpn-subsequent-
address-family",
                "bgp-flowspec:flowspec-l3vpn-ipv6-routes": {},
                "attributes": {
                  "uptodate": false
                }
              },
              {
                "afi": "bgp-types:ipv6-address-family",
                "safi": "bgp-types:mpls-labeled-vpn-subsequent-
address-family",
                "bgp-vpn-ipv6:vpn-ipv6-routes": {},
                "attributes": {
                  "uptodate": false
                }
              },
              {
                "afi": "bgp-types:ipv6-address-family",
                "safi": "bgp-types:unicast-subsequent-address-
family",
                "bgp-inet:ipv6-routes": {},
                "attributes": {
                  "uptodate": false
                }
              },
              {
                "afi": "bgp-types:ipv4-address-family",
                "safi": "bgp-flowspec:flowspec-l3vpn-subsequent-
address-family",
                "bgp-flowspec:flowspec-l3vpn-ipv4-routes": {},
                "attributes": {
                  "uptodate": false
                }
              },
              {
                "afi": "bgp-linkstate:linkstate-address-family",
                "safi": "bgp-linkstate:linkstate-subsequent-
```

```
          address-family",
                    "bgp-linkstate:linkstate-routes": {},
                    "attributes": {
                      "uptodate": false
                    }
                },
                {
                    "afi": "bgp-types:ipv4-address-family",
                    "safi": "bgp-types:mpls-labeled-vpn-subsequent-
          address-family",
                    "bgp-vpn-ipv4:vpn-ipv4-routes": {},
                    "attributes": {
                      "uptodate": false
                    }
                },
                {
                    "afi": "bgp-types:ipv4-address-family",
                    "safi": "bgp-types:unicast-subsequent-address-
          family",
                    "bgp-inet:ipv4-routes": {},
                    "attributes": {
                      "uptodate": false
                    }
                },
                {
                    "afi": "bgp-types:ipv6-address-family",
                    "safi": "bgp-labeled-unicast:labeled-unicast-
          subsequent-address-family",
                    "bgp-labeled-unicast:labeled-unicast-ipv6-routes":
          {},
                    "attributes": {
                      "uptodate": false
                    }
                },
                {
                    "afi": "bgp-types:ipv4-address-family",
                    "safi": "bgp-flowspec:flowspec-subsequent-address-
          family",
                    "bgp-flowspec:flowspec-routes": {},
                    "attributes": {
                      "uptodate": false
                    }
                },
                {
                    "afi": "OpenDaylight-bgp-evpn:l2vpn-address-
          family",
                    "safi": "OpenDaylight-bgp-evpn:evpn-subsequent-
          address-family",
```

```
                    "OpenDaylight-bgp-evpn:evpn-routes": {},
                    "attributes": {
                      "uptodate": false
                    }
                  },
                  {
                    "afi": "bgp-types:ipv6-address-family",
                    "safi": "bgp-flowspec:flowspec-subsequent-address-
      family",
                    "bgp-flowspec:flowspec-ipv6-routes": {},
                    "attributes": {
                      "uptodate": false
                    }
                  }
                ]
              },
              "effective-rib-in": {
                "tables": [
                  {
                    "afi": "bgp-types:ipv4-address-family",
                    "safi": "bgp-labeled-unicast:labeled-unicast-
      subsequent-address-family",
                    "bgp-labeled-unicast:labeled-unicast-routes": {},
                    "attributes": {}
                  },
                  {
                    "afi": "bgp-types:ipv6-address-family",
                    "safi": "bgp-flowspec:flowspec-l3vpn-subsequent-
      address-family",
                    "bgp-flowspec:flowspec-l3vpn-ipv6-routes": {},
                    "attributes": {}
                  },
                  {
                    "afi": "bgp-types:ipv6-address-family",
                    "safi": "bgp-types:mpls-labeled-vpn-subsequent-
      address-family",
                    "bgp-vpn-ipv6:vpn-ipv6-routes": {},
                    "attributes": {}
                  },
                  {
                    "afi": "bgp-types:ipv6-address-family",
                    "safi": "bgp-types:unicast-subsequent-address-
      family",
                    "bgp-inet:ipv6-routes": {},
                    "attributes": {}
                  },
                  {
                    "afi": "bgp-types:ipv4-address-family",
```

```
                "safi": "bgp-flowspec:flowspec-l3vpn-subsequent-
address-family",
                "bgp-flowspec:flowspec-l3vpn-ipv4-routes": {},
                "attributes": {}
            },
            {
                "afi": "bgp-linkstate:linkstate-address-family",
                "safi": "bgp-linkstate:linkstate-subsequent-
address-family",
                "bgp-linkstate:linkstate-routes": {},
                "attributes": {}
            },
            {
                "afi": "bgp-types:ipv4-address-family",
                "safi": "bgp-types:mpls-labeled-vpn-subsequent-
 address-family",
                 "bgp-vpn-ipv4:vpn-ipv4-routes": {},
                "attributes": {}
             },
            {
                "afi": "bgp-types:ipv4-address-family",
                "safi": "bgp-types:unicast-subsequent-address-
 family",
                "bgp-inet:ipv4-routes": {},
                "attributes": {}
            },
            {
                "afi": "bgp-types:ipv6-address-family",
                "safi": "bgp-labeled-unicast:labeled-unicast-
subsequent-address-family",
                "bgp-labeled-unicast:labeled-unicast-ipv6-routes":
 {},
                "attributes": {}
            },
            {
                "afi": "bgp-types:ipv4-address-family",
                "safi": "bgp-flowspec:flowspec-subsequent-address-
 family",
                 "bgp-flowspec:flowspec-routes": {},
                "attributes": {}
            },
            {
                "afi": "OpenDaylight-bgp-evpn:l2vpn-address-
 family",
                "safi": "OpenDaylight-bgp-evpn:evpn-subsequent-
 address-family",
                "OpenDaylight-bgp-evpn:evpn-routes": {},
                "attributes": {}
```

```
              },
              {
                "afi": "bgp-types:ipv6-address-family",
                "safi": "bgp-flowspec:flowspec-subsequent-address-
family",
                 "bgp-flowspec:flowspec-ipv6-routes": {},
                 "attributes": {}
              }
          ]
        }
      },
      {
        "peer-id": "bgp://192.168.20.56",
        "adj-rib-out": {
          "tables": [
              {
                "afi": "bgp-types:ipv4-address-family",
                 "safi": "bgp-types:unicast-subsequent-address-
family",
                "bgp-inet:ipv4-routes": {},
                "attributes": {}
              }
          ]
        },
        "peer-role": "ibgp",
        "adj-rib-in": {
          "tables": [
              {
                "afi": "bgp-types:ipv4-address-family",
                "safi": "bgp-types:unicast-subsequent-address-
family",
                "bgp-inet:ipv4-routes": {
                  "ipv4-route": [
                    {
                      "path-id": 0,
                      "prefix": "172.16.0.0/24",
                      "attributes": {
                        "ipv4-next-hop": {
                          "global": "192.168.20.56"
                        },
                        "origin": {
                          "value": "igp"
                        },
                        "multi-exit-disc": {
                          "med": 1
                        },
                        "as-path": {},
                        "local-pref": {
```

```
                          "pref": 100
                        }
                      }
                    }
                  ]
                },
                "attributes": {
                  "uptodate": true
                }
              }
            ]
          },
          "effective-rib-in": {
            "tables": [
              {
                "afi": "bgp-types:ipv4-address-family",
                "safi": "bgp-types:unicast-subsequent-address-
family",
                "bgp-inet:ipv4-routes": {
                  "ipv4-route": [
                    {
                      "path-id": 0,
                      "prefix": "172.16.0.0/24",
                      "attributes": {
                        "ipv4-next-hop": {
                          "global": "192.168.20.56"
                        },
                        "origin": {
                          "value": "igp"
                        },
                        "multi-exit-disc": {
                          "med": 1
                        },
                        "as-path": {},
                        "local-pref": {
                          "pref": 100
                        }
                      }
                    }
                  ]
                },
                "attributes": {
                  "uptodate": true
                }
              }
            ]
          },
          "supported-tables": [
```

```
                    {
                      "afi": "bgp-types:ipv4-address-family",
                      "safi": "bgp-types:unicast-subsequent-address-family"
                    }
                  ]
                }
              ],
              "loc-rib": {
                "tables": [
                  {
                    "afi": "bgp-types:ipv6-address-family",
                    "safi": "bgp-types:mpls-labeled-vpn-subsequent-address-
        family",
                    "bgp-vpn-ipv6:vpn-ipv6-routes": {}
                  },
                  {
                    "afi": "bgp-types:ipv4-address-family",
                    "safi": "bgp-flowspec:flowspec-l3vpn-subsequent-
         address-family",
                      "bgp-flowspec:flowspec-l3vpn-ipv4-routes": {}
                  },
                  {
                    "afi": "bgp-types:ipv4-address-family",
                    "safi": "bgp-flowspec:flowspec-subsequent-address-
        family",
                    "bgp-flowspec:flowspec-routes": {}
                  },
                  {
                    "afi": "bgp-types:ipv6-address-family",
                    "safi": "bgp-flowspec:flowspec-subsequent-address-
        family",
                    "bgp-flowspec:flowspec-ipv6-routes": {}
                  },
                  {
                    "afi": "bgp-types:ipv4-address-family",
                    "safi": "bgp-labeled-unicast:labeled-unicast-
        subsequent-address-family",
                    "bgp-labeled-unicast:labeled-unicast-routes": {}
                  },
                  {
                    "afi": "bgp-types:ipv6-address-family",
                    "safi": "bgp-flowspec:flowspec-l3vpn-subsequent-
        address-family",
                    "bgp-flowspec:flowspec-l3vpn-ipv6-routes": {}
                  },
                  {
                    "afi": "bgp-types:ipv6-address-family",
                    "safi": "bgp-types:unicast-subsequent-address-family",
```

```json
          "bgp-inet:ipv6-routes": {}
        },
        {
          "afi": "bgp-linkstate:linkstate-address-family",
          "safi": "bgp-linkstate:linkstate-subsequent-address-
family",
          "bgp-linkstate:linkstate-routes": {}
        },
        {
          "afi": "bgp-types:ipv4-address-family",
          "safi": "bgp-types:mpls-labeled-vpn-subsequent-address-
family",
          "bgp-vpn-ipv4:vpn-ipv4-routes": {}
        },
        {
          "afi": "bgp-types:ipv4-address-family",
          "safi": "bgp-types:unicast-subsequent-address-family",
          "bgp-inet:ipv4-routes": {
            "ipv4-route": [
              {
                "path-id": 0,
                "prefix": "172.16.0.0/24",
                "attributes": {
                  "ipv4-next-hop": {
                    "global": "192.168.20.56"
                  },
                  "origin": {
                    "value": "igp"
                  },
                  "multi-exit-disc": {
                    "med": 1
                  },
                  "as-path": {},
                  "local-pref": {
                    "pref": 100
                  }
                }
              }
            ]
          },
          "attributes": {
            "uptodate": true
          }
        },
        {
          "afi": "bgp-types:ipv6-address-family",
          "safi": "bgp-labeled-unicast:labeled-unicast-
subsequent-address-family",
```

```
                        "bgp-labeled-unicast:labeled-unicast-ipv6-routes": {}
                    },
                    {
                        "afi": "OpenDaylight-bgp-evpn:l2vpn-address-family",
                        "safi": "OpenDaylight-bgp-evpn:evpn-subsequent-address-
family",
                        "OpenDaylight-bgp-evpn:evpn-routes": {}
                    }
                ]
            }
        }
    ]
}
```

Security - user management

OpenDaylight security is a very wide context; it includes different components and technologies. The security framework of OpenDaylight is mainly based on the Apache Shiro Java security framework. The main configuration file of AAA is located at `etc/shiro.ini`, which is relative to the OpenDaylight Karaf home directory.

AAA can be enabled for each SDN module or application by simply adding a specific set of parameters to the servlet `web.xml` file, which is an advanced topic that we will not cover in this book.

User management in OpenDaylight is provided via the same framework. OpenDaylight has multiple Realm implementations; however, the main implementation that can be used widely for modules is TokenAuthRealm.

TokenAuthRealm provides the following features:

- It is AuthorizingRealm built to bridge the Shiro-based AAA service with the h2-based AAA implementation.
- It exposes a RESTful web service to manipulate the IdM policy on a per-node basis. If identical, the AAA policy is desired across a cluster and the backing data store must be synchronized using an out-of-band method.
- It provides a Python script at `etc/idmtool`, and it is included to help manipulate data contained in TokenAuthRealm.
- It is enabled out of the box.

TokenAuthRealm stores IdM data in an `h2` database on each node. Thus, the configuration of a cluster requires you to configure the desired IdM policy on each node. There are two supported methods to manipulate the TokenAuthRealm IdM configuration:

- The `idmtool` configuration
- The RESTful web service configuration
- The `idmtool` configuration

A utility script located at `etc/idmtool` is used to manipulate the TokenAuthRealm IdM policy. Now `idmtool` assumes a single domain (SDN) since multiple domains are not leveraged in the Boron release.

Using `idmtool`, you can perform basic user management operations, such as listing, adding, deleting, changing password, and adding roles and role assignments to users.

Let's discuss the examples that will help you get familiar with user management. First is list users: `python/opt/OpenDaylight/boron/etc/idmtooladminlist-users`. Once you run this command, `idmtool` will ask for the admin password in order to perform the user listing:

```
list_users
command succeeded!
json:
{
    "users": [
        {
            "description": "admin user",
            "domainid": "sdn",
            "email": "",
            "enabled": true,
            "name": "admin",
            "password": "**********",
            "salt": "**********",
            "userid": "admin@sdn"
        },
        {
            "description": "user user",
            "domainid": "sdn",
            "email": "",
            "enabled": true,
            "name": "user",
            "password": "**********",
```

```
            "salt": "**********",
            "userid": "user@sdn"
        }
    ]
}
```

To add a new user, use the following command:

```
python /opt/OpenDaylight/boron/etc/idmtool admin add-user NEW-USER
```

Once you enter this command, OpenDaylight will first ask you for the admin password to ensure you are an administrator and have rights to add a new user. Then it will ask for the new user password:

```
learningOpenDaylight@OpenDaylight01:/opt/OpenDaylight/boron$ python
/opt/OpenDaylight/boron/etc/idmtool admin add-user NEW-USER
Password:
Enter new password:
Re-enter password:
add_user(admin)
command succeeded!
json:
{
    "description": "",
    "domainid": "sdn",
    "email": "",
    "enabled": true,
    "name": "NEW-USER",
    "password": "**********",
    "salt": "**********",
    "userid": "NEW-USE
```

To delete the same user, use the following command:

```
python /opt/OpenDaylight/boron/etc/idmtool admin delete-user NEW-USER
@sdn
```

Remember that for deleting a user, you need to type the full user ID; this includes @ and the domain name, which is SDN by default.

You can use the REST interface to communicate with the AAA module. Here, we have the postman REST client listing the OpenDaylight users, using the following REST call:

```
http://192.168.20.51:8181/auth/v1/users
```

The method you use in this case is GET.

As you can see, the same output, which was provided by `idmtool`, is provided here:

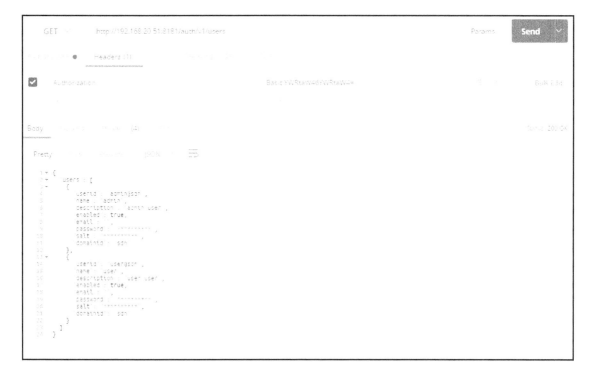

Link aggregation

Another important basic L2 feature that is available in most switches is link aggregation.

In the networking industry, there are other names for link aggregation, such as EtherChannel (Cisco term), Trunk (Brocade, HP, and Huawei), LAG (Juniper), Bond (Linux), LACP, and Port Channel (Cisco), but they all refer to the same link aggregation.

OpenDaylight supports link aggregation by supporting **Link Aggregation Control Protocol (LACP)**.

The LACP module within OpenDaylight implements LACP as an MD-SAL service module. It is used to autodiscover and aggregate multiple links between an OpenDaylight-controlled network and LACP-enabled endpoints or switches. The result is the creation of a logical channel, which represents the aggregation of the links. Link aggregation provides link resiliency and bandwidth aggregation.

Configuring LACP

LACP can be enabled in the OpenDaylight Karaf console of the OpenDaylight Karaf distribution by issuing the following command:

```
feature:install OpenDaylight-lacp-ui
```

To test this feature, let's run the following command in Mininet; we do this to run a single switch:

```
sudo mn --controller=remote,ip=192.168.20.51 --topo=linear,1 --switch
ovsk,protocols=OpenFlow13
```

Note that we are specifying the OpenFlow version 1.3 protocol. After enabling the LACP module on OpenDaylight, it will inject a flow into the OpenFlow-enabled switches in the SDN domain to forward Ethernet frames destined to `01:80:c2:00:00:02` and `ether_type =0x8809` to be forwarded to the OpenDaylight controller:

```
mininet@mininet-vm:~$ sudo ovs-ofctl -O OpenFlow13 dump-flows s1
OFPST_FLOW reply (OF1.3) (xid=0x2):
 cookie=0x3000000000000003, duration=313.446s, table=0, n_packets=0,
n_bytes=0, priority=5,dl_dst=01:80:c2:00:00:02,dl_type=0x8809
actions=CONTROLLER:65535
```

Since we have started our first OpenFlow version 1.3 switch in this example, let's have a very quick comparison between OpenFlow v1.0 (which we were using until now) and OpenFlow version 1.3 (used in this example).

Have a look at what happens when the following OpenFlow v1.0 `OpenFlow_Modify` message:

```
    Frame 94: 146 bytes on wire (1168 bits), 146 bytes captured (1168 bits)
on interface 0
Ethernet II, Src: Vmware_44:f0:0c (00:0c:29:44:f0:0c), Dst: Vmware_69:36:bc
(00:0c:29:69:36:bc)
Internet Protocol Version 4, Src: 192.168.20.51, Dst: 192.168.20.55
Transmission Control Protocol, Src Port: 6633, Dst Port: 36017, Seq: 441,
Ack: 17745, Len: 80
OpenFlow 1.0
    .000 0001 = Version: 1.0 (0x01)
    Type: OFPT_FLOW_MOD (14)
    Length: 80
    Transaction ID: 9
    Wildcards: 3678439
    In port: 0
    Ethernet source address: 00:00:00_00:00:00 (00:00:00:00:00:00)
    Ethernet destination address: Slow-Protocols (01:80:c2:00:00:02)
```

```
Input VLAN id: 65535
Input VLAN priority: 0
Pad: 00
Dl type: 34825
IP ToS: 0
IP protocol: 0
Pad: 0000
Source Address: 0.0.0.0
Destination Address: 0.0.0.0
Source Port: 0
Destination Port: 0
Cookie: 0x3000000000000002
Command: New flow (0)
Idle time-out: 0
hard time-out: 0
Priority: 5
Buffer Id: 0xffffffff
Out port: 65535
Flags: 0
```

As you can see when we use OpenFlow v1.0 , the `OpenFlow_Modify` messages, has only source and destination addresses (MAC and IP).

Now let's have a look at what happens when we use OpenFlow v1.3 to modify a packet:

```
    Frame 96: 162 bytes on wire (1296 bits), 162 bytes captured (1296 bits)
on interface 0
Ethernet II, Src: Vmware_44:f0:0c (00:0c:29:44:f0:0c), Dst: Vmware_69:36:bc
(00:0c:29:69:36:bc)
Internet Protocol Version 4, Src: 192.168.20.51, Dst: 192.168.20.55
Transmission Control Protocol, Src Port: 6633, Dst Port: 36019, Seq: 613,
Ack: 7813, Len: 96
OpenFlow 1.3
    Version: 1.3 (0x04)
    Type: OFPT_FLOW_MOD (14)
    Length: 96
    Transaction ID: 16
    Cookie: 0x3000000000000003
    Cookie mask: 0x0000000000000000
    Table ID: 0
    Command: OFPFC_ADD (0)
    Idle timeout: 0
    Hard timeout: 0
    Priority: 5
    Buffer ID: OFP_NO_BUFFER (0xffffffff)
    Out port: OFPP_ANY (0xffffffff)
    Out group: OFPG_ANY (0xffffffff)
    Flags: 0x0000
```

```
            .... .... .... ...0 = Send flow removed: False
            .... .... .... ..0. = Check overlap: False
            .... .... .... .0.. = Reset counts: False
            .... .... .... 0... = Don't count packets: False
            .... .... ...0 .... = Don't count bytes: False
    Pad: 0000
    Match
        Type: OFPMT_OXM (1)
        Length: 20
        OXM field
            Class: OFPXMC_OPENFLOW_BASIC (0x8000)
            0000 011. = Field: OFPXMT_OFB_ETH_DST (3)
            .... ...0 = Has mask: False
            Length: 6
            Value: Slow-Protocols (01:80:c2:00:00:02)
        OXM field
            Class: OFPXMC_OPENFLOW_BASIC (0x8000)
            0000 101. = Field: OFPXMT_OFB_ETH_TYPE (5)
            .... ...0 = Has mask: False
            Length: 2
            Value: Slow Protocols (0x8809)
        Pad: 00000000
    Instruction
        Type: OFPIT_APPLY_ACTIONS (4)
        Length: 24
        Pad: 00000000
        Action
            Type: OFPAT_OUTPUT (0)
            Length: 16
            Port: OFPP_CONTROLLER (0xfffffffd)
            Max length: OFPCML_NO_BUFFER (0xffff)
            Pad: 000000000000
```

As you can see, in `OpenFlow v1.3 OpenFlow_Modify` message is very different from the basic `OpenFlow v1.0 OpenFlow_Modify` message and it includes EtherType as well.

Run the following commands in Mininet:

```
    py net.addLink(s1, net.get('h1'))
py s1.attach('s1-eth2')

h1 bash
echo "alias bond0 bonding" > /etc/modprobe.d/bonding.conf
echo "options bonding mode=4" >> /etc/modprobe.d/bonding.conf
cat /etc/modprobe.d/bonding.conf
exit
```

```
py net.get('h1').cmd('modprobe bonding')
py net.get('h1').cmd('ip link add bond0 type bond')
py net.get('h1').cmd('ip link set bond0 address <bond-mac-address>')
py net.get('h1').cmd('ip link set h1-eth0 down')
py net.get('h1').cmd('ip link set h1-eth0 master bond0')
py net.get('h1').cmd('ip link set h1-eth1 down')
py net.get('h1').cmd('ip link set h1-eth1 master bond0')
py net.get('h1').cmd('ip link set bond0 up')
```

To verify link aggregation, use the following command in Mininet:

```
py net.get('h1').cmd('cat /proc/net/bonding/bond0')
    Number of ports: 2
    Actor Key: 33
    Partner Key: 8
    Partner Mac Address: 00:00:00:00:01:01

Slave Interface: h1-eth0
MII Status: up
Speed: 10000 Mbps
Duplex: full
Link Failure Count: 0
Permanent HW addr: 9e:a2:95:7e:ef:f5
Aggregator ID: 1
Slave queue ID: 0

Slave Interface: h1-eth1
MII Status: up
Speed: 10000 Mbps
Duplex: full
Link Failure Count: 0
Permanent HW addr: a6:4e:68:1e:ee:b5
Aggregator ID: 1
Slave queue ID: 0
```

Summary

In this chapter, we took a journey from legacy L2/L3 networking to SDN. We learned how basic VLANs are implemented in OpenDaylight and SDN, how BGP communication happens between OpenDaylight and external routers, and how OpenDaylight manages users.

In the next chapter, we will start writing our first SDN application.

6
Overview of OpenDaylight Applications

In this chapter, we will start looking at the structure of applications and building our first HelloWorld application in OpenDaylight. We will cover the following topics:

- OpenDaylight applications and why we use them
- Core applications
- Optional applications

OpenDaylight applications and why we use them

Now that we are familiar with ODL and understand how it operates, let's start looking at the custom applications and plugin structure that ODL offers. Building an application for ODL is a little bit different than how you do it on other platforms.

MD-SAL adds great flexibility for building applications and simplifies the communication between them. The code you build for such applications can be reused for different models if they are written in a proper way. On the other hand though, MD-SAL makes a programmer work more, as it requires them to build multiple lines of code in YANG and Java implementation codes for just a single application. Somehow, you can refer a model to a class in object-oriented programming. A class exists within a program, and you can create different objects based on this class. A model is very similar to a class. However, the context where the model lives is not inside some software; it's inside the system.

Remember that ODL is a controller, supports different southbound protocols, and is not limited only to OpenFlow. You can build an application to do a specific job and interact with the network using BGP-PCEP or NETCONF. or even with no interaction with network switches, just interacting with internal ODL components and core applications.

Some of the initial SDN controllers had their southbound APIs tightly bound to OpenFlow; however, in the ODL service abstraction, one of the major enhancements was to decouple the APIs from the southbound protocol and provide a plugin-based southbound option to support multiple protocols, such as OpenFlow, OVSDB, OpFlex, NETCONF, SNMP, and BGP.

ODL's MD-SAL provides a fully abstracted model for application developers to use and build their applications. ODL, in older versions, had an **API-Driven Service Abstraction Layer** (**AD-SAL**). AD-SAL is a method that allows APIs to directly communicate with devices. However, since devices may use different southbound protocols (some with NETCONF, OpenFlow, BGP-PCEP, and so on), you will end up with a complex method filled with different APIs for doing the same function, but using a different southbound protocol.

For example, for shutting down an interface on a switch, you can use SNMP, CLI, NETCONF, or RESTCONF methods to communicate with the device. In the AD-SAL model, you will end up with four different APIs:

- `int-shutdown-snmp($device,$int)`
- `int-shutdown-netconf($device,$int)`
- `int-shutdown-cli($device,$int)`
- `int-shutdown-restconf($device,$int)`

However, in the MD-SAL method, you just need a single API: `int-shutdown($device,$int)`.

The MD-SAL model automatically identifies the device and uses the right southbound protocol (either NETCONF, SNMP, CLI, or RESTCONF) to communicate with it.

As explained, the initial versions of ODL (prior to Hydrogen) were based on the AD-SAL model; however, after increasing the power of ODL by supporting more southbound protocols than in a single OpenFlow application, developers started realizing that the AD-SAL model is not efficient enough for ODL. That's why they started looking at a new type of SAL, which would be based on models that would interact with SDN applications and plugins rather than directly communicating with the devices on a specific protocol.

The following diagram illustrates the difference between AD-SAL and MD-SAL:

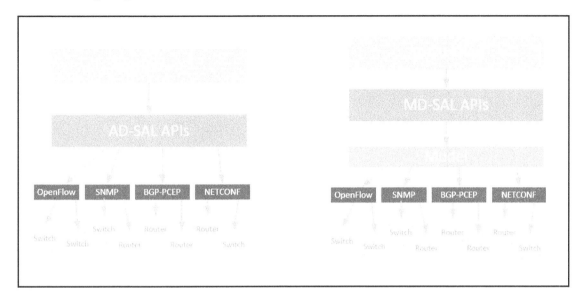

In AD-SAL, there is no model (or there might be but not with the same characteristics as that of a model in MD-SAL). Therefore, the APIs directly communicate between the SDN application and southbound plugins.

In MD-SAL, the APIs connect the SDN application to an abstract model, rather than directly with the southbound plugins. This decouples the API from the real protocol and plugin meant for communicating with the devices.

You have seen model-driven methods before. Apart from the buzz and hype surrounding MD-SAL, such a model-driven method has been there for years. If you look at monitoring tools such as Zabbix or Nagios, you will see that they also use the same MD-SAL for monitoring their devices. For example, Nagios uses `ssh` or `snmp` for monitoring and polling a network device.

When you create a device in Nagios, it is a generic object. You define its type (as a router, switch, or Linux host); based on this, Nagios knows how to deal with it. You only define that you would like to monitor its uptime.

This is exactly the same as the MD-SAL model, which has been implemented not only in Zabbix and Nagios, but also in many other monitoring applications.

In general, we can say that MD-SAL is a good approach for platforms where there are multiple southbound protocols available for communicating with the devices.

The following diagram illustrates a model-driven architecture in a type of network management software:

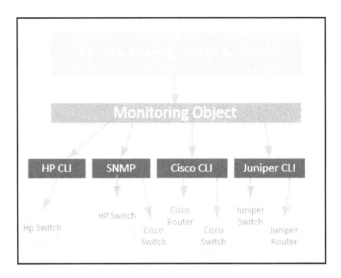

This model-driven design isolates applications and application developers from requiring knowledge of the architecture and proprietary CLI commands each network device type. As seen in the preceding diagram, CLI commands are different across manufacturers and device types, and they are hidden from the application.

Traditional network management software can read and display a device's status and bandwidth, generate graphs, and provide some kind of firmware and file management. However, they are limited and cannot deal with complex multi-protocol environments. So, MD-SAL in ODL builds on the model-driven approach of the previous systems and adds fine-tuned southbound protocols, plugins, and network agility to the solution.

Communication between modules (apps) in MD-SAL

Another benefit of using the MD-SAL model is to enhance and simplify the communication between the modules and SDN applications. Let's examine a couple of other features of MD-SAL.

Service producers and consumers

Service consumers and service producers are other terms that are used a lot in MD-SAL. A model will always have service producer APIs, which provide the plugin service to other applications. It will also have service consumers, which are used to call other services in order to utilize the service functions of other modules or functions.

Consider the following figure:

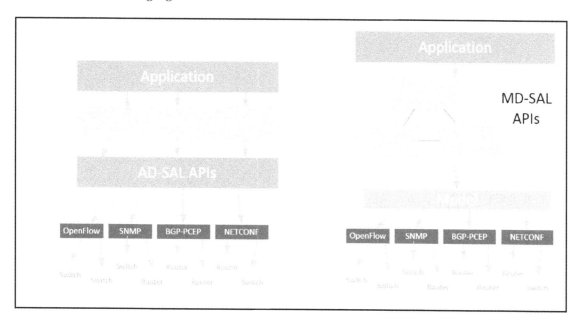

The AD-SAL model on the left-hand side illustrates an SDN application that communicates with multiple independent application modules within the SD controller.

In AD-SAL model, if the SDN application modules within the AD-SAL domain need to communicate with each other, they would need to use a message bus or an OSGi service. They would also need to manually define and implement such communication methods and interfaces.

In the MD-SAL model, on the right-hand side, each application or plugin within the MD-SAL domain is a model. Each model produces a set of APIs that other models (applications) can use to communicate with that application or model.

A model can also be a consumer of the API services provided by other applications or models at the same time. Most of the MD-SAL applications have both producer and consumer APIs.

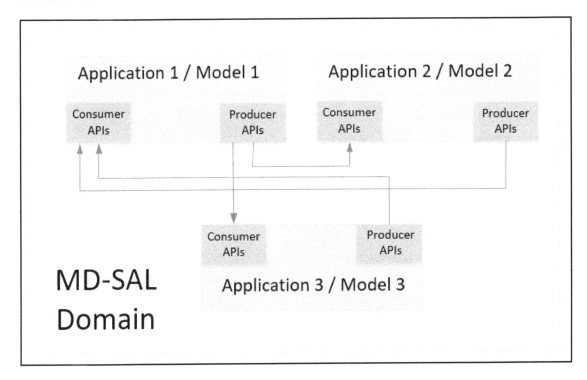

This produces an environment of producer and consumer applications living within the MD-SAL domain. The beauty of this model is that it allows you to have a method for distributing responsibilities and reusing existing applications and functions.

The following diagram shows MD-SAL: the Broker:

MD-SAL: The Brokers

Declarative versus imperative

Our network engineer readers might not be familiar with these terms, but they will understand it very well after reading the following example.

You are a network administrator in a large corporate with thousands of switches in your access layer, providing access to end client devices such as PC, IP phones, wireless access points, printers, and different workstations. There is a requirement from security to find and shut down all the ports connected to the standalone IP phones (with no PC connected) every day at 5 pm and again activate them at 6 am. How could you achieve this with a legacy network?

For achieving this task, you will probably need to run multiple commands on each switch to prepare and do this:

- Find which ports are connected to the IP phones via methods, such as resolving the MAC address, or discovery protocols, such as LLDP/CDP/FDP. (This will help to identify the ports with an IP-Phone connected to)
- Find which ports have learned that only one MAC address can help you identify the IP phones with no PC attached
- Build a script to execute this activity using your choice of southbound protocol, such as SNMP, NETCONF, or Telnet/SSH

This is a real-world example of a network engineer's life. It may take hours to build and test the code line by line, doing lots of string manipulation to reach the end result.

This is an imperative way to work. It means that you are telling the system to do different things to produce your expected result, which is your goal.

You cannot tell the system that you want all the IP phones with no PC port attached to go offline at 6 pm daily because the system does not have an understanding of what an IP phones is or what an IP phone with a connected PC port is. It is dumb.

With an imperative system, human intelligence is required to tell the system how to do a set of tasks and connect the results together to provide the end result.

Also, remember that your script needs to be intelligent enough to keep finding the IP phone ports and removing the ports that are no longer connected to an IP phone or IP phone with a PC attached from the list.

What if you could tell the system what you would like in the first place? Many of you might be familiar with SQL queries-how simple and beautiful SQL is. Imagine that your network could understand SQL and you could probably communicate the following with it:

```
UPDATE network set interface.status=disable
whereinterface.usage=ip-phone-with-connected-pc and time='05:00pm'
UPDATE network set interface.status=enable where
interface.usage=ip-phone-with-connected-pc and time='06:00am'
```

This an example of a declarative system, where you tell the system what to do and system knows what you are telling it.

Note that the preceding SQL example does not actually exist; we have used it to better explain the concept.

I know you would all love to have such a system one day to get you out of your daily Perl scripting. The good news is that the MD-SAL method helps you build declarative applications. Similar to what we imagined, using ODL to build a network discovery application could be a good exercise for you to practice MD-SAL programming, especially in ODL.

Let's summarize the difference between declarative and imperative:

- **Declarative**: In this method, you give the system what you want it to do. The system is intelligent enough to process the information and give you the desired results.
- **Imperative**: In this method, you tell the system a set of instructions to produce a result. Here, the system doesn't understand the end result.

Normally, the goal of most systems, including the network infrastructure, is that we should be able to tell the system what we want it to do and allow it to decide who would do it. We are only interested in the results.

Creating MD-SAL applications

Building MD-SAL-based applications might be a little difficult in the beginning. There are multiple steps involved for building a HelloWorld application, which we are going to explore at the end of this chapter.

In general, an application or module starts with a YANG model. YANG is a language or, better, a format used to build a model. YANG (Yet Another Next Generation) is a mark-up language similar to JSON, but used mainly for modeling.

The YANG model file is then fed to YANG tools--the YANG interpreter engine of ODL-where it generates the other source files where we need to do Java coding.

It might be difficult to get off the ground, but be patient.

The YANG tools engine automatically generates the application scripts and you can continue to code your application using the generated templates.

The following diagram shows the full process of application creation in ODL:

Again, remember that with MD-SAL, applications are created based on models. You will create a model or models, and you will interface them with other models. Your MD-SAL application will also become a service (producer) to other applications and models that are running in the MD-SAL domain within the ODL.

You might have noticed YANG in the preceding diagram. YANG is a data modeling language. MD-SAL uses YANG as the data modelling language of choice for an SDN application.

Let's have a look at the high-level steps involved for building an SDL application using MD-SAL:

1. **Defining the model**: Use YANG to define your model. In this step, you will build a YANG file to define the model of your SDN application.
2. **Compiling the model**: Once the YANG model is defined, we will use YANG tools to compile the model. YANG tools are the built-in components of ODL that can read and interpret your YANG file. The YANG compiler is used to generate multiple files that you need to code to make your MD-SAL application work.
3. **Building Artifacts**: Once the model is compiled by ODL YANG tools, there will be a number of artifact files generated by the YANG compiler. They include:
   - A model
   - A RESTCONF API
   - Provider code
   - Consumer code

The preceding files need to be coded further by you to build your real SDN application. Basically, these files form the full structure of your SDN application.

Remember that YANG tools will transform your YANG model into appropriate files and place them in different folders, then add the build instructions that will be used to compile and link your MD-SAL application.

Provider implementation

In the preceding figure, the module in green, which shows the portion of the created application code that you need to program. This is the provider implementation of your SDN application; here, you will write code and implement your application functions.

The elements in red within the MD-SAL box are created automatically for you by YANG tools during compile time.

Maven archetype

If you are not familiar with Maven archetypes, note that they are templates for creating things that are of a particular type or pattern. For MD-SAL, there is a Maven archetype that generates the framework of your project, going through the steps shown in the following diagram.

Here I've summarized the steps required to create an MD-SAL application:

1. Create a directory for your application.
2. Change the directory to the location of your newly created directory of your application.
3. Run the Maven archetype: generate a command specifying the appropriate OpenDaylight `group-id` and `artifact-id`.
4. Provide answers regarding your application's `group-id`, `artifact-id`, version, packet prefix, and so on.
5. Run the MD-SAL application generator to create your application files, folders, and build instructions.
6. Build your application.

Because of this process, the application generator will automatically create the following files:

Karaf features directory	Includes a list of sample features to enable provider, consumer, and web applications
YANG model	A simple YANG model that can be modified to specify the attributes of a model
Provider	A sample provider application that implements the RPC service defined in the Yang model
Consumer	A sample consumer application that can be extended to consume other model implementations within MD-SAL
Web	A sample implementation of a custom REST interface (note that this is in addition to the REST interfaces automatically generated for your application)

You can remove the unneeded files and projects if they are unnecessary.

What is YANG?

Published as RFC 6020, YANG is a data modeling language. Its function is similar to other data modeling languages, such as UML and XML; however, it has superior features, such as being human-readable and having support for configuration management.

It was created to be used for the definition of the data sent over the NETCONF protocol. It became popular after the success and rapid adoption of NETCONF.

Its configuration management capabilities are:

- Development support and versioning
- Supports submodules
- Grouping and structured types
- Supports the definition of operations (RPCs)
- Reusable types
- Hierarchical configuration for data models
- Easy-to-learn representation, human-readable

About 25 years ago, SNMP was introduced as a protocol between networking management and control systems devices for exchanging configurations, operations, and statistical information. SNMP started using a data modeling language called **Structure of Management Information** (**SMI**). SMI evolved and became SMIv2, but people began looking for a next generation data modeling language to support new network management protocols, such as NETCONF, which can support configuration management features and are more human-readable.

NETCONF started becoming popular and became the successor of SNMP. With more popularity of NETCONF, the need for a new data modeling language increased-a language that could deal with today's environment and could define new specifications of data models, such as RPC/APIs, to be called and notifications to be sent out from the data model to the subscribers. Therefore, YANG was developed and created and was chosen as the modeling language of NETCONF.

YANG was also found useful in non-NETCONF contexts as it had a good model to define the attributes, APIs, and notifications of a model. One of the non-NETCONF contexts that found YANG as the data modeling language of choice was MD-SAL.

MD-SAL applications use YANG to:

- Define the APIs and RPCs that will become RESTCONF APIs
- Specify the information contained in the object being modeled
- Specify any notification to be sent to the receivers or listeners

What exactly is YANG?

We have talked a lot about YANG; let's look at a sample YANG model. It can give you some idea about how the language is used. The following example is taken from the YANG-central web site (`http://www.YANG-central.org`).

The following YANG model defines a model for a module that defines the system's hostname and interfaces:

```
module acme-system {
    namespace "http://acme.example.com/system";
    prefix "acme";

    organization "ACME Inc.";
    contact "joe@acme.example.com";
    description
        "The module for entities implementing the ACME system.";

    revision 2007-11-05 {
        description "Initial revision.";
    }

    container system {
        leaf host-name {
            type string;
            description "Hostname for this system";
        }
    }


    list interface {
        key "name";
        description "List of interfaces in the system";
        leaf name {
            type string;
        }
            leaf type {
                type string;
            }
            leaf mtu {
                type int32;
            }
        }
    }
}
```

The preceding example is a model of a system that can be used for creating multiple network or host objects, such as routers, switches, and hosts.

As started in beginning of this chapter, a model is very similar to a class in object-oriented programming. You may run the YANG to Java generator to get the simple Java code represented by the sample YANG.

How does ODL use YANG?

As mentioned in the previous sections of this chapter, YANG is the base for building an SDN application in ODL, as ODL utilizes YANG and the YANG compiler.

The YANG compiler of ODL can generate a simple, skeletal MD-SAL application, using the Maven archetype functionality. Once you have done this, you will have YANG models created for you in each of the relevant modules, as follows:

- **Model:** `model/src/main/YANG/task.YANG`
- **Provider:** `provider/src/main/YANG/task-provider-impl.YANG`
- **Consumer:** `consumer/src/main/YANG/task-consumer-impl.YANG`

Examining these autogenerated YANG files for your MD-SAL application will give you an idea of how they used in the definition and creation of model-based applications in ODL.

Our very first application, HelloWorld

In this section, we will learn how to deploy our first HelloWorld application on ODL. In this example, we will perform the following steps to develop an app:

1. Create a local repository for the code using a simple build process.
2. Start the OpenDaylight controller.
3. Test a simple remote procedure call (RPC) that you would have created based on the principle of HelloWorld.

In order to build an application, we need the following tools to be installed on our ODL application or any machine that you would like to use for building applications.

You can use an Ubuntu machine as your development environment with the following setup:

- Maven 3.1.1 or later

    You probably don't have Maven installed; use the following command on your Ubuntu machine to install Maven. You can use Yum to install maven on a RedHat or CentOS platform:

```
sudo apt-get install maven
```

- Java 7- or Java 8-compliant JDK

    Since we were using `openjdk-8` as JRE, let's install JDK 8 from OpenJDK, as follows:

```
sudo apt-get install openjdk-8-jdk
```

- Create a woking directory to place all our files there:

```
mkdir   /home/learningodl
```

- Set up an appropriate Maven `settings.xml` file. A simple way to get the default OpenDaylight `settings.xml` file is as follows:

```
mkdir   /home/learningodl/.m2
wget -q -O - https://raw.githubusercontent.com/OpenDaylight
/odlparent/stable/boron/settings.xml > /home/learningodl/.m2/settings.xml
```

This will download the Maven `settings.xml` file to your `.m2` directory.

Create an example project using Maven and an archetype called `OpenDaylight-startup-archetype`. If you are downloading this project for the first time, it will take some time to pull all of the code from the remote repository.

Run the following command:

```
    mvn archetype:generate "-DarchetypeGroupId=org.OpenDaylight.controller"
"-DarchetypeArtifactId=OpenDaylight-startup-archetype" \
"-
DarchetypeRepository=https://nexus.OpenDaylight.org/content/repositories/pu
blic/" \
"-
DarchetypeCatalog=https://nexus.OpenDaylight.org/content/repositories/publi
c/archetype-catalog.xml" \
"-DarchetypeVersion=1.2.0-Boron"
```

After running the preceding command you will see the following questions.
Answer the questions with highlighted answers:
Define value for property 'groupId': org.OpenDaylight.example
Define value for property 'artifactId': example
[INFO] Using property: version = 0.1.0-SNAPSHOT
Define value for property 'artifactId': example
Define value for property 'package' org.OpenDaylight.example: :   JUST
PRESS ENTER
Define value for property 'classPrefix' Example: :
${artifactId.substring(0,1).toUpperCase()}${artifactId.substring(1)}
Define value for property 'copyright': learningodl
[INFO] Using property: copyrightYear = 2016
Y: : Y
Confirm properties configuration: Y
groupId: org.OpenDaylight.example
artifactId: example
version: 0.1.0-SNAPSHOT
package: org.OpenDaylight.example
classPrefix:
${artifactId.substring(0,1).toUpperCase()}${artifactId.substring(1)}
copyright: learningodl
copyrightYear: 2016
 Y: : Y
[INFO] --

[INFO] Using following parameters for creating project from Archetype:
OpenDaylight-startup-archetype:1.2.0-Boron
[INFO] --

[INFO] Parameter: groupId, Value: org.OpenDaylight.example
[INFO] Parameter: artifactId, Value: example
[INFO] Parameter: version, Value: 0.1.0-SNAPSHOT
[INFO] Parameter: package, Value: org.OpenDaylight.example
[INFO] Parameter: packageInPathFormat, Value: org/OpenDaylight/example
[INFO] Parameter: classPrefix, Value: Example
[INFO] Parameter: package, Value: org.OpenDaylight.example
[INFO] Parameter: version, Value: 0.1.0-SNAPSHOT
[INFO] Parameter: copyright, Value: learningodl
[INFO] Parameter: groupId, Value: org.OpenDaylight.example
[INFO] Parameter: artifactId, Value: example
[INFO] Parameter: copyrightYear, Value: 2016
[WARNING] Don't override file /home/learningodl/example/pom.xml
[INFO] Project created from Archetype in dir: /home/learningodl/example
[INFO] --

[INFO] BUILD SUCCESS
[INFO] --

```
[INFO] Total time: 02:48 min
[INFO] Finished at: 2017-03-21T14:43:24-07:00
[INFO] Final Memory: 22M/220M
[INFO] ------------------------------------------------------------------------
----
learningodl@ODL01:~$
```

```
learningodl@ODL01:~$ mvn archetype:generate "-DarchetypeGroupId=org.opendaylight.controller" "-Da
tps://nexus.opendaylight.org/content/repositories/public/" "-DarchetypeCatalog=https://nexus.open
Version=1.2.0-Boron"
[INFO] Scanning for projects...
[INFO]
[INFO] ------------------------------------------------------------------------
[INFO] Building Maven Stub Project (No POM) 1
[INFO] ------------------------------------------------------------------------
[INFO]
[INFO] >>> maven-archetype-plugin:3.0.0:generate (default-cli) > generate-sources @ standalone-po
[INFO]
[INFO] <<< maven-archetype-plugin:3.0.0:generate (default-cli) < generate-sources @ standalone-po
[INFO]
[INFO] --- maven-archetype-plugin:3.0.0:generate (default-cli) @ standalone-pom ---
[INFO] Generating project in Interactive mode
[INFO] No catalog defined. Using internal catalog
[WARNING] Archetype not found in any catalog. Falling back to central repository (http://repo.mav
[WARNING] Use -DarchetypeRepository=<your repository> if archetype's repository is elsewhere.
Define value for property 'groupId': org.opendaylight.example
Define value for property 'artifactId': example
[INFO] Using property: version = 0.1.0-SNAPSHOT
Define value for property 'package' org.opendaylight.example: :
Define value for property 'classPrefix' Example: : ${artifactId.substring(0,1).toUpperCase()}${ar
Define value for property 'copyright': learningodl
[INFO] Using property: copyrightYear = 2016
Confirm properties configuration:
groupId: org.opendaylight.example
artifactId: example
version: 0.1.0-SNAPSHOT
package: org.opendaylight.example
classPrefix: ${artifactId.substring(0,1).toUpperCase()}${artifactId.substring(1)}
copyright: learningodl
copyrightYear: 2016
 Y: : Y
```

```
[INFO]   -------------------------------------------------------------------
[INFO]   Using following parameters for creating project from Archetype: opendayli
[INFO]   -------------------------------------------------------------------
[INFO]   Parameter: groupId, Value: org.opendaylight.example
[INFO]   Parameter: artifactId, Value: example
[INFO]   Parameter: version, Value: 0.1.0-SNAPSHOT
[INFO]   Parameter: package, Value: org.opendaylight.example
[INFO]   Parameter: packageInPathFormat, Value: org/opendaylight/example
[INFO]   Parameter: classPrefix, Value: Example
[INFO]   Parameter: package, Value: org.opendaylight.example
[INFO]   Parameter: version, Value: 0.1.0-SNAPSHOT
[INFO]   Parameter: copyright, Value: learningodl
[INFO]   Parameter: groupId, Value: org.opendaylight.example
[INFO]   Parameter: artifactId, Value: example
[INFO]   Parameter: copyrightYear, Value: 2016
[WARNING] Don't override file /home/learningodl/example/pom.xml
[INFO]   Project created from Archetype in dir: /home/learningodl/example
[INFO]   -------------------------------------------------------------------
[INFO]   BUILD SUCCESS
[INFO]   -------------------------------------------------------------------
[INFO]   Total time: 31.502 s
[INFO]   Finished at: 2017-05-18T14:01:17-07:00
[INFO]   Final Memory: 16M/167M
[INFO]   -------------------------------------------------------------------
learningodl@ODL01:~$
```

This process will automatically create a folder called `example` in your home directory.

To compile and continue, enter the following commands:

```
cd /home/learningodl/example
ls
```

Ensure you have the following:

```
api  artifacts  cli  deploy-site.xml  features  impl  it  karaf
pom.xml  src
```

```
learningodl@ODL01:~$ cd example
learningodl@ODL01:~/example$ ls
api  artifacts  cli  deploy-site.xml  features  impl  it  karaf  pom.xml  src
learningodl@ODL01:~/example$
```

Let's build the project for the first time. Depending on your development machine's specification, this might take a little while. Ensure that you are in the project's root directory, `example/`, and then issue the `build` command, as shown here:

```
cd /home/learningodl/example
mvn clean install
```

This command will result in the downloading of lots of files, which are required to compile the application for OpenDaylight.

You should get the following result:

```
        [INFO] Reactor Summary:
[INFO]
[INFO] example-api ...................................... SUCCESS [07:00
min]
[INFO] example-impl ..................................... SUCCESS [
34.403 s]
[INFO] example-cli ...................................... SUCCESS [
15.841 s]
[INFO] example-features ................................. SUCCESS [07:47
min]
[INFO] example-karaf .................................... SUCCESS [04:53
min]
[INFO] example-artifacts ................................ SUCCESS [
1.111 s]
[INFO] example-it ....................................... SUCCESS [01:16
min]
[INFO] example .......................................... SUCCESS [
21.729 s]
[INFO] ------------------------------------------------------------------
----
[INFO] BUILD SUCCESS
[INFO] ------------------------------------------------------------------
----
[INFO] Total time: 26:12 min
[INFO] Finished at: 2017-03-21T15:13:47-07:00
[INFO] Final Memory: 230M/675M
[INFO] ------------------------------------------------------------------
----
learningodl@ODL01:~/example$
```

```
enderer/resources/default-site-macros.vm
[INFO]
[INFO] --- maven-site-plugin:3.5.1:attach-descriptor (generate-site) @ example-aggregator ---
[INFO] -------------------------------------------------------------------------
[INFO] Reactor Summary:
[INFO]
[INFO] example-api ........................................ SUCCESS [01:22 min]
[INFO] example-impl ....................................... SUCCESS [ 36.386 s]
[INFO] example-cli ........................................ SUCCESS [ 36.794 s]
[INFO] example-features ................................... SUCCESS [07:29 min]
[INFO] example-karaf ...................................... SUCCESS [01:39 min]
[INFO] example-artifacts .................................. SUCCESS [  3.384 s]
[INFO] example-it ......................................... SUCCESS [03:23 min]
[INFO] example ........................................... SUCCESS [01:13 min]
[INFO] -------------------------------------------------------------------------
[INFO] BUILD SUCCESS
[INFO] -------------------------------------------------------------------------
[INFO] Total time: 16:35 min
[INFO] Finished at: 2017-05-18T14:21:43-07:00
[INFO] Final Memory: 226M/721M
[INFO] -------------------------------------------------------------------------
learningodl@ODL01:~/example$
```

Once compiled, we can test it by running the ODL Karaf.

 Remember that this process downloads and compiles the ODL application, and you don't need to go back to your originally installed ODL.

Enter the following command to launch the ODL Karaf:

```
cd /home/learningodl/example/karaf/target/assembly/bin
./karaf
```

This will start ODL, and I know you are familiar with this interface.

To ensure the example application has been loaded, enter the following command in the Karaf CLI:

```
OpenDaylight-user@root>log:display | grep Example
```

You should get a result similar to the following command:

```
    2017-03-20 15:23:24,992 | INFO  | rint Extender: 2 | ExampleProvider
| 169 - org.OpenDaylight.example.impl - 0.1.0.SNAPSHOT | ExampleProvider
Session Initiated
OpenDaylight-user@root>
```

```
learningodl@ODL01:~/example/karaf/target/assembly/bin$ ./karaf
Apache Karaf starting up. Press Enter to open the shell now...
100% [=====================================================================]

Karaf started in 51s. Bundle stats: 284 active, 284 total




  <tab>' for a list of available commands
and '[cmd] --help' for help on a specific command.
Hit '<ctrl-d>' or type 'system:shutdown' or 'logout' to shutdown OpenDaylight.

opendaylight-user@root>log:display | grep Example
2017-05-18 14:23:43.640 | INFO  | rint Extender: 2 | ExampleProvider          | 169 - org
.opendaylight.example.impl - 0.1.0.SNAPSHOT | ExampleProvider Session Initiated
```

Now we need to create the HelloWorld application. Enter the following commands to generate the project:

```
    mvn archetype:generate "-DarchetypeGroupId=org.OpenDaylight.controller"
"-DarchetypeArtifactId=OpenDaylight-startup-archetype" \
"-
DarchetypeRepository=https://nexus.OpenDaylight.org/content/repositories/pu
blic/" \
"-
DarchetypeCatalog=https://nexus.OpenDaylight.org/content/repositories/publi
c/archetype-catalog.xml" \
"-DarchetypeVersion=1.2.0-Boron"
```

Once you run the preceding code, it will ask you the same questions:

```
    Define value for property 'groupId': org.OpenDaylight.hello
Define value for property 'artifactId': hello
[INFO] Using property: version = 0.1.0-SNAPSHOT
Define value for property 'package' org.OpenDaylight.hello: :
Define value for property 'classPrefix' Hello: :
${artifactId.substring(0,1).toUpperCase()}${artifactId.substring(1)}
Define value for property 'copyright': learningodl
[INFO] Using property: copyrightYear = 2016
Confirm properties configuration:
groupId: org.OpenDaylight.hello
```

```
artifactId: hello
version: 0.1.0-SNAPSHOT
package: org.OpenDaylight.hello
classPrefix:
${artifactId.substring(0,1).toUpperCase()}${artifactId.substring(1)}
copyright: learningodl
copyrightYear: 2016
 Y: : Y
[INFO] ----------------------------------------------------------------
--------
[INFO] Using following parameters for creating project from Archetype:
OpenDaylight-startup-archetype:1.2.0-Boron
[INFO] ----------------------------------------------------------------
--------
[INFO] Parameter: groupId, Value: org.OpenDaylight.hello
[INFO] Parameter: artifactId, Value: hello
[INFO] Parameter: version, Value: 0.1.0-SNAPSHOT
[INFO] Parameter: package, Value: org.OpenDaylight.hello
[INFO] Parameter: packageInPathFormat, Value: org/OpenDaylight/hello
[INFO] Parameter: classPrefix, Value: Hello
[INFO] Parameter: package, Value: org.OpenDaylight.hello
[INFO] Parameter: version, Value: 0.1.0-SNAPSHOT
[INFO] Parameter: copyright, Value: learningodl
[INFO] Parameter: groupId, Value: org.OpenDaylight.hello
[INFO] Parameter: artifactId, Value: hello
[INFO] Parameter: copyrightYear, Value: 2016
[WARNING] Don't override file /home/learningodl/hello/pom.xml
[INFO] Project created from Archetype in dir: /home/learningodl/hello
[INFO] ----------------------------------------------------------------
----
[INFO] BUILD SUCCESS
[INFO] ----------------------------------------------------------------
----
[INFO] Total time: 36.050 s
[INFO] Finished at: 2017-03-21T15:22:40-07:00
[INFO] Final Memory: 18M/162M
[INFO] ----------------------------------------------------------------
----
learningodl@ODL01:~$
```

Once you run the preceding code, the system will create the `hello` folder. Make sure you have the following:

```
    Cd hello
Ls
api  artifacts  cli  deploy-site.xml  features  impl  it  karaf  pom.xml
src
```

Now build the `hello` project using the following command:

```
cd /home/learningodl/hello
mvn clean install
```

This will take some time as `mvn` will download the full ODL again and build the `hello` project:

```
[INFO] ------------------------------------------------------------------------
[INFO] Reactor Summary:
[INFO]
[INFO] hello-api .......................................... SUCCESS [
21.059 s]
[INFO] hello-impl ......................................... SUCCESS [
12.295 s]
[INFO] hello-cli .......................................... SUCCESS [
14.958 s]
[INFO] hello-features ..................................... SUCCESS [01:50
min]
[INFO] hello-karaf ........................................ SUCCESS [
23.730 s]
[INFO] hello-artifacts .................................... SUCCESS [
0.923 s]
[INFO] hello-it ........................................... SUCCESS [
43.468 s]
[INFO] hello .............................................. SUCCESS [
17.463 s]
[INFO] ------------------------------------------------------------------------
[INFO] BUILD SUCCESS
[INFO] ------------------------------------------------------------------------
[INFO] Total time: 04:06 min
[INFO] Finished at: 2017-03-21T15:28:33-07:00
[INFO] Final Memory: 224M/610M
[INFO] ------------------------------------------------------------------------
learningodl@ODL01:~/hello$
learningodl@ODL01:~/hello$
```

Enter the following command to start the ODL Karaf:

```
cd /home/learningodl/hello/karaf/target/assembly/bin
./karaf
```

Enter the following command to ensure it is loaded:

```
    OpenDaylight-user@root>log:display | grep Hello
2017-03-20 15:55:00,879 | INFO  | rint Extender: 2 | HelloProvider
| 172 - org.OpenDaylight.hello.impl - 0.1.0.SNAPSHOT | HelloProvider
Session Initiated
  OpenDaylight-user@root>
```

Exit the Karaf by running the shutdown command:

```
    shutdown -f
```

Enter the following command to edit the YANG model file of our HelloWorld project:

```
    nano /home/learningodl/hello/api/src/main/YANG/hello.YANG
```

Make sure the YANG file has the following contents:

```
    module hello {
        YANG-version 1;
        namespace "urn:OpenDaylight:params:xml:ns:YANG:hello";
        prefix "hello";

        revision "2015-01-05" {
            description "Initial revision of hello model";
        }

      rpc hello-world {
            input {
                leaf name {
                    type string;
                }
            }
            output {
                leaf greeting {
                    type string;
                }
            }
        }



    }
```

Now start compiling it again:

```
    Cd /home/learningodl/hello
Mvn clean install
```

Wait until you get this:

```
    [INFO] --- maven-site-plugin:3.5.1:attach-descriptor (generate-site) @
hello-aggregator ---
[INFO] ------------------------------------------------------------------
----
[INFO] Reactor Summary:
[INFO]
[INFO] hello-api ....................................... SUCCESS [
21.933 s]
[INFO] hello-impl ...................................... SUCCESS [
13.746 s]
[INFO] hello-cli ....................................... SUCCESS [
12.871 s]
[INFO] hello-features .................................. SUCCESS [01:53
min]
[INFO] hello-karaf ..................................... SUCCESS [
26.652 s]
[INFO] hello-artifacts ................................. SUCCESS [
1.351 s]
[INFO] hello-it ........................................ SUCCESS [
48.758 s]
[INFO] hello ........................................... SUCCESS [
17.397 s]
[INFO] ------------------------------------------------------------------
----
[INFO] BUILD SUCCESS
[INFO] ------------------------------------------------------------------
----
[INFO] Total time: 04:18 min
[INFO] Finished at: 2017-03-21T16:08:59-07:00
[INFO] Final Memory: 225M/665M
[INFO] ------------------------------------------------------------------
----
learningodl@ODL01:~/hello$
```

Enter the following command to edit the Java implementation file of our HelloWorld project:

```
nano /home/learningodl/hello/impl/src/main/java/org/
OpenDaylight/hello/impl/HelloWorldImpl.java
```

Be careful about the header (the section that starts with /* and ends with */); it must be exactly the same as what's presented in the following code:

```
/*
 * Copyright © 2016 learningodl and others.  All rights reserved.
 *
 * This program and the accompanying materials are made available
under the
 * terms of the Eclipse Public License v1.0 which accompanies this
distribution,
 * and is available at http://www.eclipse.org/legal/epl-v10.html
 */

package org.OpenDaylight.hello.impl;

import java.util.concurrent.Future;

import  org.OpenDaylight.YANG.gen.v1.urn.OpenDaylight
.params.xml.ns.YANG.hello.rev150105.HelloService;
import org.OpenDaylight.YANG.gen.v1.urn.OpenDaylight
.params.xml.ns.YANG.hello.rev150105.HelloWorldInput;
import org.OpenDaylight.YANG.gen.v1.urn.OpenDaylight
.params.xml.ns.YANG.hello.rev150105.HelloWorldOutput;
import org.OpenDaylight.YANG.gen.v1.urn.OpenDaylight
.params.xml.ns.YANG.hello.rev150105.HelloWorldOutputBuilder;
import org.OpenDaylight.YANGtools.YANG.common.RpcResult;
import org.OpenDaylight.YANGtools.YANG.common.RpcResultBuilder;

public class HelloWorldImpl implements HelloService {

    @Override
    public Future<RpcResult<HelloWorldOutput>>
 helloWorld(HelloWorldInput input) {
        HelloWorldOutputBuilder helloBuilder = new
 HelloWorldOutputBuilder();
        helloBuilder.setGreeting("Hello " + input.getName());
        return
RpcResultBuilder.success(helloBuilder.build()).buildFuture();
    }

}
```

Edit the `impl-blueprint.xml` file:

```
nano
/home/learningodl/hello/impl/src/main/resources/org/OpenDaylight/bluepr
int/impl-blueprint.xml.
```

Make it as shown here:

```
<?xml version="1.0" encoding="UTF-8"?>
<!-- vi: set et smarttab sw=4 tabstop=4: -->
<!--
Copyright © 2016 Copyright(c) 2017 and others. All rights reserved.

This program and the accompanying materials are made available
under the
terms of the Eclipse Public License v1.0 which accompanies this
distribution,
and is available at http://www.eclipse.org/legal/epl-v10.html
-->
<blueprint xmlns="http://www.osgi.org/xmlns/blueprint/v1.0.0"
  xmlns:odl="http://OpenDaylight.org/xmlns/blueprint/v1.0.0"
  odl:use-default-for-reference-types="true">

  <reference id="dataBroker"

interface="org.OpenDaylight.controller.md.sal.binding.api.DataBroker"
    odl:type="default" />


  <reference id="rpcRegistry"

interface="org.OpenDaylight.controller.sal.binding.api.RpcProviderReg
istry"/>'''

    <bean id="provider"
      class="org.OpenDaylight.spark.impl.HelloProvider"
      init-method="init" destroy-method="close">
      <argument ref="dataBroker" />
      <argument ref="rpcRegistry" />
    </bean>


  </blueprint>
```

Edit the `HelloProvider.java` file:

nano
/home/learningodl/hello/impl/src/main/java/org/OpenDaylight/hello/impl/HelloProvider.ja
va

Then add the following:

```
/*
 * Copyright © 2016 learningodl and others.  All rights reserved.
 *
 * This program and the accompanying materials are made available
under the
 * terms of the Eclipse Public License v1.0 which accompanies this
distribution,
 * and is available at http://www.eclipse.org/legal/epl-v10.html
 */

package org.OpenDaylight.hello.impl;

import org.OpenDaylight.controller.md.sal.binding.api.DataBroker;
import
org.OpenDaylight.controller.sal.binding.api.RpcProviderRegistry;
import
org.OpenDaylight.controller.sal.binding.api.BindingAwareBroker.RpcReg
istration;
import
org.OpenDaylight.YANG.gen.v1.urn.OpenDaylight.params.xml.ns.YANG.hell
o.rev150105.HelloService;
import org.slf4j.Logger;
import org.slf4j.LoggerFactory;

public class HelloProvider {

    private static final Logger LOG =
LoggerFactory.getLogger(HelloProvider.class);

    private final DataBroker dataBroker;
    private final RpcProviderRegistry rpcProviderRegistry;

    public HelloProvider(final DataBroker dataBroker,
RpcProviderRegistry rpcProviderRegistry) {
        this.dataBroker = dataBroker;
        this.rpcProviderRegistry = rpcProviderRegistry;
    }


    private RpcRegistration<HelloService> serviceRegistration;
```

```
    /**
     * Method called when the blueprint container is created.
     */
    public void init() {
    serviceRegistration =
rpcProviderRegistry.addRpcImplementation(HelloService.class, new
HelloWorldImpl());
        LOG.info("HelloProvider Session Initiated");
    }

    /**
     * Method called when the blueprint container is destroyed.
     */
    public void close() {
        serviceRegistration.close();
        LOG.info("HelloProvider Closed");
    }
  }
```

Now we will compile the following:

```
    cd /home/learningodl/hello/impl
  mvn clean install
```

You will get an output that will be similar to this:

```
    [INFO]
[INFO] --- maven-bundle-plugin:3.0.1:install (default-install) @ hello-impl
---
[INFO] Installing org/OpenDaylight/hello/hello-impl/0.1.0-SNAPSHOT/hello-
impl-0.1.0-SNAPSHOT.jar
[INFO] Writing OBR metadata
[INFO] ----------------------------------------------------------------
----
[INFO] BUILD SUCCESS
[INFO] ----------------------------------------------------------------
----
[INFO] Total time: 6.893 s
[INFO] Finished at: 2017-03-21T16:19:52-07:00
[INFO] Final Memory: 61M/498M
[INFO] ----------------------------------------------------------------
----
```

Now go one folder up and compile the whole thing:

```
        cd /home/learningodl/hello
mvn clean install
[INFO] --- maven-site-plugin:3.5.1:attach-descriptor (generate-site) @
hello-aggregator ---
[INFO] -----------------------------------------------------------------
----
[INFO] Reactor Summary:
[INFO]
[INFO] hello-api ....................................... SUCCESS [
20.851 s]
[INFO] hello-impl ...................................... SUCCESS [
13.026 s]
[INFO] hello-cli ....................................... SUCCESS [
12.335 s]
[INFO] hello-features .................................. SUCCESS [01:51
min]
[INFO] hello-karaf ..................................... SUCCESS [
25.038 s]
[INFO] hello-artifacts ................................. SUCCESS [
0.965 s]
[INFO] hello-it ........................................ SUCCESS [
45.434 s]
[INFO] hello ........................................... SUCCESS [
17.601 s]
[INFO] -----------------------------------------------------------------
----
[INFO] BUILD SUCCESS
[INFO] -----------------------------------------------------------------
----
[INFO] Total time: 04:08 min
[INFO] Finished at: 2017-03-21T16:27:42-07:00
[INFO] Final Memory: 225M/669M
[INFO] -----------------------------------------------------------------
----
learningodl@ODL01:~/hello$
```

Now start the ODL Karaf

```
cd /home/learningodl/hello/karaf/target/assembly/bin
./karaf
```

Check to ensure the HelloWorld application is loaded:

```
    log:display | grep hello
OpenDaylight-user@root>log:display | grep hello
2017-03-21 16:28:57,676 | INFO  | Event Dispatcher |
YANGTextSchemaContextResolver     | 55 - org.OpenDaylight.YANGtools.YANG-
parser-impl - 1.0.0.Boron | Provided module name /META-
INF/YANG/hello.YANG@0000-00-00.YANG does not match actual text
hello@2015-01-05.YANG, corrected
2017-03-21 16:29:02,608 | INFO  | Event Dispatcher | BlueprintBundleTracker
| 147 - org.OpenDaylight.controller.blueprint - 0.5.0.Boron | Creating
blueprint container for bundle org.OpenDaylight.hello.impl_0.1.0.SNAPSHOT
[172] with paths
[bundleentry://172.fwk1182461167/org/OpenDaylight/blueprint/impl-
blueprint.xml]
2017-03-21 16:29:02,631 | ERROR | Event Dispatcher | BlueprintContainerImpl
| 15 - org.apache.aries.blueprint.core - 1.6.1 | Unable to start blueprint
container for bundle org.OpenDaylight.hello.impl/0.1.0.SNAPSHOT
OpenDaylight-user@root>
```

Now, from your browser, access the OpenDaylight Dlux web interface. Click on the YANG UI on the left-hand side. You should be able to see the `hello` application listed on the right-hand side of the screen. Also, you will see the `hello` services listed at the bottom of the screen:

```
[INFO]
[INFO] --- maven-bundle-plugin:3.0.1:install (default-install) @ hello-impl ---
[INFO] Installing org/opendaylight/hello/hello-impl/0.1.0-SNAPSHOT/hello-impl-0.1.0-SNAPSHOT.jar
[INFO] Writing OBR metadata
[INFO] ------------------------------------------------------------------------
[INFO] BUILD SUCCESS
[INFO] ------------------------------------------------------------------------
[INFO] Total time: 37.733 s
[INFO] Finished at: 2017-05-18T14:29:32-07:00
[INFO] Final Memory: 57M/460M
[INFO] ------------------------------------------------------------------------
learningodl@ODL01:~/hello/impl$
```

Summary

In this chapter, you learned about the basics of MD-SAL and how ODL utilizes MD-SAL for its applications. We developed a basic HelloWorld application and saw how the YANG tools engine convert the YANG model into multiple files.

In next chapter, we will study a full SDN application.

7
Building SDN Applications for OpenDaylight

In this chapter, you will learn how to build an SDN application on top of OpenDaylight. We will have a detailed review of an SDN NAC application. You will also learn the application framework of OpenDaylight and understand how to build plugins, applications and how to integrate them to the OpenDayLight packet processing engine.

Along with building this OpenDaylight application, we will cover the following topics:

- What is NAC?
- Understanding the OpenDaylight SAL
- Difference between plugins and applications
- Building a practical SDN app

Introduction to network access control via OpenDaylight

In the previous chapter, you learned how OpenDaylight's MD-SAL works. You learned how to build a basic HelloWorld application based on OpenDaylight MD-SAL and build the model using YANG. We also reviewed how to use tools to process the YANG model file of our application in which to generate multiple Java source code files.

In this chapter, we will look at building a more practical SDN application for OpenDaylight. We are going to look at OpenFlow switches again and see how we can implement an **Network Access Control** (**NAC**) solution.

NAC is one of the well-known use cases for SDN. With SDN, network access control could become easier to deploy.

 Note to remember: OpenDaylight is an SDN controller; it is not a data plane component and does not process packets in terms of forwarding or alternation.

What is NAC?

NAC is a method to control and allow only authorized devices to be connected to the network. It is more common for wired network and devices connecting with a hard-wire or a virtual interface to the network. Most wireless networks already have certain access controls available and enforced via 802.1X, WPA to ensure only authorized users or devices can connect to the wireless network.

In a wired network or a standard Ethernet switch, by default, you can connect any device to the network and obtain access. Most networks have a DHCP infrastructure running which provides an IP address to a newly connected device. This makes a wired network vulnerable as an intruder also can physically connect to the network once they get physical access to the premises. An intruder even can find the IP address details of the network in case of absence of a DHCP server in the network.

As per enterprise security best practices and ISO 27001 standards, network policies should be in place and enforced to only allow authorized devices to be connected to the network. Any unauthorized device must be denied or controlled and their access must be isolated.

To cope with this requirement, there are a couple of technologies and methods available as a security feature on most enterprise switches. Some of them are:

- **Port security**: This technology is available on most enterprise Ethernet switches and allow only a specific MAC address to be connected to a certain port. (by binding a MAC address to a switch port)
- **802.1x authentication**: In this method, the enterprise Ethernet switch enforces an authentication challenge to the connected device to be authenticated against a credential repository, such as Active Directory or a RADIUS servers.
- **MAC address authentication**: In this method, the enterprise Ethernet switch authenticates the MAC address of the connected device against an external RADIUS server. This feature is also called **MAC Address Bypass** (MAB) in Cisco terms.

- **Web authentication**: In this method, the enterprise Ethernet switch keeps the new connected device in an isolated VLAN, where NAC server also reside. When user opens a browser to access any website, the NAC device will redirect the user's browser to an internal web portal (hosted on NAC) for registration or authentication. This method doesn't work if the connected device doesn't have a browser, for example a printer.
- **Inline NAC**: In this method, the NAC device will be inline. Imagine that the user traffic passes through a transparent NAC device.

In most cases, NAC needs to be deployed for network edge or access where end user computers will be connecting. NAC is not very popular in data centers since usually there are tight physical security available that disallows people from bringing or connecting their devices to the network. In campus access, since there is limited or, in some cases, no physical security, anyone can bring a laptop, connect it to the network, and access internal resources of enterprise. NAC solves the problem of securing the access network by authenticating each device that tries to connect to the network, however, it comes with its own pains and troubles and extra work that is mainly forced on the IT service desk.

If you have ever deployed NAC in a large environment, you know the pain associated with 802.1X and EAP authentication, as it relies on client devices and operating system. The dream of every network administrator is to have a hassle-free NAC solution. Any of NAC methods we explained previously can be deployed based on the business and technical requirements of the enterprise.

We will not compare the NAC methods, but we will explore how NAC works in an SDN environment. Out of the five NAC methods mentioned previously, some of them are not implementable in a pure SDN network. For example, 802.1X, requires a piece software in the switch operating system to act as an authenticator (to terminate EAP, send RADIUS packets to the NAC server), which is not an out-of-the-box option in a pure OpenFlow based Ethernet switch which only run an OpenFlow agent.

In 802.1X, the network switch acts as an authenticator proxy and establishes an **Extensible Authentication Protocol over LAN** (**EAPOL**) point-to-point communication with the end user device. The switch uses this secure protocol to ask the client for their credentials (username and password), which in most cases is supplied as a single sign-on via user's operating system. The switch uses these details and embeds them to RADIUS access request packets and send to the NAC server to check the authenticity of the supplied credentials.

The NAC server either has a database of credentials or it is integrated into an external database such as Active Directory or an LDAP server to authenticate the received credentials from Ethernet switch. NAC sends an Access-Reject to just deny the access of the connected device or an Access-Accept response with a VLAN attribute, which tells the switch in which VLAN the port needs to be kept.

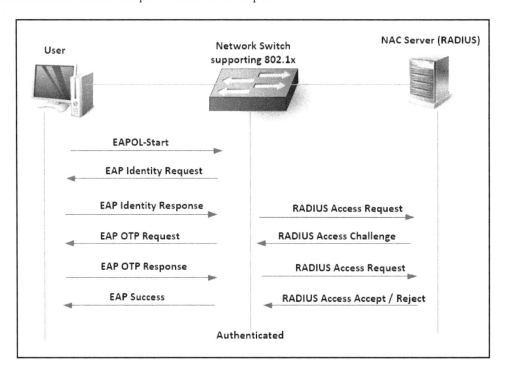

Since this piece of software doesn't exist in a pure OpenFlow switch (running only the OpenFlow agent) , we need to use other methods to authenticate the connected device.

The following methods could be used for running a NAC in an SDN environment;

- MAC address authentication (MAB/MAC address bypass)
- Web authentication
- Inline

We will look at the web authentication method to see how we can leverage SDN and OpenDaylight to secure the access network.

Building the NAC SDN application (web authentication method)

In this section, we will review the NAC application for OpenDaylight controller. The NAC SDN consists of the following components:

- OpenFlow-based switch.
- NAC plugin for OpenDaylight.
- NAC server (REST API enabled).

The following diagram illustrates the topology of NAC in an SDN enabled network with OpenDaylight controller.

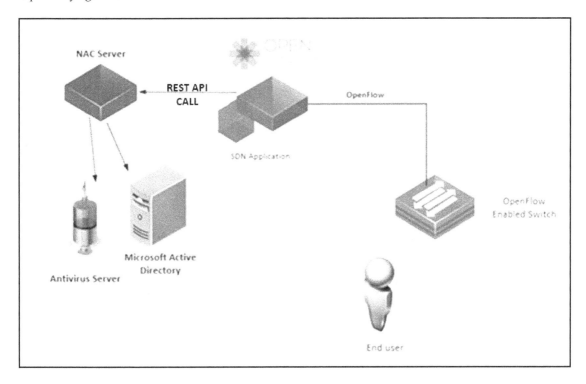

In a nutshell, we need to build an application on top of OpenDaylight to authenticate the user devices that would connect to the network. This application should detect any new device joining the network and should be able to communicate with the NAC server to check the authenticity of the users.

The NAC server will then return either an access-accept or access-reject response back to our SDN application, which needs to be translated into a flow to be installed on the OpenFlow switches in the network (SDN domain).

Let's review the steps for connecting a new device to the network for the first time:

1. The user device connects to the OpenFlow-enabled network switch.
2. The user device sends a DHCP DISCOVER broadcast to find the IP address.
3. Normally, there is a flow in the flow tables of OpenFlow switch that allows DHCP requests to go to the DHCP server. This flow normally matches with any source and destination as `FF:FF:FF:FF:FF:FF` and UDP port `67`. With this flow enabled, the packet will be forwarded to the DHCP server by the SDN switches.
4. DHCP server receives the request from a new client device, processes the request, and allocates an IP address. Then it sends back a DHCP reply along with the allocated IP address for new device, default gateway, and DNS server details to the client device.
   1. The OpenFlow switch forwards back the received DHCP reply from DHCP server to the client device based on already populated flow in its flow table.
5. The client receives the IP address and will now be able to communicate. At this stage, the client device may send any packet based on the applications running on the machine however no packet will be forwarded until the client is authenticated. Client needs to authenticate via web, which means the user must launch a browser and try to open a website. In this example, imagine the client device has a Internet browser and would like to go to `www.packtpub.com`.
6. The client device needs to send a DNS request to resolve `www.packtpub.com` as it doesn't have the IP address of this URL.
7. Before sending the DNS packet out to DNS server as normally DNS servers are located in different layer 3 networks, the client needs to find the MAC address of the default gateway; it sends an ARP request to find the MAC address of its default gateway. The ARP packet is L2 broadcast and will come to the OpenFlow switch.
8. The OpenFlow switch forwards the ARP packet to OpenDaylight.
9. The OpenDaylight L2 switch application has an ARP handler, which will prepare an ARP response based on the IP address of the router in the client device network. OpenDaylight encapsulates this packet in an `OpenFlow Packet-Out` message and sends it to the OpenFlow switch who forwarded this message.
10. The OpenFlow switch decapsulates and forwards the packet to the client device. At this stage our client gets an ARP reply message which contains the MAC address of the default router. Now it should be able to send the DNS request.

11. The client device prepares a DNS packet with the following details:

- **L2 source address**: The client's MAC address
- **L2 destination address**: The MAC address of the default gateway
- **L3 Source IP address**: The client IP address, received from DHCP
- **L3 destination IP address**: The DNS server's IP address, received from DHCP
- **L3 next protocol**: UDP
- **L4 source port**: A random port chosen by the client OS
- **L4 destination port**: `53` (DNS)

13. The client operating system sends out this packet on the wire.
14. The OpenFlow switch receives the packet, but it doesn't find any flow matching with Layer 2 and Layer 3 attributes of this packet.
15. The OpenFlow switch encapsulates and ends this packet as an `OpenFlow Packet_IN` message to OpenDaylight.
16. OpenDaylight receives this packet and analyses it. At this stage, our SDN-NAC application comes to play. SDN-NAC is attached to OpenDaylight and listens for any DNS packet. In this case, since the packet is DNS, OpenDaylight gives the control to process this packet to our SDN-NAC application.
17. Our SDN-NAC application running on OpenDaylight has packet handler which only looks for DNS packets. If there is any other packet sent by OpenDaylight to our SDN-NAC module that will be ignored. In this case, our SDN-NAC plugin has received a DNS packet and starts processing.
18. Our SDN-NAC application on OpenDaylight prepares all the information required for NAC Server to process the request. It will prepare a REST call with the following information:

- Device MAC address
- Device IP address
- Switch ID, where the client device is connected
- Switch port, where the client device is connected
- Full packet payload

19. The SDN-NAC application on OpenDaylight sends a REST API call to NAC server supplying all the preceding details.
20. The NAC server receives the details from OpenDaylight and looks in its session table to find whether the client is already registered or not. However, this is the first time this client device is connecting and there is no previous record.

21. The NAC server sends a REST API to OpenDaylight, calls the SDN-NAC northbound API, and tells that this device is accepted but needs to be isolated in order to complete the authentication.

22. The SDN-NAC application on OpenDaylight processes this REST call and installs two flows in OpenFlow switches:
    - Flow 1: This is to send DNS-generated traffic from new client device to the NAC server. This is simply a flow in one or multiple switches in the path to enable all DNS request packets form the client to be sent to the NAC server. (from Client to NAC sever)
    - Flow 2: This is to send traffic from NAC server destined to the MAC address of the client device . (From NAC sever to client)

23. The NAC server starts receiving DNS packets on its network interface that are originated from the client device. By default, NAC server should ignore and drop these DNS packets as they are not destined to MAC address and IP address of NAC server. However, the NAC server runs a simple IP tables rule, which redirects all DNS packets to one of the processes of the NAC server.

24. Just to remind you, in this long process and steps that the NAC server is already aware that the host is not yet authenticated as it happened during step 20 and 21.

25. The NAC server has a DNS poison component, which processes the DNS packet and replies. DNS poison module in the NAC server simply generates a DNS reply packet with the source IP address of the original DNS server (finds it from the DNS query) and its own IP address (NAC Server IP) as the A record for the query. In our example, this will be a DNS response with the following details:

    - Query: `www.packtpub.com`
    - Response: Type A, the address IP address of the NAC server

26. The NAC server sends this packet on wire. The packet reaches the OpenFlow switch first, and since there is a flow installed to forward such a packet back to the client, packet will be sent to the client port.

27. The client receives the DNS response and finds the IP address of `www.packtpub.com`, which is the IP address of the NAC server; however, the client is not aware of this. The client Internet browser builds an HTTP request packet toward the NAC server with the following details:

    - Destination IP: the NAC server
    - Protocol: TCP
    - Port: `80`
    - Request method: `GET`

- Request URI: /
- Host: www.packtpub.com

The client device sends this HTTP request packet on wire. Note that there will be a three-way TCP handshake, which will happen prior to sending this packet. This three-way TCP handshake will happen between the NAC server and the client.

28. The NAC server receives the HTTP request. It has a mechanism to redirect the HTTP request to its internal secure (HTTPS), based on the web authentication form. The client will be redirected to the web authentication form of the NAC server and will also have a form to enter username and password. The client would then need to enter username and password and submit the form.

29. The NAC server receives the credentials and handles the authentication against the active directory or other databases, using its own protocols, such as LDAP. If the username and password were correct, it creates a record for the client in its database as authenticated.

   If the credentials are rejected by the active directory, the client will be informed via a web page and will not be able to access the network until a successful authentication is completed.

30. If the authentication is successful, the NAC server will send a REST API call to OpenDaylight, its a call to northbound API of our SDN-NAC application. This API call will be received by OpenDaylight and the SDN-NAC application. It will push a trigger to remove the previously installed DNS flows from the OpenFlow switches. The flows will be deleted, and from then onward, the SDN-NAC application on OpenDaylight will not install any DNS flows for this client until the authentication timer is expired.

31. Upon the expiry of the timer, the SDN-NAC application will be able to identify whether the host is still on the network by checking the flow tables and asking the NAC server to check whether the user is authenticated or not.

32. Upon disconnection or shutdown, SDN-NAC must be able to identify the event and inform the NAC server that the host no longer exists in the network. The NAC server will then close the session of the user accordingly.

This was a complete breakdown of the steps related to what needs to be done in our NAC and SDN-NAC application running on OpenDaylight.

Which NAC software can be used to integrate with OpenDaylight?

The good news is that the NAC software and its OpenDaylight SDN-NAC software are available as open source by Inverse software. It is called PacketFence (www.packetfence.org).

PacketFence is an open source NAC designed to be compatible with all legacy networking equipment as well as SDN-based networks, including OpenDaylight. It already have the SDN-NAC application for OpenDaylight and we will analyze this plugin in details.

PacketFence has a module for OpenDaylight; we call it in the SDN-NAC application. This application is a plugin for OpenDaylight, where it enforces user authentication via a web portal and manages SDN flows in OpenFlow switches.

The following illustration diagram shows the flow chart of PacketFence SDN application.

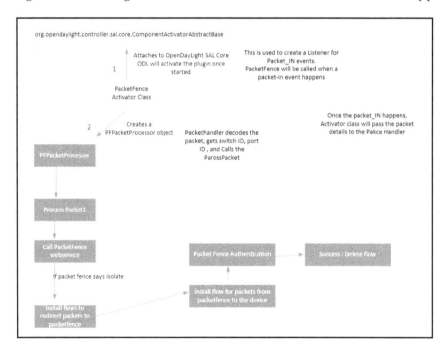

The SDN-NAC application is a SAL application (not MD-SAL), and in this chapter, you will find the differences in building basic SAL applications.

To start with, you need to download the PacketFence OpenDaylight components. You can get them from
`https://github.com/inverse-inc/packetfence/tree/feature/OpenDaylight/addons/OpenDaylight/src/main/java/ca/inverse/OpenDaylightpf`.

Here, you will find the source files of the plugin, which we will analyze. This is the SDN-NAC module of PacketFence, which includes the following Java classes:

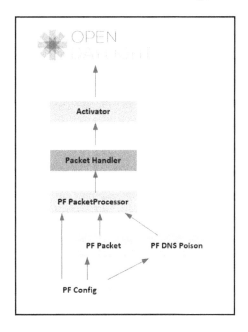

- `Activator`: This is the main class that attaches the NAC SDN plugin to OpenDaylight. It uses `org.OpenDaylight.controller.sal.core.ComponentActivatorAbstractBase` to do this.
- `PacketHandler`: This class is called by `Activator`. It manages the incoming packets and processes them.
- `PFPacketProcessor`: This class is called by `PacketHandler`. It implements the functions for authentication of the user, communicating back to the PacketFence REST API, and installing DNS redirection flows.
- `PFDNSPoisin`: This class is called by `PFPacketprocessor` and has functions for installing and removing the DNS redirection flows in OpenFlow switches.

- `PFPacket`: This class is a function utility that PacketFence uses to help in packet processing. It includes functions such as integer to MAC address converter, layer 4 payload extractor, layer 3 payload extractor, source port finder, source and destination finder, and so on.
- `PFConfig`: This module has a configuration file. It includes the functions for reading and parsing the configuration file.

Attaching the NAC plugin to OpenDaylight

This application uses the `Activator` class to attach itself to OpenDaylight. This class creates an `Activator` class that is extended from `org.OpenDaylight.controller.sal.core.ComponentActivatorAbstractBase`.

As we discussed in previous chapters, OpenDaylight is based on Apache Karaf OSGi container. The NAC plugin is an OSGi component, and in order to implement this, we need two other class files:

- **OSGi activator**: This is to register the component with the OSGi framework.
- **PacketHandler**: This is the control logic to process the packets in the event of packet-in and when the packets are handed over to PacketHandler.

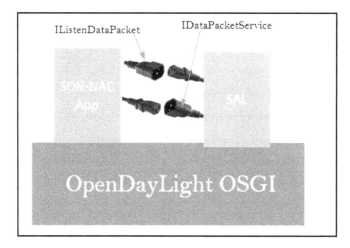

Lets have a closer look at the Activator.java source code :

```
01 package ca.inverse.odlpf;
02
03 import java.util.Dictionary;
04 import java.util.Hashtable;
05 import org.apache.felix.dm.Component;
06 import
org.opendaylight.controller.sal.core.ComponentActivatorAbstractBase;
07 import org.opendaylight.controller.sal.packet.IDataPacketService;
08 import org.opendaylight.controller.sal.packet.IListenDataPacket;
09 import
org.opendaylight.controller.sal.flowprogrammer.IFlowProgrammerService;
10 import org.slf4j.Logger;
11 import org.slf4j.LoggerFactory;
12
13 public class Activator extends ComponentActivatorAbstractBase {
14
15     private static final Logger log =
LoggerFactory.getLogger(PacketHandler.class);
16
17     public Object[] getImplementations() {
18         log.trace("Getting Implementations");
19
20         Object[] res = { PacketHandler.class };
21         return res;
22     }
23
24     public void configureInstance(Component c, Object imp, String
containerName) {
25         log.trace("Configuring instance");
26
27         if (imp.equals(PacketHandler.class)) {
28
29             // Define exported and used services for PacketHandler
component.
30
31             Dictionary<String, Object> props = new Hashtable<String,
Object>();
32             props.put("salListenerName", "PacketFence packet
handler");
33
34             // Export IListenDataPacket interface to receive packet-
in events.
35             c.setInterface(new String[]
{IListenDataPacket.class.getName()}, props);
36
37             // Need the DataPacketService for encoding, decoding,
```

```
sending data packets
    38                c.add(createContainerServiceDependency(containerName)
.setService(IDataPacketService.class).setCallbacks("setDataPacketService",
        "unsetDataPacketService").setRequired(true));
    39
    40              // Need FlowProgrammerService for programming flows
    41
              c.add(createContainerServiceDependency(containerName).
    setService(IFlowProgrammerService.class).setCallbacks(
    42                       "setFlowProgrammerService",
"unsetFlowProgrammerService").
    setRequired(true));
    43
    44        }
    45    }
    46 }
```

The activator class extends the base class `ComponentActivatorAbstractBase` from the OpenDaylight controller.

OpenDaylight is based on the OSGi framework. When a bundle component is being loaded, OSGi calls the `start()` method of that bundle; similarly, when OpenDaylight is shutting down or disabling a component, the OSGi framework calls the `stop()` method of that component.

To manage the life cycle of an OpenDaylight component, these methods are overridden in the `ComponentActivatorAbstractBase` class. In this class, the following two methods are called:

- `Line 17 : getImplementations()`: This method returns the class or classes that implement the components of this plugin, which normally is the `PacketHandler` class.
- `Line 24 :configureInstance()`: This method configures the components and sets the exported service interfaces and the services used by the component.

After this, we continue by declaring the services exported by our plugin. Remember that in order to receive packet-in events, the plugin needs to implement the `IListenDataPacket` service interface.

In line 35 of the preceding code, we registered our component as a `packet-in` listener. Also, we need to specify a name for our listener using the `salListenerName` property (see line 32 of the preceding code).

Note that the packet handlers are called sequentially, not in a specific order.

There might be many other plugin components (other OpenDaylight-SDN apps) that are registered with OpenDaylight for `packet-in` events.

We cannot specify or force OpenDaylight to call a specific listener first when a packet-in event happens. The order in which listeners are called is unspecified. However, to overcome this, we can create dependency lists using the `salListenerDependency` property.

In addition, we can define a filter using the `salListenerFilter` property. This property sets a `org.OpenDaylight.controller.sal.match.Match` object for the listener to filter packets based on different L2, L3, and L4 header details, such as MAC, IP address, DSCP values, EtherType, and so on. It is highly recommended that you use a filter; otherwise, the plugin will receive all the packets (if the previous listener did not consume that packet before reached to the packet handler).

In lines 38 and 41, we created two `ContainerServiceDependency`:

- The one in line 38: This one implemented the `IDataPacketService` interface; it is used for encoding, decoding, and sending data packets.
- The one in line 41: This one implemented the `IFlowProgrammerService` interface, which is used for programing the flows in the network.

In both the preceding `ContainerServiceDependany`, we defined two callback functions:

- `setDataPacketService()`
- `unsetDataPacketService()`

These callback functions are called with a reference to the service.

Implementation of the OSGi component - PacketHandler

The second part of our implementation is the PacketHandler, which receives packet-in events. (The class that you configured through `Activator`.) To this end, we implemented the `PacketHandler` class by creating the `PacketHandler.java` file in the directory:

```
001 package ca.inverse.odlpf;
002
003 import java.net.InetAddress;
004 import java.net.URL;
005 import java.net.UnknownHostException;
006 import java.net.HttpURLConnection;
007 import java.io.DataOutputStream;
008 import javax.net.ssl.HostnameVerifier;
009 import javax.net.ssl.HttpsURLConnection;
010 import javax.net.ssl.SSLContext;
011 import javax.net.ssl.SSLSession;
012 import javax.net.ssl.TrustManager;
013 import javax.net.ssl.X509TrustManager;
014 import javax.xml.bind.DatatypeConverter;
015 import org.opendaylight.controller.sal.core.Node;
016 import org.opendaylight.controller.sal.core.NodeConnector;
017 import org.opendaylight.controller.sal.packet.Ethernet;
018 import org.opendaylight.controller.sal.packet.IDataPacketService;
019 import org.opendaylight.controller.sal.packet.IListenDataPacket;
020 import org.opendaylight.controller.sal.packet.IPv4;
021 import org.opendaylight.controller.sal.packet.Packet;
022 import org.opendaylight.controller.sal.packet.PacketResult;
023 import org.opendaylight.controller.sal.packet.RawPacket;
024 import
org.opendaylight.controller.sal.flowprogrammer.IFlowProgrammerService;
025 import org.slf4j.Logger;
026 import org.slf4j.LoggerFactory;
027 import java.io.DataOutputStream;
028 import java.net.HttpURLConnection;
029 import java.net.URL;
030 import javax.net.ssl.*;
031 import javax.xml.bind.DatatypeConverter;
032 import org.opendaylight.controller.sal.utils.HexEncode;
033 import java.io.InputStreamReader;
034 import java.io.BufferedReader;
035 import org.json.*;
036 import java.util.Hashtable;
037 import java.util.ArrayList;
038
```

```
039 public class PacketHandler implements IListenDataPacket {
040     private static final Logger log =
LoggerFactory.getLogger(PacketHandler.class);
041     private IDataPacketService dataPacketService;
042     private IFlowProgrammerService flowProgrammerService;
043
044     /*
045      * Transforms an integer to an IP address
046      */
047     static private InetAddress intToInetAddress(int i) {
048         byte b[] = new byte[] { (byte) ((i>>24)&0xff), (byte)
((i>>16)&0xff),
    (byte) ((i>>8)&0xff), (byte) (i&0xff) };
049         InetAddress addr;
050         try {
051             addr = InetAddress.getByAddress(b);
052         } catch (UnknownHostException e) {
053             return null;
054         }
055
056         return addr;
057     }
058
059     /**
060      *  * Sets a reference to the requested FlowProgrammerService
061      *  */
062     void setFlowProgrammerService(IFlowProgrammerService s) {
063         log.trace("Set FlowProgrammerService.");
064
065         flowProgrammerService = s;
066     }
067
068     /**
069      *  * Unsets FlowProgrammerService
070      *  */
071     void unsetFlowProgrammerService(IFlowProgrammerService s) {
072         log.trace("Removed FlowProgrammerService.");
073
074         if (flowProgrammerService == s) {
075             flowProgrammerService = null;
076         }
077     }
078
079     public IFlowProgrammerService getFlowProgrammerService(){
080         return flowProgrammerService;
081     }
082
083     /*
```

```
084        * Sets a reference to the requested DataPacketService
085        */
086       void setDataPacketService(IDataPacketService s) {
087           log.trace("Set DataPacketService.");
088
089           dataPacketService = s;
090       }
091
092       /*
093        * Unsets DataPacketService
094        */
095       void unsetDataPacketService(IDataPacketService s) {
096           log.trace("Removed DataPacketService.");
097
098           if (dataPacketService == s) {
099               dataPacketService = null;
100           }
101       }
102
103       public IDataPacketService getDataPacketService(){
104           return dataPacketService;
105       }
106
107       /*
108        * Executed when receiving a Packet
109        * Will find the source mac, switch id and port number
110        * Will then call informPacketFence to trigger the new
connection events on PacketFence
111        */
112       @Override
113       public PacketResult receiveDataPacket(RawPacket inPkt) {
114           log.trace("Received data packet.");
115
116           // The connector, the packet came from ("port")
117           NodeConnector ingressConnector =
inPkt.getIncomingNodeConnector();
118           // The node that received the packet ("switch")
119           Node node = ingressConnector.getNode();
120
121           // Use DataPacketService to decode the packet.
122           Packet l2pkt = dataPacketService.decodeDataPacket(inPkt);
123
124           if (l2pkt instanceof Ethernet) {
125               Object l3Pkt = l2pkt.getPayload();
126               if (l3Pkt instanceof IPv4) {
127                   IPv4 ipv4Pkt = (IPv4) l3Pkt;
128                   int dstAddr = ipv4Pkt.getDestinationAddress();
129                   InetAddress addr = intToInetAddress(dstAddr);
```

```
130                          System.out.println("Pkt. to " + addr.toString() +
    " received by node " + node.getNodeIDString() + " on connector " +
    ingressConnector.getNodeConnectorIDString());
131                          String switchId = node.getNodeIDString();
132                          String port =
ingressConnector.getNodeConnectorIDString();
133                          PFPacketProcessor pf = new
PFPacketProcessor(switchId, port, inPkt, this);
134                          return pf.processPacket();
135                      }
136                  }
137              return PacketResult.IGNORED;
138          }
139
140  }
```

As shown in the preceding code, the handler implements `IListenDataPacket` as the listener interface. This interface declares the `receiveDataPacket()` function, which is called when a packet-in event is triggered from OpenFlow. The `receiveDataPacket()` function is called with full raw data of the packet (packet-in) as input.

We are using the OpenDaylight data packet service (`DataPacketService`) to parse raw packets. This is accomplished using two callback functions, namely `setDataPacketService()` and `unsetDataPacketService()`, which we defined in the `Activator` class.

If you look closely at the `receiveDataPacket` method of `PacketHandler`, `setDataPacketService()` is called with a reference to the data packet service, which is used for parsing raw packets.

In line 122, we used the `dataPacketService.decodeDataPacket(inPkt)` method to decode raw packets and get layer 2 information parsed, after receiving a raw packet, namely `inPkt`. Further, we checked whether the upper protocol is IPv4. Then we parsed the layer information of the packet, such as source and destination IP address.

In line 131 and 132, we determined the switch and its port number that the packet is received.

Finally, we decided whether the packet should be further processed by another ODL plugin or handler, or whether we want to consume the packet by returning a corresponding return value.

We called the `processPacket` method, which is defined in `PFPacketprocessor.java`, and this method returned `PacketResult.CONSUME`. This means no other handler should receive the packet after this handler. (ODL sorts the handlers, and they are called sequentially).

In line 137, the last IF statement in PacketHandler simply returned `PacketResult.IGNORED`, indicating that the packet is not an Ethernet frame. `PacketResult.IGNORED` tells ODL that packet processing should continue, and ODL can send this packet to other plugins and handlers since we did not handle the packet.

Lets have a look at PacketFence packet processor source code:

```
001 package ca.inverse.odlpf;
002
003 import java.net.InetAddress;
004 import java.net.URL;
005 import java.net.UnknownHostException;
006 import java.net.HttpURLConnection;
007 import java.io.DataOutputStream;
008 import javax.net.ssl.HostnameVerifier;
009 import javax.net.ssl.HttpsURLConnection;
010 import javax.net.ssl.SSLContext;
011 import javax.net.ssl.SSLSession;
012 import javax.net.ssl.TrustManager;
013 import javax.net.ssl.X509TrustManager;
014 import javax.xml.bind.DatatypeConverter;
015 import org.opendaylight.controller.sal.core.Node;
016 import org.opendaylight.controller.sal.core.NodeConnector;
017 import org.opendaylight.controller.sal.packet.Ethernet;
018 import org.opendaylight.controller.sal.packet.IDataPacketService;
019 import org.opendaylight.controller.sal.packet.IListenDataPacket;
020 import org.opendaylight.controller.sal.packet.IPv4;
021 import org.opendaylight.controller.sal.packet.UDP;
022 import org.opendaylight.controller.sal.packet.TCP;
023 import org.opendaylight.controller.sal.packet.Packet;
024 import org.opendaylight.controller.sal.packet.PacketResult;
025 import org.opendaylight.controller.sal.packet.RawPacket;
026 import org.slf4j.Logger;
027 import org.slf4j.LoggerFactory;
028 import java.io.DataOutputStream;
029 import java.net.HttpURLConnection;
030 import java.net.URL;
031 import javax.net.ssl.*;
032 import javax.xml.bind.DatatypeConverter;
033 import org.opendaylight.controller.sal.utils.HexEncode;
034 import java.io.InputStreamReader;
035 import java.io.BufferedReader;
```

```
036 import org.json.*;
037 import java.util.Hashtable;
038 import java.util.ArrayList;
039
040
041 public class PFPacketProcessor {
042
043     private static final Logger log =
LoggerFactory.getLogger(PacketHandler.class);
044
045     private static final PFConfig pfConfig = new
PFConfig("/etc/packetfence.conf");
046
047     // Keep a cache of the current transactions so we don't do work
twice
048     private static ArrayList<String> transactionCache = new
ArrayList<String>();
049     // Keep a cache of the ignored ports
050     private static ArrayList<String> ignoredCache = new
ArrayList<String>();
051     // Keep a cache of the discovered uplinks
052     private static Hashtable<String, String> uplinks = new
Hashtable<String, String>();
053     // This is the bytes representation of the PacketFence MAC to
use in the redirected
     packets
054     private static final byte[]
    PF_MAC =   pfConfig.getMacBytes(pfConfig.getElement("pf_dns_mac"));
055
056     private static Hashtable<String, String> packetBackMemory = new
Hashtable<String,
    String>();
057
058     private String sourceMac;
059     private String switchId;
060     private String port;
061     private PFPacket packet;
062     private PacketHandler packetHandler;
063
064     PFPacketProcessor(String switchId, String port, RawPacket
packet, PacketHandler
    packetHandler){
065         this.packetHandler = packetHandler;
066         this.packet = new PFPacket(packet, packetHandler);
067         this.sourceMac = this.packet.getSourceMac();
068         this.switchId = switchId;
069         this.port = port;
070     }
```

```
071
072     /*
073      * This method gets called on every packet in
074      * Queries PacketFence if needed and triggers the returned
actions
075      */
076     public PacketResult processPacket(){
077         //Handling return DNS packets if needs to be
078         //It's when a DNS packet is coming back on an uplink
079         System.out.println("Packet src port
"+this.packet.getSourcePort()+"
  packet source int "+this.port);
080         if (this.packet.getSourcePort() == 53 &&
this.port.equals("1")){
081             String key =
this.packet.getDestMac()+","+this.packet.getDestPort();
082             String value = packetBackMemory.get(key);
083             if(value != null){
084                 System.out.println("Got "+value+" for key "+key);
085                 String[] data = value.split(",");
086                 String initial_mac = data[0];
087                 String initial_ip = data[1];
088                 String initial_sw_port = data[2];
089                 initial_mac = initial_mac.replace(":", "");
090                 this.forwardMasquerade(initial_mac, initial_ip,
initial_sw_port);
091                 return PacketResult.CONSUME;
092             }
093             else{
094                 System.out.println("DNS packet came back on the
uplink but can't find a
    direct rewrite to do with it");
095             }
096         }
097
098         if( !this.alreadyInTransaction()  &&
!this.shouldIgnorePacket() ){
099             this.startTransaction();
100             JSONObject response = this.getPacketFenceActions();
101             PacketResult result =
this.handlePacketFenceResponse(response);
102             this.finishTransaction();
103             return result;
104         }
105         else if(this.alreadyInTransaction()){
106             log.info("Ignoring packet because a current transaction
is already started");
107             System.out.println("Ignoring packet because a current
```

```
transaction is
   already started");
    108            return PacketResult.IGNORED;
    109          }
    110          else if( this.shouldIgnorePacket() ){
    111            System.out.println("Ignoring packet because it was
previously declared as
   to be ignored");
    112            return PacketResult.IGNORED;
    113          }
    114          return PacketResult.IGNORED;
    115
    116      }
    117
    118      /*
    119       * Adds a port to the ignored ports by PacketFence so
processing is not duplicated
    120       */
    121      private void addToIgnoreList(){
    122          PFPacketProcessor.ignoredCache.add(this.getPortUniqueId());
    123      }
    124
    125      /*
    126       * Removes a port from the ignored list
    127       */
    128      private void removeFromIgnoreList(){
    129
PFPacketProcessor.ignoredCache.remove(this.getPortUniqueId());
    130      }
    131
    132      /*
    133       * Sets a new transaction in progress for the current packet
    134       * Based on the MAC
    135       */
    136      private void startTransaction(){
    137          PFPacketProcessor.transactionCache.add(sourceMac);
    138      }
    139
    140      /*
    141       * Sets a transaction as finished for the current packet
    142       * Based on the MAC
    143       */
    144      private void finishTransaction(){
    145          PFPacketProcessor.transactionCache.remove(sourceMac);
    146      }
    147
    148      /*
    149       * Checks if the packet should be ignored by querying the cache
```

```
150        * Reduces the number of queries to be done to PacketFence
151        */
152       private boolean shouldIgnorePacket(){
153           return
PFPacketProcessor.ignoredCache.contains(this.getPortUniqueId());
154       }
155
156       /*
157        * Checks if there is already a transaction in progress
158        *   with PacketFence for that MAC address
159        */
160       private boolean alreadyInTransaction(){
161           return
PFPacketProcessor.transactionCache.contains(sourceMac);
162       }
163
164       /*
165        * Handles the JSON response given by PacketFence
166        * Will trigger the DNS poisoning if PacketFence sends the
isolate action and
167        *   and the isolation strategy for the switch is DNS
168        * Will not do anything if the isolation strategy is VLAN (it's
controlled
     by  PacketFence)
169       * Will ignore and add the packet to the ignore list if
PacketFence send the
     ignored action
170        */
171       private PacketResult handlePacketFenceResponse(JSONObject
response){
172           try{
173               JSONArray result = response.getJSONArray("result");
174               JSONObject data = result.getJSONObject(0);
175               String action = data.getString("action");
176               if (action.equals("ignored")){
177                   this.addToIgnoreList();
178               }
179               else if(action.equals("isolate")){
180                   String method = data.getString("strategy");
181                   // We forward the DNS traffic to PacketFence
182                   if(method.equals("DNS") && packet.getDestPort() ==
53){
183                       // do dns poisoning stuff
184                       PFDNSPoison dnsPoison = new
PFDNSPoison(this.packet,
     this.packetHandler);
185                       dnsPoison.poisonFromPacket();
186                       this.forwardToPacketFence();
```

```
187                        return PacketResult.CONSUME;
188                  }
189              // This is currently broken since TCP checksum is
invalid
190               // Still doing it though so we keep the device as
isolated as possible
191               else if(method.equals("DNS") &&
packet.getDestPort() == 80){
192                  this.forwardToPacketFence();
193                  return PacketResult.CONSUME;
194              }
195              else if(method.equals("DNS") &&
packet.getDestPort() == 443){
196                  this.forwardToPacketFence();
197                  return PacketResult.CONSUME;
198              }
199              else if(method.equals("VLAN")){
200                  // pf takes care of the flows here
201                  // and packets from that device don't
202                  // need to be treated
203                  return PacketResult.CONSUME;
204              }
205              else{
206                  return PacketResult.KEEP_PROCESSING;
207              }
208          }
209          // For bad switches on which the DNS traffic always
goes through this plugin
210          else if(action.equals("accept") &&
this.packet.getDestPort() == 53){
211              this.forwardNormal();
212          }
213          System.out.println(data.toString());
214          log.debug(data.toString());
215          return PacketResult.KEEP_PROCESSING;
216      }
217      catch(Exception e){
218          e.printStackTrace();
219          return PacketResult.KEEP_PROCESSING;
220      }
221  }
222
223  /*
224   * Forwards the original packet to PacketFence by modifying the
destination MAC and IP
225   */
226  private void forwardToPacketFence(){
227
```

```
228         // Let's remember this packet in case it comes back
229         String key =
this.packet.getSourceMac()+","+this.packet.getSourcePort();
230         String value =
this.packet.getDestMac()+","+this.packet.getDestIP()+","+this.port;
231         System.out.println("Setting "+key+" "+value);
232         packetBackMemory.put(key, value);
233
234         // Set destination IP to PacketFence
235         try{
236          this.packet.getL3Packet().
  setDestinationAddress(InetAddress.getByName
  (pfConfig.getElement("pf_dns_ip")));
237          }catch(Exception e){e.printStackTrace();}
238         // Set destination MAC to PacketFence
239         this.packet.getL2Packet().setDestinationMACAddress(PF_MAC);
240
241         Packet l4Packet = this.packet.getL4Packet();
242
243         // For now we set the checksum to 0
244         // It doesn't work for TCP though
245         if(l4Packet instanceof UDP){
246             ((UDP)this.packet.getL4Packet()).setChecksum((short)0);
247         }
248         else if(l4Packet instanceof TCP){
249             ((TCP)this.packet.getL4Packet()).setChecksum((short)0);
250         }
251
252         // Find the uplink port - port 1 is hardcoded to be the
uplink for this test
253         NodeConnector outbound = NodeConnector.fromStringNoNode("1"
  , this.packet.getRawPacket().getIncomingNodeConnector().getNode());
254
255         RawPacket raw
=
packetHandler.getDataPacketService().encodeDataPacket(this.packet.getL2Pack
et());
256         raw.setOutgoingNodeConnector(outbound);
257
packetHandler.getDataPacketService().transmitDataPacket(raw);
258
259     }
260
261     private void forwardMasquerade(String mac, String ip, String
port){
262         try{
263
this.packet.getL3Packet().setSourceAddress(InetAddress.getByName(ip));
```

```
264                }catch(Exception e){e.printStackTrace();}
265
266            // Set destination MAC to initial
267
this.packet.getL2Packet().setSourceMACAddress(pfConfig.getMacBytes(mac));
268
269            Packet l4Packet = this.packet.getL4Packet();
270
271            // For now we set the checksum to 0
272            // It doesn't work for TCP though
273            if(l4Packet instanceof UDP){
274                ((UDP)this.packet.getL4Packet()).setChecksum((short)0);
275            }
276            else if(l4Packet instanceof TCP){
277                ((TCP)this.packet.getL4Packet()).setChecksum((short)0);
278            }
279
280            NodeConnector outbound =
NodeConnector.fromStringNoNode(port,
    this.packet.getRawPacket().getIncomingNodeConnector().getNode());
281
282            RawPacket raw
=
packetHandler.getDataPacketService().encodeDataPacket(this.packet.getL2Pack
et());
283            raw.setOutgoingNodeConnector(outbound);
284
packetHandler.getDataPacketService().transmitDataPacket(raw);
285
286      }
287
288      private void forwardNormal(){
289
290            // Let's remember this packet in case it comes back
291            String key =
this.packet.getSourceMac()+","+this.packet.getSourcePort();
292            String value =
this.packet.getDestMac()+","+this.packet.getDestIP()+","+this.port;
293            System.out.println("Setting "+key+" "+value);
294            packetBackMemory.put(key, value);
295
296            NodeConnector outbound = NodeConnector.fromStringNoNode
    ("1",
this.packet.getRawPacket().getIncomingNodeConnector().getNode());
297
298            RawPacket raw = packetHandler.getDataPacketService().
    encodeDataPacket(this.packet.getL2Packet());
299            raw.setOutgoingNodeConnector(outbound);
```

```
       300
packetHandler.getDataPacketService().transmitDataPacket(raw);
       301     }
       302
        303    /*
       304    * Sends an HTTP request to the PacketFence API
       305    * Will trigger the DNS poisoning depending on the node's
state
       306    */
       307    private JSONObject getPacketFenceActions() {
       308        this.setupHttpsConnection();
       309        try{
       310            JSONObject jsonBody = this.getPacketFenceJSONPayload();
       311
       312        String request =
"https://"+pfConfig.getElement("host")+":"+pfConfig.getElement("port")+"/";
       313
       314        String authentication = DatatypeConverter.printBase64Binary
       (new
String(pfConfig.getElement("user")+":"+pfConfig.getElement("pass")).getByte
s());
       315        URL url = new URL(request);
       316        HttpsURLConnection connection = (HttpsURLConnection)
url.openConnection();
       317        connection.setDoOutput(true);
       318        connection.setDoInput(true);
       319      connection.setInstanceFollowRedirects(false);
       320      connection.setRequestMethod("POST");
       321        connection.setRequestProperty("Content-Type",
"application/json-rpc");
       322        connection.setRequestProperty("charset", "utf-8");
       323        connection.setRequestProperty("Content-Length", ""
     +  Integer.toString(jsonBody.toString().getBytes().length));
        324        connection.setRequestProperty("Authorization", "Basic
"+authentication);
       325        connection.setUseCaches (false);
       326
       327        DataOutputStream wr = new
DataOutputStream(connection.getOutputStream ());
       328        wr.writeBytes(jsonBody.toString());
       329        wr.flush();
       330        wr.close();
       331        connection.disconnect();
       332        System.out.println(jsonBody.toString());
       333
       334            BufferedReader response = null;
       335            response = new BufferedReader
     (new InputStreamReader(connection.getInputStream()));
```

```
336                  String line = null;
337                  while ((line = response.readLine()) != null) {
338                      System.out.println(line);
339                  return new JSONObject(line);
340                  }
341
342          }
343       catch(Exception e){
344          e.printStackTrace();
345         return new JSONObject();
346       }
347      return new JSONObject();
348    }
349
350    /*
351     * Sets up the HTTPS connection so it ignores certificates
352     */
353    private void setupHttpsConnection(){
354      TrustManager[] trustAllCerts = new TrustManager[]{
355        new X509TrustManager() {
356              public java.security.cert.X509Certificate[]
getAcceptedIssuers() {
357                  return null;
358              }
359          public void checkClientTrusted(
360              java.security.cert.X509Certificate[] certs, String
authType) {
361              }
362          public void checkServerTrusted(
363              java.security.cert.X509Certificate[] certs, String
authType) {
364              }
365        }
366    };
367      try {
368          SSLContext sc = SSLContext.getInstance("SSL");
369          sc.init(null, trustAllCerts, new
java.security.SecureRandom());
370
HttpsURLConnection.setDefaultSSLSocketFactory(sc.getSocketFactory());
371      } catch (Exception e) {
372              e.printStackTrace();
373      }
374
375      HttpsURLConnection.setDefaultHostnameVerifier(new
HostnameVerifier()
376          {
377              public boolean verify(String hostname, SSLSession
```

```
session)
378                    {
379                        if (hostname.equals(pfConfig.getElement("host")))
380                            return true;
381                        return false;
382                    }
383            });
384
385        }
386
387        /*
388         * Creates the payload to send to PacketFence API
389         */
390        private JSONObject getPacketFenceJSONPayload(){
391            try{
392                JSONObject jsonBody = new JSONObject();
393                jsonBody.put("jsonrpc", "2.0");
394                jsonBody.put("id", "1");
395                jsonBody.put("method", "sdn_authorize");
396                JSONObject params = new JSONObject();
397                params.put("mac", sourceMac);
398                params.put("switch_id", switchId);
399                params.put("port", port);
400                params.put("controller_ip",
pfConfig.getElement("controller_ip"));
401                jsonBody.put("params", params);
402                return jsonBody;
403            }
404            catch (Exception e){
405                e.printStackTrace();
406                return new JSONObject();
407            }
408        }
409
410        /*
411         * Returns a unique ID for a given switch and port
412         * For use in the caching
413         */
414        private String getPortUniqueId(){
415            return switchId + "-" + port;
416        }
417
418 }
```

This class handles most of internal processing of PacketFence.

line 76, `processpacket` : handles the process. It prepares a packet with all the details to be sent out to the packet fence NAC server.

In line 90 , it choose to use `forwardMasquerade` to send packets to PacketFence NAC server. As we will learn there are three methods for sending clients packets to PacketFence, where it needs to be defined in this line.

In line 91: it marks the event as consumed since we have sent the details to PacketFence and we don't want the OpenDaylight OSGI to send this event to other listeners.

In line 98: it handles the response from packet fence

In line 171 , there is a function to communicate to PacketFence NAC server via REST APIs. This function reads the response from the NAC server related to the specific user and enforces the required action.

There are three different methods in this class just for sending the packets to PacketFence NAC server

It may uses any of these methods for sending the clients packets to the PacketFence NAC server. Currently it is hardcoded in line 90

In line 226 , `forwardToPacketFence` function , creates a new packet out of the client packet with following different attributes:

- Destination IP: PacketFence NAC Server IP address
- Destination MAC: PacketFence NAC server MAC address

This is required, because if the packet is just sent to PacketFence NAC server, it will drop the packet as the operating system looks at the destination IP and MAC address first, if it is not related to the server it drops the packet.

In line 261 `forwardMasquerade` : sends the packets to PacketFence server without modifying the IP address. it only changes the MAC address field to predefined source MAC address defined in PF configuration file.

In line 288 `forwardNormal` : just sends the packet as it is to the packet fence NAC server

The server needs to have redirection in place to match this packet and process it, otherwise it will be dropped.

In line 307 `getPacketFenceAction`, is the function to communicate with PacketFence NAC server REST API.

This function builds a REST API call based on a JSON prepared payload created in line 390

In line 390 `getPacketFenceJSONPayload` : builds a JSON format for all the details of the packet which require to be processed by NAC.

```
PFDNSPoison.Java
```

This class follows the simple implementation of installing and removing OpenFlow flows in switches to redirect traffic to OpenDaylight in order to enforce a web authentication portal to users:

```
001 package ca.inverse.odlpf;
002
003 import java.net.InetAddress;
004 import java.net.URL;
005 import java.net.UnknownHostException;
006 import java.net.HttpURLConnection;
007 import java.io.DataOutputStream;
008 import javax.net.ssl.HostnameVerifier;
009 import javax.net.ssl.HttpsURLConnection;
010 import javax.net.ssl.SSLContext;
011 import javax.net.ssl.SSLSession;
012 import javax.net.ssl.TrustManager;
013 import javax.net.ssl.X509TrustManager;
014 import javax.xml.bind.DatatypeConverter;
015 import org.opendaylight.controller.sal.core.Node;
016 import org.opendaylight.controller.sal.core.NodeConnector;
017 import org.opendaylight.controller.sal.packet.Ethernet;
018 import org.opendaylight.controller.sal.packet.IDataPacketService;
019 import org.opendaylight.controller.sal.packet.IListenDataPacket;
020 import org.opendaylight.controller.sal.packet.IPv4;
021 import org.opendaylight.controller.sal.packet.TCP;
022 import org.opendaylight.controller.sal.packet.UDP;
023 import org.opendaylight.controller.sal.packet.Packet;
024 import org.opendaylight.controller.sal.packet.PacketResult;
025 import org.opendaylight.controller.sal.packet.RawPacket;
026 import org.opendaylight.controller.sal.flowprogrammer.Flow;
027 import org.opendaylight.controller.sal.match.Match;
028 import org.opendaylight.controller.sal.utils.Status;
029 import org.opendaylight.controller.sal.match.MatchType;
030 import org.opendaylight.controller.sal.action.*;
031 import org.slf4j.Logger;
032 import org.slf4j.LoggerFactory;
033 import java.io.DataOutputStream;
034 import java.net.HttpURLConnection;
035 import java.net.URL;
036 import javax.net.ssl.*;
037 import javax.xml.bind.DatatypeConverter;
```

```
038 import org.opendaylight.controller.sal.utils.HexEncode;
039 import java.io.InputStreamReader;
040 import java.io.BufferedReader;
041 import org.json.*;
042 import java.util.Hashtable;
043 import java.util.ArrayList;
044 import java.util.LinkedList;
045 import java.util.List;
046 import java.net.UnknownHostException;
047
048
049 public class PFDNSPoison {
050     private static final Logger log =
LoggerFactory.getLogger(PacketHandler.class);
051     private static final PFConfig pfconfig = new
PFConfig("/etc/packetfence.conf");
052      private PFPacket packet;
053     private PacketHandler packetHandler;
054
055     // The PF mac to use when redirecting packets
056     private static final byte[] PF_MAC
  = pfconfig.getMacBytes(pfconfig.getElement("pf_dns_mac"));
057
058      PFDNSPoison(PFPacket packet, PacketHandler packetHandler){
059         this.packet = packet;
060         this.packetHandler = packetHandler;
061     }
062
063     /*
064      * Installs the required flows to forward the DNS traffic to
PacketFence
065      */
066     public void poisonFromPacket(){
067         System.out.println("Installing DNS outbound redirect
flow");
068         this.poisonOutbound();
069         System.out.println("Installing return flow");
070         this.poisonInbound();
071     }
072
073     /*
074      * Returns the outbound match based on the initial destination
of the packet
075      */
076     private Match getOutboundMatch(){
077         Match match = new Match();
078         match.setField(MatchType.DL_TYPE, (short) 0x0800);  // IPv4
ethertype
```

```
079          match.setField(MatchType.NW_PROTO, (byte) 17);
080          match.setField(MatchType.DL_SRC,
packet.getSourceMacBytes());
081           match.setField(MatchType.NW_DST,
packet.getDestInetAddress());
082          match.setField(MatchType.TP_SRC, (short)
packet.getSourcePort());
083          match.setField(MatchType.TP_DST, (short)
packet.getDestPort());
084
085        return match;
086     }
087
088     /*
089      * Returns the actions to do on packet so it's forwarded to
PacketFence
090      * Rewrites the destination IP and MAC to the ones in the
PacketFence
  configuration  file on
091      *   the controller
092      */
093     private List getOutboundActions(){
094         List actions = new LinkedList();
095         try{
096         actions.add( new SetNwDst(
InetAddress.getByName(pfconfig.getElement
   ("pf_dns_ip"))  ) );
097         }catch(Exception e){e.printStackTrace();}
098
099         actions.add( new SetDlDst( PF_MAC ) );
100         actions.add( new Flood() );
101
102         return actions;
103     }
104
105     /*
106      * Installs the flow to redirect the DNS queries to PacketFence
107      */
108     private void poisonOutbound(){
109         this.installFlow(this.getOutboundMatch(),
this.getOutboundActions());
110     }
111
112     /*
113      * Returns the inbound match based on the new destination of
the packet
114      */
115     private Match getInboundMatch(){
```

```
116          Match match = new Match();
117           match.setField(MatchType.DL_TYPE, (short) 0x0800);  // IPv4
ethertype
118          match.setField(MatchType.NW_PROTO, (byte) 17);
119
120          try{
121          match.setField(MatchType.NW_SRC,
    InetAddress.getByName(pfconfig.getElement("pf_dns_ip")) );
122          }catch(Exception e){e.printStackTrace();}
123          match.setField(MatchType.TP_SRC, (short)
packet.getDestPort());
124          match.setField(MatchType.TP_DST, (short)
packet.getSourcePort());
125          match.setField(MatchType.DL_DST,
packet.getSourceMacBytes());
126
127           return match;
128      }
129
130      /*
131       * Returns the actions to do on the packet that gets back
132       *   so it respects the initial destination of the packet
133      * Rewrites the source IP to the one that the packet
134       *   should have originally been sent to.
135       */
136      private List getInboundActions(){
137          List actions = new LinkedList();
138          try{
139          actions.add( new SetNwSrc( packet.getDestInetAddress()  )
);
140          }catch(Exception e){e.printStackTrace();}
141
142          actions.add( new SetDlSrc( packet.getDestMacBytes() ) );
143          actions.add( new Flood() );
144
145          return actions;
146      }
147
148      /*
149       * Installs the flow to rewrite the return packet so it looks
like
150       *   it came from the original destination
151       */
152      private void poisonInbound(){
153
154          this.installFlow(this.getInboundMatch(),
this.getInboundActions());
155      }
```

```
156
157     /*
158      * Generic method for this class to install a flow based on a
match
159      *    and a list of actions
160      */
161     private void installFlow(Match match, List actions){
162         Flow flow = new Flow(match, actions);
163          flow.setPriority((short)1001);
164          flow.setHardTimeout((short)30);
165          Status status = packetHandler.getFlowProgrammerService().
addFlow(packet.getIncomingConnector().getNode(), flow);
166             if (!status.isSuccess()) {
167                System.out.println("Could not program flow: " +
status.getDescription());
168             }
169         }
170
171 }
```

This class is being called by PF `PacketProcessor` class.

In line 161 we define an Install Flow function where it installs a flow in fabric using `FlowProgrammingService` of OpenDayLight. This service will manage using a southbound protocol to communicate this Flow installation to the switch using `OpenFLow OP-MODIFY` message.

All the source code of these files are also available in GitHub repository of this book. We didn't include the code of PFPacket and PF config classes; however, they are available on GitHub.

Summary

In this chapter, you learned the basics of SAL and how an SDN application connects to OpenDaylight and processes packets.

In the next chapter, we will start looking at network function virtualization and the service chaining features of OpenDaylight.

8
Network Function Virtualization

In this chapter, we will get familiar with the role of OpenDaylight and OPNFV in the **Network Function Virtualization** (**NFV**) ecosystem. We will also cover how OpenDaylight forces traffic to go through specific network functions, such as firewalls and load balancers.

Additionally, we will go through NFV basics and the existing OPNFV projects. We will discuss service chaining as well, which is one of the main use cases of SDN and OpenDaylight. And we will end this chapter by going through two real-life examples of NFV and service chaining.

Specifically, we will cover the following topics:

- NFV categories
- OPNFV projects
- Service chaining using OpenDaylight
- Examples of forcing traffic to go through a firewall and load balancer
- Example of a network traffic broker and packet capturing

Virtual network functions (VNFs)

NFV or VNF is the new buzzword in the industry. However, this technology has been around for a few years. In very simple language, NFV means virtualizing network functions, such as routers, firewalls, load balancers, traffic optimizers, IDS or IPS, web application protectors, and so on.

Out of these examples, firewalls and load balancers are the most common virtual network functions of NFV in the real world, especially for deployments inside data centers.

Data centers and enterprises

In the networking industry, the use of hardware network functions (firewalls, load balancers, and so on) is very common. We (network engineers) have always been of hesitant about relying on a virtual firewall or load balancer. However, after the establishment of production server virtualization in the last decade (from VMware ESX 3 until now), virtualization-as-technology has passed all the tests and has become a reliable resource, especially for application servers.

There are many critical application servers that run on a virtualized environment. Because of maturity of virtualization technology and its enterprise features it is considered a highly reliable and resistance technology.

In recent years, virtualization has grown more than servers and computing power (Aka compute). It started virtualizing storage first and eventually moved on to networking. After computing and servers, storage became the next revolution. Storage virtualization evolved into a massive storage market. However, the growing number of storage vendors commoditized the storage market. Storage virtualization was initiated by disaggregation of storage software and hardware. For many years, many storage vendors produced massive storage boxes with many disk shelves, combined with some software. Storage controllers were the point of contact for **Storage Area Networks** (**SANs**). This communication used to happen via a fiber channel; an Ethernet-based protocol, such as iSCSI; or a file-based protocol, such as NFS, CIFS, or SMB.

After the storage revolution settled down, virtualization started affecting network functions; it is then that we started seeing virtual firewalls, virtual load balancers, and virtual routers. The introduction of Vyatta (acquired by Brocade) was a revolution in the networking industry; its primary objective was to have a full-fledged router running on a virtual machine and competing with hardware appliance routers.

X86's processing speed and power gave a tremendous push to virtualized routers and firewalls. After realizing this power, vendors started limiting their performance through the use of licensing. A virtual firewall running on good hardware might be able to perform over 40 Gbps or more of filtering or IPS; however, with licensing, vendors started limiting this performance.

The big market players of the networking, security, and load balancing sectors followed suit and started innovating to provide new virtual appliances. Juniper started building a virtual version of their flagship, namely SRX firewall series; F5 built a virtual LTM (their local traffic manager or standard load balancer); Cisco built **Cloud Services Router** (**CSR**), which was based on IOS XE); and so on. There are many other examples of visualized systems, which we will not be able to cover, but it's important to note that a lot of traditional vendors started offering virtualized systems.

VNFs are good; they are great if there are processes available to keep the network simple, as these devices lack physical interfaces. Unlike physical appliances, where we are limited to some physical copper or fiber interfaces, virtual appliances support a much larger number of interfaces.

Flexibility, high performance, and lower **total cost of ownership** (**TCO**) are the key drivers of NFV solutions which is based on the concept of virtualizing hardware appliances.

In many large enterprises, network administrators and engineers who started building and delivering virtual network functions, such as firewalls and load balancers, found it difficult to manage a farm of virtual firewalls and load balancers. A virtual firewall lives in a cluster of computing hosts. Often, you will not be able to determine on which host it lives. What's worse than this is that sometimes, virtual appliances fly between hosts, meaning they may migrate from one computing host to another via the virtual platform server.

Keeping these complexities in mind, placing and routing traffic to virtual firewalls and load balancers will come across as pain. They are virtual functions, and sometimes, they clone themselves to support more traffic (this is common in the case of virtual load balancers as they create new instances to support higher traffic demands when there is a business requirement).

Apart from some complexities that NFV/VNF provide, they provide many great features and most important one, which is flexibility. Flexibility is the main driver for any visualization platform, either NFV, virtual storage, or computing.

The data center network itself is part of the virtualization revolution. SDN and network overlays are the key drivers for virtualizing networks in data centers.

The following diagram illustrates how server virtualization is going to host network functions such as routers, firewalls and load balancers:

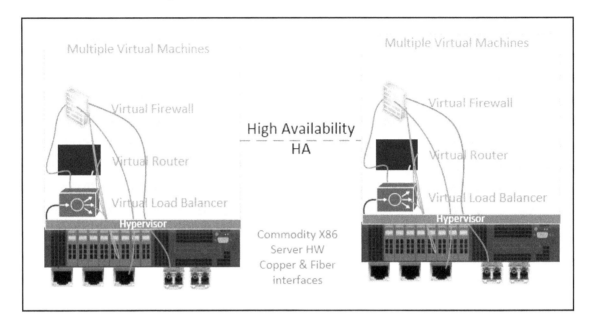

Service providers

In service provider networks, the use of NFV is a bit different from enterprises and data centers.

Note that when I talk about service providers in this section, I'm referring to MPLS and WAN. They are everywhere, in every country, providing high quality network services to their customers.

Such service providers have their networks divided into customer, provider, and edges. This is illustrated in the following diagram:

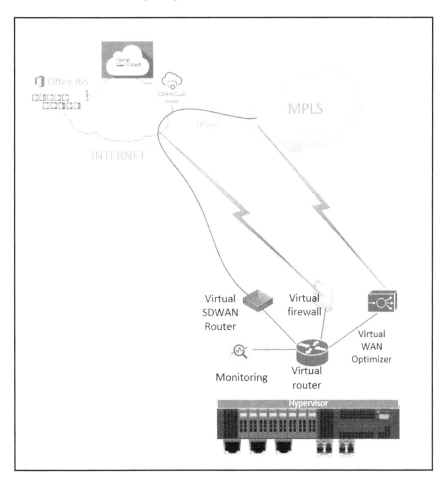

As you can see, service providers must provide the **Customer Premises Equipment** (CPE) device to all their clients. This device is normally a hardware appliance, a router with limited performance, based on the customer's requirements.

In many instances, customers may need to change their CPE or add extra features, such as a managed firewall or managed WAN optimizers, to their network. This needs to be executed by the service provider; it's their job to provide, install, and commission extra equipment to the clients.

The process of any alteration to CPE is lengthy (all the folks who have dealt with service providers know this pain).

On the other hand, the cost of hardware appliances, licensing, managed services, and support makes it more complex for the service provider to cope with the estate of CPE of many customers.

Service providers started realizing the benefits of NFV when they started offering it to their clients. One of the main use cases of NFV is **Virtual Customer Premises Equipment (vCPE)**. Service providers started deploying standard X86 compute servers to their clients as CPE. Yes, they also started realizing that by deploying two X86 servers at customer sites and running a hypervisor, they will be able to manage all the requirements of the clients without having to make any changes to the hardware or even visit the site.

The X86 server hosts a virtual router. It can also host other network functions, such as **Software-Defined WAN (SDWANN)**, WAN optimizers, Internet routers (for local Internet connection or breakouts), and firewalls.

Service providers have also built their own virtual provisioning tools to manage the whole state of virtual services. In recent years, many of them have built orchestration platforms to automate the provisioning of service for their clients.

We can categorize VNF features as follows:

- Virtual routers:
  - These are standard packet-forwarding systems. They can route and run routing protocols and other features, such as NAT,and Policy-Based Routing.
- Virtual firewalls:
  - These are standard stateful or stateless firewalls with L3-L7 filtering capabilities.
  - They may be equipped with deep packet inspection engines to provide features such as IDS and IPS.
- Virtual load balancers:
  - Layer 4 to layer 7 load balancers that are able to host virtual **IPs (VIP)** and forward (and NAT) the traffic to real servers.
  - They may be equipped with **Web Application Firewall (WAF)** features.
- Virtual WAN optimizers:
  - These include caching, TCP optimization, and protocol acceleration.

- SDWAN routers:
    - They are used for logically bounding multiple WAN and Internet connections and build VPN tunnels back to the SDWAN head-end units in data centers.
    - These are used for intelligent link measurement and application-based routing.

OPNFV and its role in service provider NFV

Open Platform for NFV (OPNFV) was announced by the Linux Foundation back in 2014. Its aim is to create a standard carrier-grade platform, mainly for NFV.

Since the Linux Foundation also hosts OpenDaylight and **Open Network Operating System (ONOS)**, the combination of a network controller such as OpenDaylight or ONOS and OPNFV can help transition industry toward virtualization of networks and network functions.

OPNFV promotes open source networking and motivates companies to work together to accelerate innovation. It can be used by service providers, data centers, cloud providers, vendors, end users, and developers to create an open source platform in order to accelerate the development and deployment of NFV.

Its main current objective to create a standard open source platform for VNF in order to run on different platforms. For example, if OpenStack and VMware vSphere are both OPNFV certified, we can load a OPNFV certified VNF (such as a virtual load balancer) on any of these certified platforms with no troubles.

The following diagram shows the current scope of OPNFV:

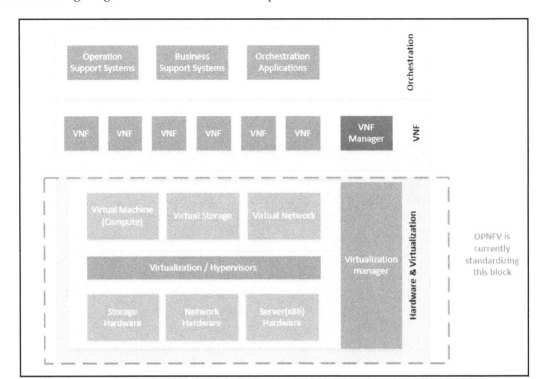

The initial phase of OPNFV is limited to building standards for **NFV infrastructure** (**NFVI**) and **Virtualized Infrastructure Management** (**VIM**).

How OpenDaylight and OPNFV integrate and implement NFVs in service provider networks

Service providers are one of the main buyer and consumers of networking hardware. They buy and deploy routers, switches, firewalls and other networking equipment much more than enterprises. They have a very large footprint of hardware appliances. This footprint grows and the burden of managing and operating it also grows (at a different rate). NFV and network virtualization can help service providers to reduce their complex management and operation as well as reducing their cost by utilizing SDN and NFV.

Many networking gurus are hesitant to trust a server to run a virtual router or firewall. They are still not comfortable with using virtualization technology to run their core networking functions. However this will change, as server administrators also had the same feeling when virtualization was starting to spread.

The key point for network specialists is reliability. A hardware appliance such as router or firewall uses a dedicated hardware to run its software. VNF can provide same or more resilient infrastructure by using high availability between two or more server hardware.

In WAN service providers, the vCPE is an early and popular use case for SDN and NFV. In order for vCPE to be successfully implemented, it is necessary to employ **Service Function Chaining** (**SFC**) to manage the traffic being passed to different network functions such as firewalls and routers.

SFC provides the ability to define an ordered list of network services (for example, firewalls or load balancers). These services are then stitched together in the network to create a service chain.

Virtualizing the CPE can help service providers to simplify and automate the network edge of their customers. Service such as routing, wan optimization, firewalling, SDWAN can be automatically provisioned as a VNF. They can be controlled by the service provider's orchestration platform. Such VNFs can run on a Hypervisor hosted by a commodity server under the service provider's control.

The functionality of a vCPE may be implemented at different locations such as headquarters, customer sites, branches, remote data centers, regional hubs, or even public cloud service providers.

vCPE or any **Virtual Network Function as a Service** (**VNFaaS**) needs to convey the same benefits as that of physical network functions, and they need to do so in geographically distributed locations. A service chain is required when a network service consists of a set of physical or virtual network functions and the traffic needs to traversed in a predefined order. Service chains can vary in complexity, from being very simple to very complex.

An example of a simple chain is a firewall and a load balancer sitting in front of a number of DNS servers. A complex service chain might be the service infrastructure sitting behind a mobile gateway device.

In the following diagram, the blue service uses the firewall, WAN optimization, and then encryption, whereas the green server uses the firewall and then has the traffic load balanced:

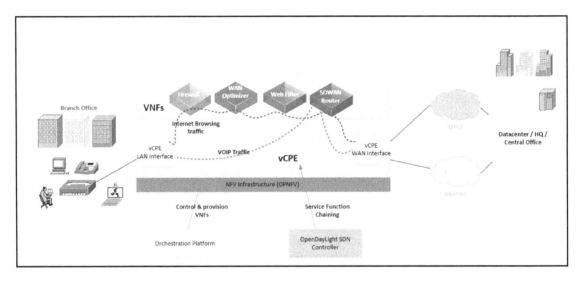

OpenDaylight is presently being investigated by OPNFV members to be used in delivering services such **Fiber to the Premise (FTTP)**, **Fiber to the Home (FTTH)**, **Gigabit Passive Optical Networks (GPON)**, and **Optical Line Termination (OLT)**.

Service chaining using OpenDaylight

As you just learned, NFV is nothing but having a virtual platform to serve network functions such as firewall, IPS, and load balancing. But what is the role of SDN and OpenDaylight in NFV?

To answer this question, let's go back to traditional networking and consider an example scenario.

We have a data center **Point Of Delivery (POD)**, or in simpler terms, a couple of racks with network connectivity with a farm of web servers and database server; this is for a sample CRM application. We would like to route the incoming traffic through a firewall and then to a load balancer in order to distribute the traffic to multiple web servers. Communication between web servers and the database must pass over the firewall. Finally, the return traffic should go from the load balancer (not directly from the servers) back to the original client.

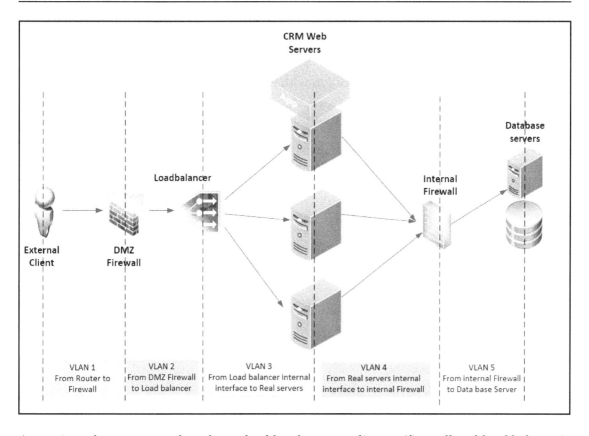

Assuming a legacy network and standard hardware appliances (firewall and load balancer), we do need to implement this solution as follows:

1. The DMZ firewall must be configured in such a way that it should allow traffic from the outside that is destined to a specific virtual IP address terminated on the load balancer. The DMZ firewall requires NAT and security policies in place to allow such traffic.

2. The network between DMZ firewall and load balancer must be configured in such a way that it should allow you to route and provide IP connectivity between these two devices.

3. The load balancer must be configured in such a way that it should host virtual IP addresses on its VIP interface and have a real server pool configured with the IP addresses of three CRM web servers. Normally, the communication between a load balancer and real servers is placed in a different VLAN.

4. The CRM web servers (real servers) should be able to receive packets from load balancers and respond. They communicate with database servers over a different interface and VLAN.
5. CRM web server communication with the database server must pass through the internal firewall.
6. The internal firewall should route and send the packets to the database server.

This process might be familiar to many network engineers as they deal with such requests on a daily basis, which is creating network platforms for new services. Configuring the underlying network to support multiple VLANs, as shown in the preceding diagram, and allowing the equipment to route the traffic from the user to the servers will return the result to the requester.

In a legacy network, we would need to build the entire design and topology in order to support this scenario. Basically, you would need to prepare a design or documentation for implementing the following:

- Multiple VLANs on different switches
- Spanning tree
- Next hop redundancy protocols (such as VRRP)
- Policy-based routing
- Static routing
- Dynamic routing protocol advertisement

This takes time. It takes time to design, implement, and test it. It could take weeks or months to do this.

Also, imagine that after a week, the business wants you to send the traffic to a **Web Application Firewall** (**WAF**) before it reaches the load balancer.

Such requirements are becoming very frequent in most organizations these days. With the growth of server and storage virtualization, developers can build an infrastructure for testing or for creating a service or application. Business demands new services, new websites, online portals, and so on; they simply can't wait for the network and security team to design and implement each requirement in this way.

Here comes service chaining. It helps solve this problem and decrease the time required to provision such services, or even the more complex ones.

Have a look at the following diagram:

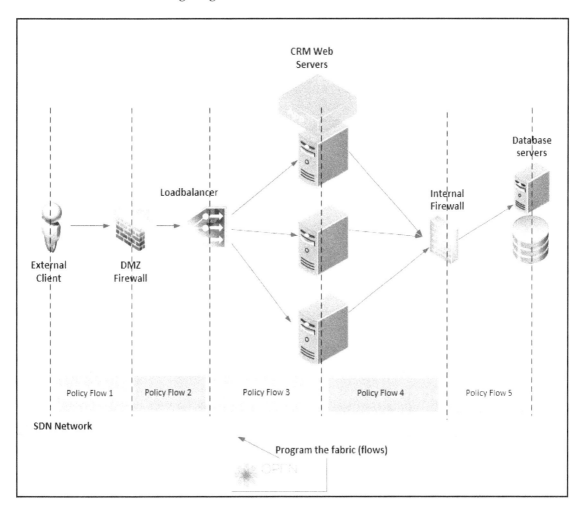

Here, we are dealing with a single SDN-enabled network and have an SDN controller (OpenDaylight) to program the flows in the network. We don't need to manually build a complex VLAN setup or a complex policy-based routing configuration to route the traffic from the user to the servers. Instead, ODL will program the network based on the service chain we define.

ODL can program the fabric in standalone mode. This means that you can define and build a topology with ODL to match the packets that are originated from an external users and destined to a VIP (Virtual IP) on a load balancer , to pass through a firewall in DMZ and then to the load balancer.

ODL can become smart and get integrated with your NFV tools. For example, it can talk to a firewall or load balancer. When you create a new configuration in a load balancer, ODL can fetch that configuration and proactively populate and program the network to support the newly configured services. Such integrations are part of Open NFV standards and they help create a standard framework for NFV services in order to get integrated with external tools, such as ODL.

Service chaining describes the delivery of multiple service functions in a specific order:

- It matches all or very specific traffic/packets to go inside a specific network function or a series of network functions
- It supports dynamic insertion of service functions
- It decouples network topology and service functions
- It creates a common model for all types of services (for example, a model of the firewall and load balancer or a model of firewall and WAF)
- It allows network service functions to share information between each other

OpenDaylight has a service chaining module. This module is designed to handle service chaining for applications and includes the following components:

- **Classifier**: This determines what traffic needs to be chained, based on a match policy
- **Service chain**: The refers to the list of network services that the matched packets need to traverse
- **Service path**: This refers to the actual instances of services traversed
- **Service overlay**: This is a topology that is created to visualize a service path
- **Metadata**: This refers to the information passed between participating services

This module uses service graphs to define service chains:

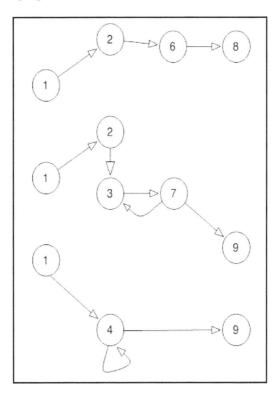

The service chaining module receives information about chains and/or paths to be constructed via a northbound API. Information about the available service nodes are contained in the node's data store.

This module constructs the service path in the following ways:

- **Simple**: Just a list
- **Complex**: Constrained list (such as bandwidth and capabilities)

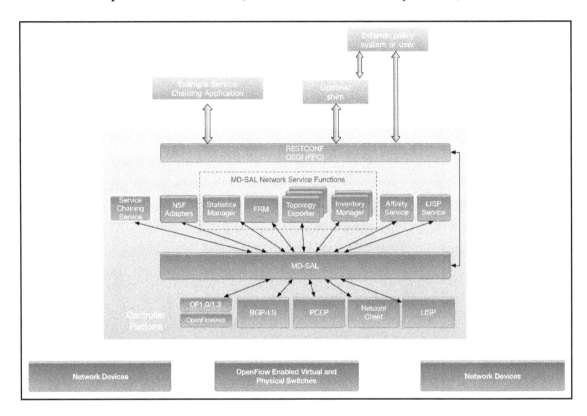

Apart from the service chaining module in ODL, there are other modules that can also be used to achieve similar function compared to service chaining:

- **LISP service**: LISP can provide the needed overlay to create a service path. It uses the LISP API to map service locators.
- **Group-based policy**: Service chains are information within a policy, or policy metadata passed along with service chain.

Examples of forcing traffic to go through a firewall and load balancer

In the previous section, we discussed how to send network traffic from a user (or a group of users or a network) to a firewall and load balancer. We evaluated the requirement of the network to support the scenario, which included designing and implementing multiple routing and switching technologies, including VLANs and routing.

Now let's use the same example in an SDN world with ODL. We would like to perform basic service chaining with ODL to redirect a specific user's traffic to a firewall, then to a load balancer, and finally to a web server.

We will not be able to explain the entire process of configuration in a firewall and load balancer, but you can build this simple lab using open source tools, such as PFSence (open source firewall: `https://www.pfsense.org/`) and HA Proxy (open source load balancer: `http://www.haproxy.org/`). In addition, you can try using the evaluation version of commercial products, such as Juniper vSRX or F5 virtual load balancer.

The following figure illustrates our service chaining scenario:

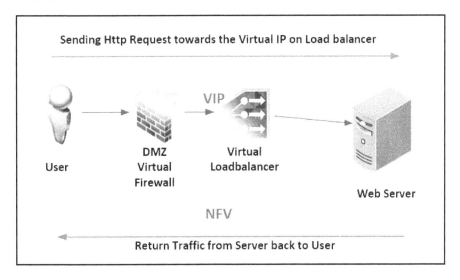

We would like to send the user's traffic to the web server; however, the traffic must pass through the firewall and load balancer.

Let's have a closer look at the implementation of this scenario in an SDN network:

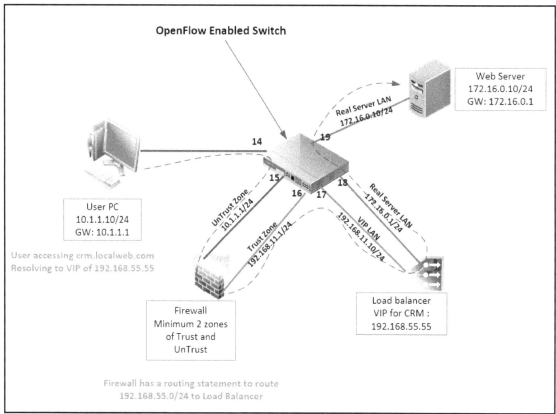

The preceding diagram explains basic connectivity between the devices: an OpenFlow-enabled switch and the equipment connected to the same switch (this is just a lab exercise; it is not a production environment).

The OpenFlow switch can be controlled by OpenDaylight. This is how this scenario should work:

1. The user sends HTTP request packets to the VIP of the CRM, which is hosted on the load balancer. This VIP is configured to send the request to a single real server at 172.16.0.10 (assuming DNS is already in place.). Your PC (Personal Computer) will generate this packet:
    - **Source IP**: 10.1.1.10
    - **Destination IP**: 192.168.55.55

2. The packet reaches the OpenFlow switch. This switch may or may not have any flow that would match the packet attributes (L2, L3 of source, or destination addresses). Assuming it doesn't have any flow, the switch will send an `OpenFlow PACKET_IN` message to the SDN controller (ODL) in order to inform the controller that it has received such a packet.

3. ODL may have a service chaining application running. This application is similar to other ODL applications; it may get informed by the controller in the event of `PACKET_IN`, and this packet may reach the service chaining application. This application can very simply identify that we need to enforce the packet to pass through the firewall and the load balancer in order to reach the web server.

4. The service chaining application will prepare and send an `OpenFlow FLOW_MODIFY` packet to the switch in order to instruct the switch to install the flows.

The flows are as follows:

- **Flow 1**:
    - **Source**: PC (`10.1.1.10`)
    - **Source Ethernet port**: `14`
    - **Destination**: VIP on load balancer (`192.168.55.55`)
    - **Out Ethernet port**: `15`

- **Flow 2**:
    - **Source**: Firewall trust interface (`192.168.11.1`)
    - **Source Ethernet port**: `16`
    - **Destination**: VIP on load balancer (`192.168.55.55`)
    - **Out Ethernet port**: `17`

- **Flow 3**:
    - **Source**: Load balancer's real server interface (`172.16.0.1`)
    - **Source Ethernet port**: `18`
    - **Destination**: Real CRM web server (`172.16.0.10`)
    - **Out Ethernet port**: `19`

The service chaining application also builds the flows for return traffic, as follows:

- **Flow 11**:
  - **Source**: Real CRM web server (172.16.0.10)
  - **Source Ethernet port**: 19
  - **Destination**: Load balancer's real server interface (172.16.0.1)
  - **Out Ethernet port**: 18

- **Flow 12**:
  - **Source**: VIP on the load balancer (192.168.55.55)
  - **Source Ethernet port**: 17
  - **Destination**: Firewall trust interface (192.168.11.1)
  - **Out Ethernet port**: 16

- **Flow 13**:
  - **Source**: VIP on the load balancer (192.168.55.55)
  - **Source Ethernet port**: 15 (Firewall untrust port)
  - **Destination**: PC (10.1.1.10)
  - **Out Ethernet port**: 14

5. Once ODL programs the switch, the packet will be sent to the firewall at its Untrust port (Ethernet `port 15`).

6. The firewall will receive the packet, and based on its internal configuration, it will route it out of its trust interface, toward the load balancer. The firewall must have policy routing in place to route the packet to the load balancer with load balancer VIP as the destination. Also, the firewall policy must be in place to allow the packet to pass from the untrust zone to the trust zone with specific access controls in place.

7. The packet will be sent from the firewall to the load balancer. Since the OpenFlow switch already has the flows in place, it will send the packet out of `port 17` toward the load balancer.

8. The packet will hit the load balancer. Since the load balancer has a VIP with 192.168.55.55, it needs to handle the request. At the same time, it will send a packet to the real CRM server at 172.16.0.10.

9. The packet will come to the OpenFlow switch, and since the flows are already installed, it will go out of `port 19` toward the real CRM server.

10. For return traffic, the same process will happen; you'll need to send the packet to the user's PC.

So, we can conclude that an SDN-enabled service chaining can save time and reduce the complexity of legacy routing and switching in a network. Building a service chaining application on ODL can help you automate the network configuration on all SDN-enabled switches. Remember, it doesn't really matter that the switches are OpenFlow-enabled; the same can be achieved using legacy switches if they are configured via NETCONF, and of course, if they support the required configuration elements to deploy this using VLANs, STP, or policy-based routing.

Standalone mode

The entire preceding scenario can be implemented using standalone flow programing via ODL.

This is a static configuration, similar to what we normally do with legacy switches. We can use the ODL `rest` API via cURL or POSTMAN to push the flows to the switches.

With Postman, do this:

- **Set headers**:
    - **Content-Type**: application/xml
    - **Accept**: application/xml
    - Authentication
- **URL**: `http://<controller IP>:8181/restconf/config/OpenDaylight-inventory:nodes/node/openflow:1/table/0/flow/1`
- **Method**: `PUT`
- **Body**:

```
01 <?xml version="1.0" encoding="UTF-8" standalone="no"?>

02 <flow xmlns="urn:OpenDaylight:flow:inventory">
03      <flow-name>Flow1</flow-name>
04      <id>258</id>
05      <instructions>
06          <instruction>
07              <order>0</order>
08              <apply-actions>
09                  <action>
10                      <order>0</order>
```

```
11                        <output-action>
12                            <output-node-connector>15</output-node-
connector>
13                        </output-action>
14                    </action>
15                </apply-actions>
16            </instruction>
17        </instructions>
18        <match>
19            <ipv4-source>10.1.1.0/24</ipv4-source>
20            <ipv4-destination>192.168.55.55/32</ipv4-destination>
21            <tcp-destination-port>80</tcp-destination-port>
22        </match>
23 </flow>
```

In this example, we configured a flow to match the packets that come from the users (whole network of `10.1.1.0/24`), destined to the VIP of the CRM. These packets are all forwarded to port `15` (look at line `12`), which is going toward the firewall.

Example of network traffic broker and capturing

Packet broker is a term used in professional traffic-monitoring tools. Imagine you have a complex campus and a data center network that consists of multiple switches, multiple routing domains, and VRFs. In this network, for any troubleshooting that requires packet capture, you would need to either bring a packet capture device to the local switch--where you need to do the capture--or use remote mirror (span) technologies to send the captured traffic to a packet analysis or monitoring tool.

Nowadays, many monitoring applications require you to set up some sort of packet duplication to appliances for analysis and monitoring. Examples of these are IDS, NAC, application performance monitoring tools, analyzers, and so on.

The following diagram illustrates the SDN monitoring fabric:

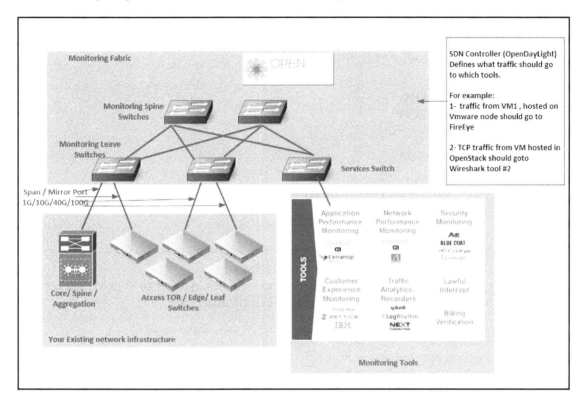

A monitoring fabric is a separate network with single or multiple switches. These switches will be connecting to enterprise network using single high bandwidth links (10G or 40G). Production switches will be configured to mirror the traffic passing from the switch over the mirror port connected to monitoring fabric switches.

Monitoring switches receive huge mirror traffic from enterprise networks. These switches can deliver a specific part of the traffic to the monitoring tools connected to the monitoring switches.

Using SDN and OpenDaylight, these switches can be programed to send specific packets based on a match and classification rule, to specific ports where monitoring tools are connected.

We can define a detailed conditions list to match the packets, based on the multiple parameters of packets, such as:

- MAC address (source and destination)
- IPv4 and IPv6 address (source and destination)
- Ethertype
- Input port number
- IP DSCP and ECN
- ARP
- 802.1q parameters
- MPLS labels
- TCP port (source and destination)
- UDP port (source and destination)
- Metadata
- VXLAN VNID

The following sample XML code can push a flow to switches in order to match a packet based on multiple parameters, such as MAC address, IP, and DSCP:

```
01 <?xml version="1.0" encoding="UTF-8" standalone="no"?>
02 <flow xmlns="urn:OpenDaylight:flow:inventory">
03     <strict>false</strict>
04     <table_id>2</table_id>
05     <id>131</id>
06     <cookie_mask>255</cookie_mask>
07     <match>
08         <ethernet-match>
09             <ethernet-type>
10                 <type>2048</type>
11             </ethernet-type>
12             <ethernet-destination>
13                 <address>ff:ff:29:01:19:61</address>
14             </ethernet-destination>
15             <ethernet-source>
16                 <address>00:00:00:11:23:ae</address>
17             </ethernet-source>
18         </ethernet-match>
19         <ipv4-source>17.1.2.3/8</ipv4-source>
20         <ipv4-destination>172.168.5.6/16</ipv4-destination>
21         <ip-match>
22             <ip-protocol>6</ip-protocol>
23             <ip-dscp>2</ip-dscp>
24             <ip-ecn>2</ip-ecn>
```

```
25              </ip-match>
26              <tcp-source-port>25364</tcp-source-port>
27              <tcp-destination-port>8080</tcp-destination-port>
28              <in-port>0</in-port>
29          </match>
30  </flow>
```

Apart from ODL, to build a packet broker network, there are SDN-based commercial tools available, such as BigSwitch Big Monitoring Fabric. This tool also has a community edition, which can support a minimal number of match rules. Big Monitoring Fabric comes from BigSwitch networks and is based on FloodLight (another SDN controller).

Summary

In this chapter, you learned about the basics of NFV and service chaining. We walked through scenarios related to service chaining and explored the complexities involved in designing and implementing service chaining in traditional networks. We also looked at how SDN can help simplify service chaining in NFV.

In the next chapter, we will explore how the integration of OpenDaylight and OpenStack can help us build a software-defined datacenter.

9
Building a Software-Driven Data Center with OpenDaylight

In this chapter, we will use all that you have learned in this book and integrate it to a responsive software-driven data center use case. We will explore the integration of OpenDaylight into OpenStack as a complete private cloud solution. Also, you'll learn how to integrate and automate the networking tasks from OpenStack to OpenDaylight as well as understand and integrate OpenStack orchestration services with OpenDaylight to build a fully automated data center and private cloud.

Specifically, we will cover the following topics:

- The integration of OpenStack into OpenDaylight
- Automatic network provisioning
- Network orchestration

Data center designs that exist in most organizations are common silo-based architectures of compute, storage, and network.

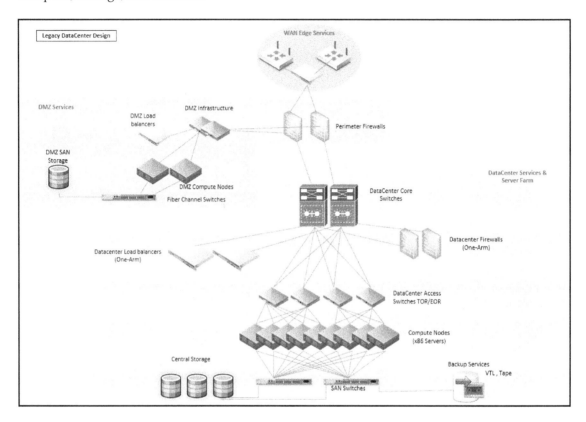

With the popularity of mobile apps, many organizations have started deploying mobile app servers and mobility and mobile databases. The trend to big data and the birth of Hadoop (free) have influenced many organizations to start exploring this new big data platform. Business managers now demand more services from in-house developers and the IT infrastructure team.

Suddenly, Docker and containers born, and since then, developers have started exploring to build containerized apps. Containers have their own specific requirements: networking, storage, and so on.

Developers who are familiar with public clouds, such as Amazon, Azure, and Google, want the same cloud experience for their on-premise data center. They want the ability to provision, alter, and kill server instances with their choice of OS on their fingertips.

It is very common in most organizations that businesses and developers are behind in rush demands on IT infrastructure to support their needs.

Software-defined data center

The idea of an **Software-Defined Data Center** (**SDDC**) started a couple of years ago.

Giant Web 2.0 Cloud companies, such as Amazon, Microsoft, Facebook, and Google started deploying the concept of a cloud orchestration platform. This platform has a web interface where you can log in, create and kill virtual servers, spin them up, create a virtual private network between them, add a virtual firewall in between, and so on. This infrastructure is a dream for every enterprise who runs a data center. It is a highly integrated self-serviced platform with no dependency on hardware, and it can scale out.

The launch and growth of Amazon's AWS public cloud was the tipping point for enterprise IT. Everyone loved the new way of provisioning infrastructure from a web interface. (Although there were multiple public and private cloud launches prior to Amazon, Amazon AWS was one of the most successful and emerging cloud offerings.)

Enterprise IT wanted to build something similar to provide identical experience, that is, the ability to control the whole data center infrastructure from a single console.

The server industry changed a long time ago. There was a time when vendors used to sell server hardware bundled with their own proprietary operating system.

A server is a fully integrated system that consists of a motherboard, CPUs, RAM, disks, and interfaces. There are thousands of vendors and models out there, but they run *YOUR* choice of operating system: either Windows or some flavor of Unix/Linux or a Hypervisor. Your application runs on top of an operating system and is not aware of what is happening in the hardware.

In the storage world, the revolution happened just recently. The use of massive fiber channel central storage systems are declining. Storage is getting closer to servers. With the introduction of storage virtualization systems, every server with a bunch of disks becomes a storage node and participates in the virtual storage area network. In effect, storage virtualization disrupted the storage market.

In fact, storage virtualization was another example of separation of hardware and software. It doesn't matter what kind of storage hardware you have. A **JBOD** (server with **Just a Bunch of Disks**) or a fiber channel can store many **Disk Array Units** (**DAE**s); all you need to manage is access to your virtual storage console. It manages your disks, raid groups, LUNs, volumes, replication, backups, and so on.

The move to hyper-convergence (shifting storage next to compute) started the introduction and birth of **Nutanix**, followed by VMware VSAN and VXRAIL and DataCore, which led to **Software-defined Storage** (**SDS**).

This reduced the use of SAN and central storage. Servers promoted having faster and cheaper hard disks and SSD drives. The use of blade servers declined, as they do not support multiple hard disks and they have proprietary architecture.

Slowly, storage moved to IP, eliminating the use of a fiber channel. Then, multiple 10G interfaces were introduced for network and storage traffic. **Fibre Channel over Ethernet** (**FCoE**) slowed down due to its limitation (single hop) and DCB protocols complexity.

Storage got virtualized, and started running on bare metal servers with high quantity disks.

This revolution gave birth to storage benefits, such as scale-out (not limited to the legacy storage controller's maximum supported capacity), and helped them get integrated into the virtualization engine (VMware vSphere and OpenStack) to better manage storage.

What happened to compute and storage?

Using the generic x86 commodity bare-metal servers as storage nodes makes the data center more standardized in order to make x86 run both storage and compute.

The rise of x86 servers from OEM vendors, such as Quanta and Super Micro, led to an increase in the rack mount server purchases. Data centers limited the use of proprietary blade servers and started standardizing them on rack mount Dual/Quad CPU servers.

The server networking technology changed, and silicon companies-such as Mellanox, Chelsio, and Intel-started building 40G, 100G, and also, 10G-Base-T network adapters. The prices are not sky-high; you can purchase a single port 100 GBps network adapter (PCIe x16) for around $1,500 from Amazon.

Servers and storage started getting equipped with faster processors, more memory, and faster network adapters. But is the network capable enough of supporting 40G or 100G for server connectivity?

Hyper-converged infrastructure

Storage virtualization added an extra load to the network, using IP and Ethernet as files and the block delivery platform. So your network is the same and business demands more bandwidth to support the new servers with 100G NIC cards.

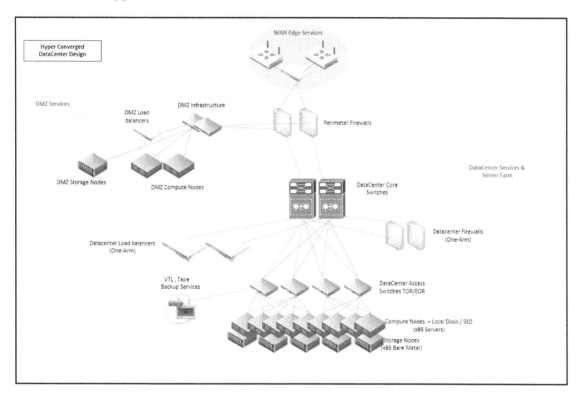

The networking industry is being pushed by multiple trends toward its limits, and it needs to re-examine the legacy networking architecture.

Some of the key computing trends driving the need for a new network paradigm are as follows:

- Increase in mobile devices (smart phones/watches, tablets, wearables, IoT devices)
- Cloud services
- Server-to-server communication (changing traffic patterns to *east-west*)
- The increased use of cloud services
- Big data

- Rise of servers with high-speed NIC cards (40G/100G)
- The consumerization of IT
- Need to create virtual isolated networks between VMs and containers
- Competition with the public cloud feature set

The limitations of current networking technologies

Traditional networking architecture and equipment are mostly built to be managed by human, on a device by device using annual processes. They are not built to be centrally managed, programmed, or even automated.

The new trends in enterprises, data centers, and service providers requires the network to reconfigure fast to adopt fast changes. The demand for changes is beyond the capabilities of manual processes and human.

- As a basic enterprise example, to add or move any device in campus or data center, IT teams need to configure multiple switches, routers, and firewalls, and update ACLs, VLANs, and **Quality of Services** (**QoS**).
- Such manual process will lead to inconsistent policies, where some policies or configuration don't apply (are forgotten) which leads to more time-consuming troubleshooting sessions.
- Considering the manual processes involved for applying such changes, it is obvious that it is a time-consuming process and won't scale. IT teams will not be able to cope with changes quickly and normally the change request SLAs are beyond weeks.

Can SDN solve the problem?

As you learned, the software-defined networking method is based on a controller, which communicates with networking equipments, such as switches and routers. Using an SDN controller at least can help the networking to only deal with a single console, which is SDN controller. There is no need to manage individual networking equipment in a pure SDN-enabled network.

This can solve many problems of a network to cope with high demand changes, reduce the provisioning and changes, and reduce manual work.

By building some custom SDN applications or scripts to call different APIs on OpenDaylight SDN controller, you can achieve some automation. However, networking team still requires to trigger that small amount of manual work to execute the scripts or SDN applications with the required arguments to execute a specific task.

For example, you can create an SDN application for ODL to find the ports with and IP-phone connected and shut them down at 6 pm everyday. This sounds simple, and you enjoy automating such tasks.

But with more complex requirement to provision network for a new application in data center, which requires to creating new VLAN in the network, VRFs in routers and configure IP interfaces on routers, that might not sound simple even with an SDN controller.

The key for solving the provisioning automation is to integrate the network with your cloud orchestration platform, in a more simple and practical language, to integrate your network with VMware vSphere or OpenStack/CloudStack.

This integration will help you automate the provisioning right from cloud orchestration platform toward network. This integration must be implemented at API level between the cloud and SDN platforms. Any newly created environment in the cloud orchestration platform will trigger an API call to SDN controller (ODL) with specific parameters to create and provision required networking.

The integration of OpenStack into OpenDaylight

OpenStack is a popular open source private cloud or **Infrastructure as a Service** (**IaaS**) project, covering compute, storage, and network management. OpenStack was introduced in 2010 by Rackspace and NASA, and its initial code came from NASA's Nebula and Rackspace Cloud Files platform.

OpenStack was born after a joint effort between NASA and Rackspace, who decided to take Nebula to the next level. It became popular and got many developer resources from different countries and large companies.

Red Hat, Canonical, and Mirantis started building their own OpenStack distribution with easy-to-use installer and provisioning tools. OpenStack is growing, with two releases per year.

OpenStack is a combination of tightly integrated tools that provides a virtual infrastructure as a service. OpenStack consists of multiple components and projects; important ones are as follows:

- **Nova compute**: Server virtualization
- **Swift object storage and Cinder block storage**: Storage virtualization
- **Neutron**: Network virtualization

There are many other projects and components; however, the preceding are just the key components of OpenStack for server, storage, and network virtualization.

OpenStack networking was initially based on Nova networking (basic flat layer 2). However, slowly, in the past few years, Neutron has taken over Nova as a network virtualization platform for OpenStack. Unlike Nova, Neutron was a kind of next-generation network virtualization technology where it could use layer 2 over layer 3 encapsulation, and it can build virtual overlay networks between hosts to provide a layer 2 network to virtual machines over a layer 3 underlay network.

Neutron can also provide a legacy network based on Linux Bridges without building an overlay. It is a modular project that can be integrated with other networking products, such as OpenDaylight, Cisco ACI, VMware NSX, Big Switch BIG Cloud Fabric, and other commercial and open source networking products.

Neutron is based on **Open Virtual Switch** (**OVS**). OVS is a virtual switch that runs on hypervisor hosts, providing networking services to virtual machines in a host. OVS has legacy L2 capabilities (features, such as spanning tree, link aggregation, LLDP, and so on); also, it has an OpenFlow-capable agent, which can be integrated with an SDN controller such as ODL that supports OVSDB as a southbound protocol.

Neutron itself provides network virtualization using the VXLAN overlay on top of legacy underlay network. This means that OpenStack Neutron brings software-defined networking through network virtualization and overlays.

By default, Neutron's scope is limited only to hosts.

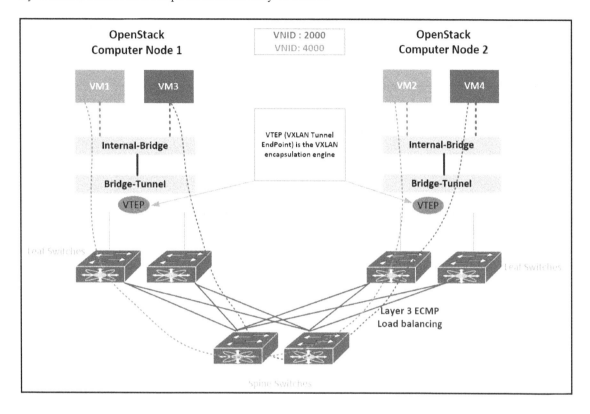

Neutron, by default, only controls networking on hosts. It runs and manages OVS on hosts to provide network connectivity between virtual machines. If virtual machines are located on different hosts, Neutron builds host-to-host tunnels using VXLAN to provide the same layer 2 network to virtual machines. However, they are located on different hosts, placed on an L3-routed network (no layer 2 connectivity between the hosts).

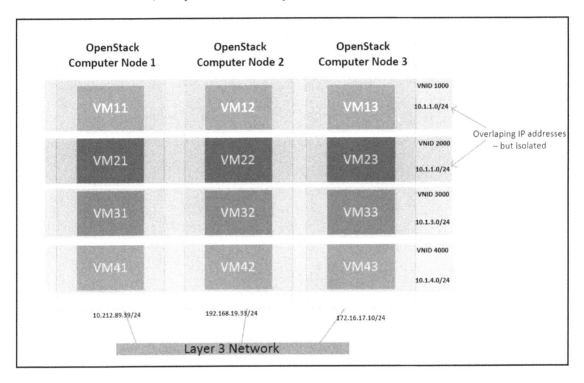

Neutron is modular and has an open source plugin that can be used to allow Neutron to control external networking platforms or underlay networks. The plugin system of Neutron is named **Modular Layer 2** (**ML2**). Third-party networking vendors have built plugins for OpenStack to integrate their networking product with OpenStack. For example, Cisco has built an ML2 plugin for OpenStack to allow OpenStack to use Cisco networking products in order to integrate their network equipment and OpenStack.

Alternatively, another interesting networking vendor has built ML2 plugin to integrate with their network platform is Big Switch Networks. Their product's big cloud fabric integrates with OpenStack via an ML2 plugin. Big cloud fabric runs the physical network as well as virtual networks on the hosts by installing an OVS agent in each host to manage the virtual switches in each host.

Now that you have learned about OpenStack and Neutron, let's explore how OpenStack integrates with OpenDaylight.

OpenDaylight has also built an ML2 plugin for OpenStack. This plugin is written and maintained by OpenDaylight:

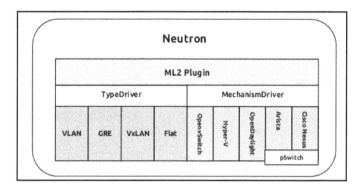

OpenStack can use OpenDaylight as it's a network management provider through the ML2 northbound plugin. OpenDaylight manages the network flows for the OpenStack compute nodes via the OVSDB southbound plugin.

At this level, this plugin allows OpenDaylight to use southbound protocols, such as OVSDB, to manage the OVS running on compute hosts within the OpenStack domain as well as the SDN underlay network (physical network) connecting the compute hosts to the network.

Multi-tenancy

If you are familiar with OpenStack, you know that it is based on isolated projects (also known as Tenants). Tenants are a way to isolate the computer, storage, and networking between the entities of OpenStack.

For example, an OpenStack platform can serve multiple tenants; you can imagine tenants as different companies. Each company (tenant) will have its own isolated and dedicated virtual infrastructure. Each tenant can create its own virtual infrastructure, including virtual machines and NFVs, such as firewall and load balancers. Each tenant has its own monitoring and management tools to manage its virtual infrastructure.

Each tenant has its own virtual networks. Tenants can create different networks and have them access their respective virtual machines. They will not be able to communicate with the outside world unless they go through a gateway.

Tenants may have overlapping IP addresses and subnets in their virtual networks.

For example, tenant 1 may have the subnet `192.168.10.0/24`; the same subnet is used in tenant 2 (`192.168.10.0/24`). Virtual networks are local to each tenant; they do not route to the outside world. To do this, tenants have to go through a virtual gateway/firewall, which will NAT the internal IP addresses to a global network of that particular tenant.

As discussed, ODL can provide networking to the OpenStack platform; this means ODL should be able to support tenants and the network isolation between them.

If we technically look at the supporting tenants in a network from a technical perspective, it is mainly implemented by policies and access lists. Using the tools available in legacy networking, such as VLANs (layer 2 isolation), virtual routing forwarding (layer 3 isolation), and L2/L3/L4 access lists, can help build isolation.

In an SDN network, implementing such isolation and restrictions are much easier as the SDN controller decides who should be able to talk to whom.

OpenDayLight's Virtual Tenant Networks

To support and better integrate with OpenStack's tenants, ODL has a specific module named **Virtual Tenant Network** (**VTN**).

VTN is one of the very interesting modules in ODL; we haven't discussed this yet. VTN integrates with OpenStack through the ML2 plugin. Technically, VTN is an SDN policy manager. It builds a list of tenants and their resources (virtual machines, networks, IP addresses, MAC addresses, policies, NAT, and so on).

Once we connect ODL and OpenStack using the ML2 plugin, any newly created tenant in OpenStack will be created in ODL's VTN too.

VTN allows users to design a virtual legacy L2/L3 network. Once the network design is finalized in VTN, it will get automatically mapped to the underlying physical network. This mapping is done via the ODL controller by injecting the required configuration to each individual switch or networking equipment, based on the southbound protocol supported by that networking gear.

The following picture from ODL illustrates how VTN maps a virtual network to a physical network:

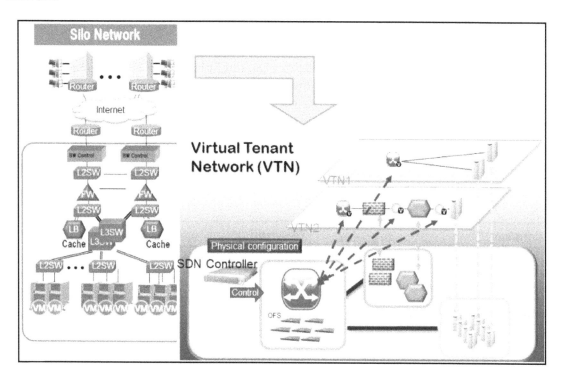

As you can see in the preceding diagram, VTN builds an **Over The ToP** (**OTT**) virtual networks on top of physical networks. This may sound complex; but to better understand VTN, always consider it as a simple policy set. As a policy set living within ODL, VTN has full visibility of all the virtual machines, their MAC addresses, IP addresses, and the project (tenant) they belong to. With this visibility, VTN simply defines policies related to what device should be able to communicate with others and how traffic routing or service chaining must be in place.

Once these policies are defined, VTN uses the MD-SAL concept to program the underlying network. VTN might not be aware of what protocol is used to configure the underlying switches, as this is a model-driven activity. ODL injects the related configuration via the supported southbound protocol to the underlying switch; it can be OVSDB, OpenFlow, NETCONF, or even CLI over SSH.

Unlike the previous ODL modules we learned, VTN consists of two main components:

1. **VTN manager**: This is the main component of the VTN plugin, which resides inside ODL (similar to all other plugins you have learned).

   VTN manager is a standard OpenDaylight plugin, which is again similar to other plugins you have learned so far. It provides a REST interface to configure VTN components, such as create/update/delete of vBridge, vRouter, and so on. (We will explore the components later in this chapter.)

   To install VTN manager, you need to enter the following commands in the ODL Karaf prompt:

Command	Description
feature:install odl-vtn-manager	VTN Manager's Java API
feature:install odl-vtn-manager-rest	VTN manager's REST API
feature:install odl-vtn-manager-neutron	Integration with the Neutron interface

2. VTN coordinator is an external application that runs on a separate host (or on an ODL host) and provides a web interface GUI for the user to interact with VTN.

   VTN coordinator interacts with the VTN manager plugin through VTN manager's REST APIs to implement the user configuration. It is also capable of communicating with multiple ODL controllers.

   VTN coordinator will use the REST interface exposed by VTN manager to read the policies and details from VTN manager and visualize the virtual network.

User interaction with the web GUI of VTN coordinator is translated as the REST API to VTN manager by the OpenDaylight controller driver component.

VTN coordinator can be downloaded from the ODL website download page as a separate downloadable application.

Virtual network components

As already discussed, VTN builds an overlay virtual network. This network is based on virtual components. Virtual components, such as virtual bridge (virtual switch) and virtual routers, are then connected to virtual interfaces on hosts or connected to each other via virtual links.

The following table lists and describes virtual components:

Virtual Component	Description
vBridge	This is a virtual layer 2 switch. It is normally implemented as a Linux bridge.
vRouter	This is a virtual layer 3 router with IP routing functions.
vTunnel	This is a representation of a virtual tunnel. It consists of vTEPs and vBypass.
vTep	This is virtual tunnel end point. It's a gateway to an overlay network, which normally encapsulates/decapsulates VXLAN packets.
vBypass	This refers to the logical representation of connectivity between controlled networks or tunnel endpoints.
Virtual interface	This is the virtual interface on a virtual device (such as vBridge or vRouter).
Virtual Link (vLink)	This refers to virtual cables used to connect virtual interfaces to each other. (Imagine it as a virtual CAT6 patch cord.)

The following figure shows an example of a constructed virtual network between two virtual machines. They are connected via a virtual bridge to a virtual router. vRouter performs routing between the 10.1.1.0/24 and 10.2.2.0/24 networks:

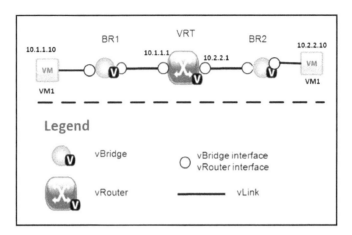

vBridge functions

vBridge provides the standard layer 2 switching (bridging) function, which transfers a frame to the output of a virtual port according to the destination MAC address or other policies.

Its functionality is similar to the standard layer 2 switch. It supports MAC learning and keeping up-to-date MAC address table per vBridge.

This feature is very intensively implemented in VTN coordinator as well as VTN manager.

vBridges are created in VTN coordinator by user or through an external application such as OpenStack via API call. VTN coordinator then will translate the requirement and calls the VTN manager API to create the vBridges. The other functions of vBridge such as adding MACs, interfaces, and flow filter are all performed in the same way.

VTN manager created the virtual bridges in ODL. The following diagram illustrates the vBridge:

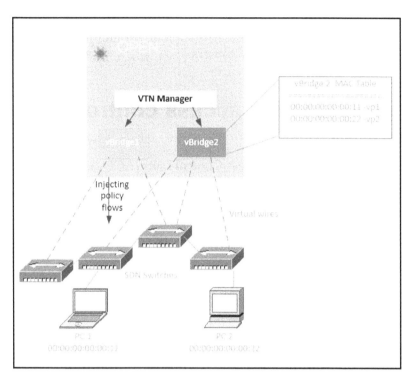

vRouter functions

vRouter is a basic layer 3 router that can have multiple virtual interfaces connected to different virtual devices, such as vBridges.

It is designed to support basic layer 3 features such as routing (between interfaces and static routing) and DHCP relay agent.

It is very important to mention that vRouter functions are all implemented in VTN coordinator. There is no code for vRouter inside the VTN manager module inside ODL.

Also, please note that the vRouter feature is still under development, and it is barely documented.

Currently, VTN coordinator has implementation for provisioning and managing vRouters. This means that it has capability to create vRouters, create virtual interfaces for vRouter and assign and connect them and other provisioning and management features.

Future releases of ODL will have the implementation of vRouter in VTN manager module, which allows the VTN to provision the vRouters.

Flow filter functions - access control and policy-based routing

The flow filter function is similar to **Access Control Lists** (ACL) or **Policy-based Routing (PBR)** in legacy networking.

Flow filter is implemented in both VTN coordinator and VTN manager.

The function of flow filter is to apply filters in networking equipment (physical, virtual) and take an action against the matched traffic.

A filter can be created by a user or via APIs in VTN coordinator. The Flow filter implementation in VTN coordinator then will translate the high-level requirement, which user has requested to VTN manager's flow filter APIs.

VTN manager's flow filter implementation finally executes the required configuration using relevant southbound protocol (mainly OpenFlow) to the network switches.

Flow filter can match packets based on the following single or multiple parameters:

- MAC address
- Ether type
- VLAN priority
- IP address
- DSCP
- IP protocol
- TCP/UDP port
- ICMP type, code

The action of a flow filter follows this pattern: accept, reject, or redirect.

This is very similar to a policy-based routing feature. It uses the same concept of flow management to redirect the matched packets to a specific ports or accept (allow the packet to be processed by routing/ switching) or just drop the packet.

Redirection is used for service chaining to send a packet to a different destination. Redirection can send a packet out of its predefined out port, or it can send and also modify packet attributes, such as MAC addresses.

Action	Function
Pass	If the packet matches the condition, just pass it. This means that in vBridge, the frame will continue the processing to identify the output port based on lookups in the MAC address table. In a vRouter, the process continues to route the packet-based on the routing table and determines the output port.
Drop	This drops the packet that match in the condition.
Redirection	This redirects the packet to a desired virtual interface/port. It can either just redirect the packet or redirect and change the MAC addresses in the packet.

VTN coordinator

VTN coordinator is an external application that provides a REST interface to the user to use VTN. It interacts with the VTN manager module within the ODL to implement the user configuration.

The following diagram illustrates the relationship between VTN manager and coordinator:

The table identifies the functions and interfaces used by VTN components:

Component	Interface	Purpose
VTN manager	RESTful API	To configure VTN components in OpenDaylight
VTN manager	Neutron API implementation	To communicate with OpenStack Neutron
VTN coordinator	RESTful API	To provide a web interface and REST interface for users to configure virtual networks

VTN coordinator provides web GUI as well as REST APIs. Users can use the web GUI to create, delete, and change the virtual network components, such as vRouter, vBridges, and the connectivity between them.

External applications also can use the REST interface of VTN coordinator to perform operations such as GET/PUT/POST/DELETE against virtual network components.

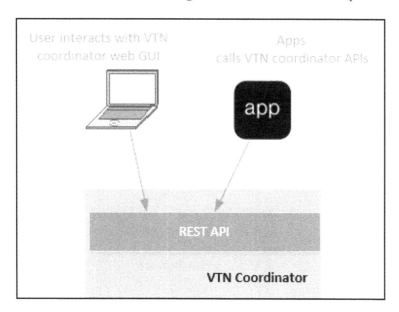

VTN installation

To install VTN manager, enter the following commands in your ODL Karaf:

```
Feature:install odl-vtn-manager
Feature:install odl-vtn-manager-rest
```

To install VTN coordinator based on the version available on the ODL website, follow the installation guide. It is recommended that you rather use a different virtual machine or host than your ODL machine to install VTN coordinator.

How ODL's ML2 plugin works

The ML2 mechanism driver, which has been built by OpenDayLight to be used in OpenStack, passes all OpenStack's Neutron API calls to Open Daylight's NeutronAPIService via REST calls.

The `NeutronAPIService`, which is one of the components of the VTN manager (installed as `Feature:install odl-vtn-manager-neutron`), is a service broker. This means it receives information from OpenStack and makes it available for OpenDaylight modules.

> Neutron API Service also communicates to OVSDB southbound plugin in order to implement the required changes requested by OpenStack, for example, to create VXLAN tunnels.

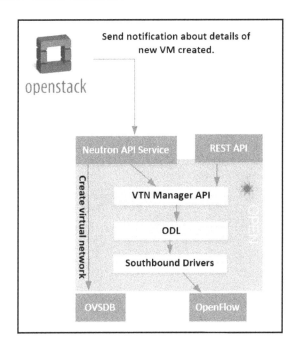

Automatic network provisioning

After the successful integration of ODL and OpenStack, all the network-provisioning actions will be automated inside OpenStack and ODL. When a tenant creates a virtual network in OpenStack, the same network will be created in OpenStack. This happens via the ML2 plugin as the Neutron API calls from OpenStack will be sent to ODL's Neutron Service REST module. This service makes the API calls available to other services, such as VTN, which pick up the request and build their virtual network in VTN.

Because ODL manages the underlay physical network as well as the OpenStack virtual network, it becomes a big source of all networking information. It will know all the virtual machines, where they are running (which host), and other attributes, such as the owning tenants, service chains, and so on.

This integration makes the network fully integrated with the data center and cloud management and orchestration tools, such as OpenStack. This helps you build a fully integrated software-defined data center with a single web console for provisioning tenants, virtual machines, network services, firewalls, load balancers, and service chaining. This forces traffic to go through specific network services.

VTN manager receives interface creation requests from OpenStack via the OVSDB plugin. Using information provided by OpenStack, VTN manager automatically creates a virtual tenant network in the OpenDaylight controller. All the detailed information from OpenStack is stored in OpenDaylight's VTN manager, as they are learned via OVSDB.

You can view the configuration of VTN using the VTN coordinator web UI. The network created in OpenStack is mapped to a vBridge in VTN. The tenant itself is mapped to a VTN object.

The UID of the network in OpenStack is mapped to the v-bridge identifier in VTN.

The network name from OpenStack is mapped to a description of v-bridge.

Network orchestration

Network orchestration is our last section of this book.

There are different definitions available for orchestration, but all different ideas and designations have a common concept for orchestration, and that is, automation and integration of a network with other systems.

Especially in data centers and cloud platforms, network orchestration is the ability of self-service applications and services to program the network in order to provide the required networking functions. For example, consider you have a self-service portal in order to purchase a new virtually routed network or load balancer; after the completion of the purchase, the system provisions the required services without administrator or human interaction.

Network orchestration can start with customer service orders that are generated manually or through automatic actions, such as ordering a service through a website. The application or service would then use network orchestration to automatically provision the required services.

Automation is the key of network orchestration.

You might be thinking that we have already achieved some sort of network orchestration via integrating OpenStack and OpenDaylight. This is true. In fact, the integration between OpenStack and ODL is a good example of network orchestration in a private cloud or data center environment.

End users interact with a portal (for example, the OpenStack portal) and create virtual machines, virtual networks, and virtual network services, such as Firewall or Load balancer. Ideally, this process is fully automated without human interaction.

We can also scale out the data center orchestration to multiple data centers, this can help organization with multiple data centers to have a single orchestration console to log in and provision services in different data centers.

Another important use case of network orchestration, which is related to service providers.

Service providers

Connectivity and WAN service providers also require network orchestration to automatically provision services to their customers.

Service providers already have some sort of processes for their business. You may have heard about **Operation Support Systems** (**OSS**) and **Business Support Systems** (**BSS**).

BSS is a combination of complex processes for provisioning services to both existing or new customers. The BSS process is one of the lengthy processes in service provider networks. For example, when a customer requires a new circuit to be delivered to its new site in London, the BSS process of the service provider creates multiple tickets in different systems to provision the service. This includes provisioning of physical connectivity medium (fiber, DSL, Docsis, and so on) and providing **Customer Premises Equipment** (**CPE**) and configuration of devices.

The same might apply in the case of OSS, which is mainly for maintaining and servicing a service provider network in order to provide services. OSS includes internal service provider networks as well as the maintenance of CPE. Any change should be automated via orchestration to reduce time to market.

Tier 1 and Tier 2 service providers are under pressure from both their existing large, aging technology networks and competition from new, smaller service providers providing low price connectivity with high bandwidth and **Service Level Agreement** (**SLA**). Managing their networks is expensive and complex, which makes them hard to move.

Automation is one of the solutions to increase service providers' speed for provisioning services; it also simplifies the operation, which also results in reduction of operation costs.

In a service provider environment, OSS always grows as a new service, with devices added to the service portfolio. It's very common that older, larger service providers are more complex, heavy, expensive, and slow moving. OSS is a set of processes and tools to support the services. Many service providers have a common OSS for all services (mobile, Internet, WAN, wireless, and so on); some modern service providers have different OSSes for each function with tight integration between each other to resolve dependency issues.

Every time a service provider adds a new service or device, it needs to change the OSS code and processes, which makes the OSS slower and slower in the long run.

The promise of network service orchestration is to evolve OSS by making it agile and decoupling the network services from specific components (hardware appliances and software). This allows the network service orchestration to automatically configure the network based on the service requirement, regardless of the underlying hardware.

Network service orchestration uses modeling (similar to what you have learned in OpenDaylight) to create high-level models without the need for building code to configure custom hardware or appliances. It uses appliance drivers or southbound protocols to communicate with the underlying hardware and automatically provision the services.

A network orchestration platform can help service providers automate all the configuration activities of the network. In addition, they are slowly being able to provision a virtual CPE on a standard x86 server at the customer's premises. This helps service providers untie the hardware and software and provide a more flexible service using network service functions. Nowadays, they can virtualize a router-a virtual router with performance better than a physical router.

Service providers require a different type of network orchestration platform in order to provide automated WAN services. OpenStack is not an orchestration tool for such service providers as it will not be able to provision the CPE or configure the service provider network.

Different types of tools available, such as Glue Networks and NSO (from Tail-f, which was acquired by Cisco):

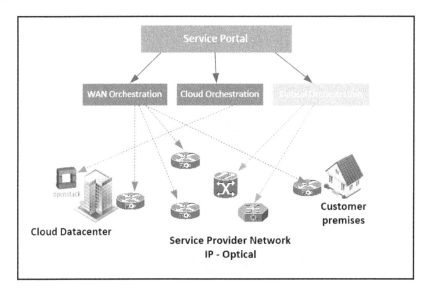

A network orchestration platform in service should be able to support different vendors and legacy equipment. Such tools are more complex when compared to standard data center network orchestration tools as service provider networks are majority very large and wide supporting hundreds and thousands of routers and switches.

In future, SDN orchestration systems will provide the important *glue* between a wide range of technologies that would enable cloud-based networks and communication services. It is expected that they will provide the coordination and automation technology that would bridge the gap between telecom systems, data center resources, OSS systems, and the customers looking to purchase cloud-based technologies and network services.

Open Network Automation Platform

Open Network Automation Platform (**ONAP**) is a very new project in Linux foundation related to SDN, NFV, and orchestration for service providers.

Started in April 2017 to combine two projects, open source ECOMP and **Open Orchestrator Project** (OPEN-O) to allow service providers to automate, design, orchestrate, and manage services and virtual functions.

Enhanced Control, Orchestration, Management, and Policy (ECOMP) was a project started by **AT&T** , but it become open source and transferred to Linux foundation.

ECOMP is a set of tools designed for BSS and OSS functions, with a portal to design and build new services as well as maintain and manage the current services. It also has an analytic platform.

OPEN-O is an orchestration platform for SDN, NFV, and legacy networks all under a single orchestration umbrella.

As combination of the ECOMP and OPEN-O projects, ONAP is created as an open source software platform to deliver capabilities for the design, creation, orchestration, monitoring, and life cycle management of SDN, NFV (VNFs), and higher level combination services based on SDN, NFV, and service chaining.

Although ONAP is new, but the subprojects were mature. ONAP provides a common standard platform with potential to be tested and adopted by global operators.

Software-defined optical networking

Optical networking is another area that can be automated by orchestration. **Wavelength Division Multiplexing** (WDM) systems and where switches are used in service providers to provide fiber connectivity to different clients. Similar to all other silo-based systems, the WDM platforms are also managed and operated individually.

One of the key points of OpenDaylight is its modularity, which allows integrating and building plugins and modules to manage other systems.

New optical networking products mostly support NETCONF and YANG where the vendor allows an SDN controller such as OpenDayLight or ONOS to manage the optical switch.

Optical networking doesn't have a large footprint in service providers comparing to CPE devices. Therefore, it might not be in interest of service providers to transform their WDM platform to a software-defined era.

We may see more software-defined optical networking in future.

Summary

In this chapter, we discussed the automation of the last block (Networking) in a data center. The future of all data centers is toward automation. Automation is the foundation of cloud orchestration platforms. Hardware is becoming more standard and commoditized, and will be managed by software. Software-defined networking is slowly progressing in service providers and enterprises with many deployments of commercial products.

OpenDaylight is a great foundation to manage not only a software-defined Ethernet network but also other aspects, such as IoT and city.

Index

Enhanced Control, Orchestration, Management, and Policy (ECOMP) 309
enterprise switches, security features
    802.1x authentication 222
    inline NAC 223
    MAC address authentication 222
    port security 222
    web, authentication 223
Extensible Authentication Protocol over LAN (EAPOL) 223

F

fabric
    as service 57
    controlling 11
    direct fabric programming 11
    direct fabric programming, and overlay
        differences between 12
    overlay 12
federation 59
Fiber to the Home (FTTH) 266
Fiber to the Premise (FTTP) 266
Fibre Channel over Ethernet (FCoE) 286
firewall
    standalone mode 277
    traffic forcing, example 273
flow entry 14
flow filter
    functions 300
flow table 14
flows
    handling 146

G

Genius generic network interfaces 60
Gigabit Passive Optical Networks (GPON) 266
Group-Based Policy (GBP) 44

H

HA Proxy
    URL 273
HelloWorld application
    deploying, on ODL 201
host isolation
    implementing, in ODL 150

hyper-converged infrastructure 287
hypervisor
    Mininet OVF file, importing 116, 117, 118

I

imperative method 195
Infrastructure as a Service (IaaS) 289
Internet of Things Data Management (IoTDM) 44, 61
IP address
    setting 85, 119

J

Java Development Kit (JDK) 85
Java interfaces 81
Java Runtime Environment (JRE) 82
Java
    installation 86
Jupiter 7
Just Bunch of Disks (JBOD) 285

L

L2 switch
    about 62
    AddressTracker 63
    Flow Writer Service 63
    PacketHandler 62, 256
    Path Computation Service 63
    STP Service 63
Layer 2 switching
    about 144
    flows, handling 146
    in ODL 144
    link aggregation 181
    topology, building 147
Link Aggregation Control Protocol (LACP)
    about 65, 181
    configuring 182
link aggregation
    about 181
    LACP, configuring 182
Link Layer Discovery Protocol (LLDP) 148
Linkstate (LS) 51
load balancer
    traffic forcing, example 273

M

N